Militancy, Market Dynamics, and Workplace Authority

SUNY Series in American Labor History
Robert Asher and Amy Kesselman, editors

Militancy, Market Dynamics, and Workplace Authority

The Struggle over Labor Process Outcomes in the U.S. Automobile Industry, 1946 to 1973

James R. Zetka, Jr.

State University of New York Press

Published by
State University of New York Press, Albany

Printed in the United States of America

For information, address State University of New York Press,
State University Plaza, Albany, NY 12246

Production by Bernadine Dawes • Marketing by Bernadette LaManna

Library of Congress Cataloging-in-Publication Data

Zetka, James R., 1957–
Militancy, market dynamics, and workplace authority : the struggle over labor process outcomes in the U.S. automobile industry, 1946–1973 / James R. Zetka, Jr.
p. cm. — (SUNY series in American labor history)
Includes bibliographical references and index.
ISBN 0–7914–2065–5. — ISBN 0–7914–2066–3 (pbk.)
1. Strikes and lockouts—Automobile industry—United States--History. 2. Trade-unions—Automobile industry workers—United States—History. 3. Automobile industry and trade—United States--Management—History. 4. Labor discipline—United States--History—20th century. 5. Industrial relations—United States--History—20th century. I. Title. II. Series.
HD5325.A8Z47 1995
331.89'28292'0973—dc20 93–48155
CIP

10 9 8 7 6 5 4 3 2 1

In dedication to the memories of
William B. Parker,
Rudolph Zetka,
Walter Lind,
and
Georgia Lind

Contents

List of Tables

Acknowledgments

My first debt is to the workers from an automotive stamping plant whom I interviewed for their willingness to describe their work processes to me in a very frank and open way, when they, themselves, were experiencing trying times. For confidentiality reasons, I cannot disclose their names. However, I especially want to thank my key informants for arranging interviews and for providing rich and detailed information that was very useful in generating hypotheses for what turned out to be a historical study.

I want to also thank Arnold S. Feldman for supporting the very unusual and long dissertation that served as the foundation for this book. Throughout my graduate career in the sociology department at Northwestern University, Feldman had an uncanny knack for knowing what I needed most and for delivering it—whether it be unrelenting criticism, coffee and paternal direction, or praise and support.

I also owe a debt to Arthur Stinchcombe for supporting my work in general and for serving as the interim chair of my dissertation committee when Ackie was on leave. Stinchcombe's willingness to be critical, honest, and frank in evaluating my work made it better.

I also thank Howard S. Becker, Charles Ragin, and Allan Schnaiberg for their encouragement and support throughout the course of this project and my graduate training. The ongoing conversations with John P. Walsh, Paula Rossow, and other members of Ackie Feldman's seminars at Northwestern University from 1983 to 1989 were very helpful in shaping the work in its formative stages.

Input from Larry J. Griffin on the National Science Foundation proposal, from John R. Logan regarding my statistical analyses, from Charles Tilly regarding marketing and publication prospects, and from the participants in the Historical Sociology Group at the State University of New York at Albany also proved helpful. I especially thank Robert Asher, the editor of the University's series on labor history, for his insightful and useful comments on later drafts of the manuscript. Having a labor historian working in the area to serve as editor proved to be an unusual benefit to me as an industrial sociologist. I thank Clay Morgan as well, the editor at the State University of New York Press, for taking the manuscript through the various stages of the publication process quickly and painlessly.

This research was supported financially by National Science Foundation Dissertation Grant No. SES-8706712 and by a Northwestern University graduate fellowship. The able assistance of the staff at the Transportation Library at Northwestern University, the Archives of Labor and Urban Affairs at Wayne State University, and the Wisconsin Historical Society all proved to be helpful to the project. I also thank Terri Melrose, my research assistant, for helping me find and compile statistical data.

Finally, I thank my family for their continued support as I pursued an unconventional career path—Lois Parker, Bill Zetka, James R. Zetka, Sr., and Betty Zetka. Most of all, I thank my wife, Janet Feldgaier, for her patience and warm emotional and intellectual encouragement throughout the years which I have spent laboring on this project.

An early abbreviated version of chapters 3 and 4 was published as "Work Organization and Wildcat Strikes in the U.S. Automobile Industry, 1946 to 1963," *American Sociological Review* 57, 2 (1992):214–226. An abbreviated version of chapter 9 was published as "Mass-Production Automation and Work-Group Solidarity in the Post–World War II Automobile Industry," *Work and Occupations* 19, 3 (1992):255–271.

Introduction

The Hegemony Model

Two interrelated crises plagued industrial development in the United States prior to the post-World War II period. One was centered on the shop floor and involved struggles between managers and workers over control of work organization and production outcomes. The other was centered in the market arena and involved destructive price competition among firms. These interrelated crises became most chronic during the Great Depression. All told, they threatened capitalism's future.

How did the major U.S. industries resolve these interrelated crises? This question was a critical concern of industrial analysis in the decades following World War II. During the late 1970s, a popular explanatory model emerged from this debate which argued that the intensification of the market and shop-floor-level crises during the 1930s and 1940s forced managements to develop and install regulatory structures, both in the workplace and in the market arena.[1]

These structures were hegemonic. They won the active commitment and consent of their participants—managers, labor unions, and workers—to courses of action consistent with monopoly capitalist interests. These participants willingly pursued such courses of action because they believed that it was in their best interests to do so, given the alternatives open to them. These hegemonic structures allegedly resolved capitalism's crisis tendencies and created an industrial environment that delivered desirable investment returns from the 1950s into the 1970s.

In the popular hegemony model, the workplace structures linked to the decline of shop-floor-control crises are plant-level status hierarchies, internal labor markets governed by seniority, and collective bargaining systems. These structures allegedly arrested the deskilling tendencies that had created masses of unskilled workers with homogenized interests in conflict with those of management. By differentiating jobs by status and reward criteria at the plant level, and by forcing workers to compete for placement in the better positions, these structures divided worker interests and secured managements' shop-floor control. By offering workers tangible rewards for staying with the firm, and by legitimating themselves through democratically ratified collective bargaining agreements, these structures allegedly won workers' active participation and consent to the postwar industrial regime.[2]

The market structures that enabled these shop-floor developments to occur are labeled *monopoly capitalist* in the popular model and include informal price-maintenance arrangements among firms, and horizontally and vertically integrated production and marketing organizations. These structures purportedly arrested destructive price competition among firms, thereby creating environments conducive to stable and predictable profit making. Such structures lessened pressure by firms to cut production costs and increase productivity, allowing managements to institute and maintain the types of shop-floor structures already mentioned.[3]

Recent Challenges

During the renaissance of labor-process scholarship in the late 1970s and 1980s, many found the logic of this simple hegemony model to be appealing. However, a number of developments have taken place of late to challenge the hegemony model's viability. A largely unanswered challenge comes from revisionist accounts of labor militancy. Historians and historical sociologists—conducting fine-grained analyses of the social origins of those initiating militant collective action—have concluded that low-skilled factory workers were rarely at the forefront of militant struggle in the past. Low-skilled factory workers were most affected by managerial structures of domination in the factory. The fragmented and atomized relationships which they experienced there did not facilitate collective action in opposition to managerial authority. Militancy researchers have identified artisans and skilled craft workers as the active agents of the militant struggles of the late nineteenth century. These artisans and skilled craft workers were either beyond managements' sphere of domination and control, or held resources within it that granted them autonomy and power.[4]

While the focus of such research is on typically late-nineteenth century struggles, recent evidence suggests that the militants of the 1930s and 1940s also held positions that differed markedly from the low-skilled workers that were numerically dominant in the mass-production industries. Research conducted by Lichtenstein and others suggest that those initiating militant activities during the 1930s and 1940s worked on nonassemblyline jobs, controlled key aspects of their work organization, and held higher status positions than did other workers on the lines.[5]

These findings challenge the hegemony model at its core, for its proponents have depicted the rise of factory militancy as a mass movement initiated by deskilled and formerly atomized mass-production workers.[6] If future research confirms considerable occupational variation in factory-level militancy—especially if it shows that the militancy was led by a minority of specific occupational groups—the hegemony model will have to be revised drastically. It is not likely that managements tamed these militants' demands with general-level concessions affecting all workers, nor with concessions affecting primarily the majority of low-skilled assemblers. It is more likely that managements recognized the identity of those most active in shutting down their product lines and dealt with them in specific ways. Managements' responses to the control crises took the form of multiple strategies. Most were targeted to occupationally specific shop-floor environments.

The notion of monopoly market control that is central to the model of monopoly capitalist hegemony has also become untenable in light of the chronic economic crises since 1973. With the demise of the myth of market control, many have become disillusioned with the viability of the model's "monopoly-capitalism" thesis in explaining earlier postwar developments.[7] If this thesis explains market developments during the 1950s and 1960s, how did monopoly firms lose their grips on their markets so quickly and so pervasively by the 1980s? The monopoly-capitalism thesis does not answer this question adequately. Its conceptualization of the structures guiding postwar market development lacks the specificity required for pinpointing fault lines in the system and for developing a cogent understanding of the monopoly market structure's rather sudden and pervasive breakdown.

Responses

Industrial analysts have responded to the second challenge in numerous ways. Some have located the source of the breakdown in changes in the structure of the global market. They specify a global economy shattered by the destruction of World War II and a U.S. industrial base left untouched by that destruction as the twin foundations for the effective emergence and functioning of postwar monopoly capitalist structures in the United States. This historical situation gave U.S. industries a strategic advantage over others in the world market. It also insulated their domestic markets from international competition, thereby supporting weak forms of monopolistic market control. This situation changed dramatically, however, as Europe and Asia rebuilt their industrial infrastructures and reentered the global economy.[8]

This account contains considerable insight that must be incorporated into an explanation of industrial developments in the United States. Yet, its focus turns us away from internal dynamics and contradictions within the regulatory system that might also have played a role in its breakdown. It allows us to leave our glossing conceptualizations of monopoly-capitalist regulation intact and diverts our energies from the critical task of building more fine-grained conceptual distinctions that would enable us to pinpoint with precision when this structure functioned and why, as well as when it broke down and why.

A second and related response attempts to incorporate the hegemony model's insights into ambitious stage theories of industrial development. These delimit the hegemony model's generalizability to the period spanning World War II to the 1970s and define the current crises as marking a new stage of advanced capitalist industrialization driven by distinct—but, as of yet, vaguely specified—developmental dynamics.[9]

The stage models view market-regulating structures as developing along cyclical trajectories. About every forty years or so, a given structure is prone to breakdowns, generating severe market instability and shop-floor crises in the process. Then a new structure emerges, resolves the accumulation crises generated by the breakdown of the old structure, stabilizes and grows. After about forty years, this structure exhausts its capacities and breaks down, generating a new one in its place.

Such stage models seem to work best when they embrace Marx's general model of capitalist development. Gordon, Edwards, and Reich, for example, use Marx's model effectively in explaining the regulatory transformation occurring in U.S. industries during the period spanning 1870 to the early twentieth century.[10] They document empirically the developments Marx's model predicts: declining rates of profit, increasing shop-floor control struggles, intensifying business cycles and prolonged depressions, and so on. The resolution to the accumulation crisis of the late nineteenth century was the one which Marx's model predicts as well: the shift from industrial organizations using traditional forms of work organization and maintaining profits through increasing the length of the working day, to those securing profits with productivity increases gained from the labor-process innovations associated with mass production.

In the model which Gordon, Edwards, and Reich borrow from Marx, the dynamics driving this structural transformation are clear, as are the features of the new system linked to the crisis' resolution. In other words, price competition forced the breakdown, as it increasingly threatened the very survival of capitalists dependent upon the old form of work organization for their surplus. Increasingly fierce competition in the product market selected out those capitalists who could sell their products at lower prices. As capitalists drove their workforces to the natural limits of the working day, this cutthroat competitive environment favored those who could produce greater value with less input and thereby profit on lowered prices. The survivors of the crisis period were driven to adopt the organizational form in the factory—the mass-production system—that facilitated constantly increasing productivity. This new factory organization, coupled with newly emerging forms of market control—such as mergers, and horizontally and vertically integrated firms—enabled capitalists to prosper and expand until the next crisis wave was ushered in by the 1929 stock market crash and the Depression which followed it.

The new stage theories run into trouble, however, when they are forced to leave Marx's classic model of competitive capitalism. The drive to increase productivity in order to survive in a market with tendencies driving down the overall rate of profit is not necessarily the primary drive of monopoly capitalism. Instead, profits are stabilized by administered prices, markets are rigged, and production is planned and scheduled so as to assure stability. What are the dynamics propelling this system to collapse? What is it about monopoly dynamics that force this collapse every forty years? What conjuncture of social forces selects a new regulatory system and enables it to function effectively?

Marx's model could predict such outcomes within the parameters of systems driven by competitive capitalist dynamics. The stage theories of the 1980s have not adequately specified the dynamics propelling monopoly capitalism through its successive changes. This leads to an ad hoc form of theorizing that leaves much to be desired. We must develop models of the market/shop-floor relationship with far greater specificity than those currently in vogue.

The Weberian Response

For the most part, American industrial scholars have ignored Max Weber's classic attempt to steer a path between the extremes of radical historicism and sweeping but facile deductive generalization. On the one hand, Weber accepts radical historicism's critique of positivist sociology and rejects the view that human relations are predictably determined by external developments. Historical outcomes are viewed in Weber's sociology as contingent responses to conjunctural forces. They occur in a realm of multiple possibilities and display a complexity and uniqueness that can only be glossed in deterministic models. In Weber's view, actors are also the subjects authoring these outcomes, and his sociology attempts to account for the influence of meaning and motive upon them as well.

Yet, Weber desires to achieve more than descriptive accounts of important historical outcomes. Weber is attracted to the model of a predictive science and attempts to achieve the precision and rigor championed by its adherents. He defines a role for logical deduction, prediction, and functional analysis in his historical sociology.

To reconcile these seemingly contradictory positions, Weber radically separates the theoretical from the historical realm. In the realm of theory—the ideal typical realm—Weber makes simplifying assumptions that enable deductive logic to reign supreme as a determining force. In this realm, actors rationally pursue courses of action consistent with values specified in a singular meaning frame. Structures emerge logically in response to the willful pursuit of such rational action. These assumptions enable Weberian scholars to: (1) deduce and predict courses of action which actors will take under a variety of objective circumstances confronting them; (2) trace the consequences of rational action in these varying circumstances for the emergence and functioning of structures; and (3) establish functional linkages between the structures emerging from stable commitments to courses of rational action. In this ideal typic realm, the power of logical deduction can operate effectively and predict outcomes with precision.

However, this theoretical realm is only imaginary. Weber does not assume that the logic specified in his ideal types drives historical development. Rather, deductive theoretical constructions must be humbled before the march of history. They do not predict it, nor are they to be used as a substitute for detailed, painstaking historical description and analysis. In Weber's historical sociology, ideal types are used primarily for interpretation. When well-constructed, they point to the course of development that would have unfolded had actors pursued rationally the singular ends specified in an ideal-type definition of the situation. Such ideal types are used as reference guides for assessing the extent to which development followed their logic and for specifying other forces at play in determining unanticipated outcomes.

The Major Argument and Chapter Outline

This book addresses the central questions of the popular hegemony model in reference to a single case of industrial development—that followed by the U.S. automobile industry in post-World War II years. With Weberian ideal types, I examine how the U.S. auto industry arrested both the labor militancy and market instability plaguing its development prior to World War II. In doing so, this book addresses the challenges to the hegemony model already discussed. To better fit developments in auto manufacturing, the hegemony model's basic conceptual imagery is reconstructed as a set of interconnected ideal types. The decline of shop-floor militancy is linked to the development of distinctive workplace-level managerial practices which were, themselves, made possible by the institution of a market-regulating structure arresting interfirm price competition.

How did the automobile manufacturers tame the shop-floor militancy that was disrupting production schedules throughout the 1940s and 1950s? This study develops a response to this question that challenges popular theories. It shows that specific occupational groups initiated most of the labor militancy of the late 1940s and 1950s, and that the everyday work experiences of these groups differed considerably from those working on machine-paced assembly lines. This book argues that management eventually decoupled these occupational groups from those without militant structural capacities and responded to them in different ways. Dual authority structures emerged in the industry after 1958 as a result of this decoupling.

The authority system responsible for the decline of shop-floor militancy among the militant occupational groups was quite different than the drive system legitimating management's prerogative to set and change production expectations at will—the system thought to characterize industrial relations in auto manufacturing. This authority system legitimated preset production quotas as the standard setting managerial expectations regarding production output. Rather than management's arbitrary command, the output quota—or production standard—became the accepted definition of a fair day's work. After a period of struggle and unrest, auto managements came to respect the legitimacy of production quotas established through custom and precedent, and chose not to drive workers on vital operations for more production than these quotas specified.

Once the output quota became legitimated—and contractual provisions were instituted to protect it—workers consented to deliver predictable production outputs. They developed shopfloor game cultures similar to those which Burawoy described in *Manufacturing Consent.*[11] These cultures rewarded workers for using their initiative and cunning in beating production quotas and "earning time" on the job. Once management accepted this quota-based authority system in key auto plants, workers who were inclined to initiate unauthorized work stoppages in the past, now chose not to do so.

While functioning effectively to reduce militant workers' propensities to initiate wildcat strikes, this quota-based authority system affected only a minority of the industry's workforce. Those workers bucking production on the machine-paced lines were not protected from management's tendency to drive them with the dreaded speedup.

This book specifies the market structure enabling this limited form of shop-floor stabilization to emerge and persist after 1958. This structure was partially successful in enabling competing auto firms to avoid destructive price competition and to accept a labor process system on vital operations that produced stable and predictable production outputs, rather than one that drove workers constantly for higher levels of productivity. The success of this market-stabilizing structure was limited, however. The structure's failures to stabilize market relations in key market segments—and its failure to protect profit margins—blocked the spread of the quota-based authority system throughout the industry. In response to market pressures, auto managements continued to drive workers for more production in those plants, such as final assembly where workers' capacities for resistance were limited.

There are three parts to this book. Parts I and II develop and defend a theoretical framework for understanding the market/workplace relationship of interest. Part III uses this framework to interpret developments in the industry from 1946 to 1973.

Part I consists of two chapters. Chapter 1 sketches features of a market-regulating structure that I label *Sloanist* because it embodies the marketing policies that General Motors pursued in the 1920s under the leadership of Alfred P. Sloan. Sloanism involves a set of marketing strategies that steer firms away from head-on price competition with one another. When pursuing this set of strategies, firms do not act as profit maximizers in the classic sense. Rather, they attempt to maintain high rates of return on investment by balkanizing the market ,and by avoiding overcrowding and price competition. When this set of strategies becomes hegemonic in a given product market—when the major competitors there embrace it as their action-orienting definition of the situation—a structure emerges that regulates competitive relations. Chapter 1 also discusses developments that conditioned the auto firms to embrace Sloanism by the end of World War II.

Chapter 2 defines the essential characteristics of the labor-relations structure that is functionally compatible with Sloanist market regulation. It defines the demands that Sloanist market strategies made on the labor process, and shows how the labor-relations structure that developed during the 1940s was intentionally designed to meet these demands. On paper, this structure rationalized industrial conflict so that the labor process would deliver calculable results. This structure committed workers and their labor representatives to procedural rules that signaled in advance when work stoppages would occur. This structure, thus, granted management time for strategically planned responses to labor demands and the option of resolving disputes peacefully on the basis of rational cost-benefit analysis. On paper, this structure gave management the leverage for strategic planning that it had lost during the turbulent 1930s and 1940s. The chapter then traces the historical conditions that led managements, union leaders, and rank-and-file workers to accept this formal structure by the onset of the postwar period.

After spelling out these functional linkages, chapter 2 concludes with a presentation of descriptive data on wildcat strikes which challenges their validity. The data show that, within a formal structure outlawing unauthorized strike action, auto workers wildcatted well into the late 1950s with a frequency that was threatening to management. These data suggest that the Sloanist labor-relations structure failed to manufacture consent to its prescriptions. These data force a shift in the analysis from the formal labor relations structure to the shop floor.

Part II lays the theoretical groundwork for this conceptual shift. In chapter 3, the conditions enabling workers to act collectively on the shop floor in militant opposition to management are defined and illustrated. Following Lichtenstein and Sayles,[12] the source of such militancy is located in the immediate organization of work tasks on particular operations in the factory. Work groups with militant capacities worked in labor processes that (1) granted them control over work outcomes and pacing, and (2) forced them to coordinate their actions with one another on a moment-by-moment basis to accomplish valued work ends. These conditions generated in-group solidarity and commitment to group goals that were independent of those which managements defined. Such conditions held for only a minority of the blue-collar labor force in auto manufacturing. These militancy-generating labor processes are contrasted in descriptive detail with the atomizing final assembly line—the more typical work organization in auto manufacturing.

Chapter 4 tests the effects of this type of solidarity-generating labor process on the likelihood of workers initiating wildcat activity. The results of logistic regression analyses strongly support the theory. Documenting the different effects of solidary, atomizing, and other labor processes on wildcat-strike activity sets the stage for a historical account of the decline of worker militancy which focuses, not on the evolution of general work structures setting employment conditions for all, but on those that affected the particular shop-floor experiences of the militants.

Chapter 5 links the theoretical distinctions made in chapter 3 to those made in chapter 1. The chapter defines two distinct types of shop-floor authority which are legitimated by very different definitions of a fair day's work. The first is compatible with both the interests of managements operating in Sloanist-regulated market environments and the solidary work groups defined in chapter 3. This authority system is labeled *quota-based* because a predetermined production standard or quota established through custom and past practice is recognized by both managers and workers as the standard for assessing the legitimacy of current work expectations. This authority system is contrasted with a drive system granting management the prerogative to command compliance to any work-related demand that does not injure or harm the health of the worker.

The chapter then links these very different types of authority to market developments. Quota-based authority is hypothesized as being functionally compatible with Sloanist-regulated markets. The drive system is hypothesized as being largely determined by competitive product market conditions. The chapter concludes with the development of two sets of conjunctures linking market conditions, authority systems, and levels of shop-floor militancy. The first is theorized to produce high levels of militancy. It consists of fiercely competitive markets; management's insistence upon its managerial prerogative to set and change production standards at will; and the centralization of decision-making in the hands of a finance-oriented managerial faction far removed from the shop floor. The second is theorized to produce stable production outcomes and low levels of militancy. It consists of Sloanist-regulated markets; the legitimation of a quota-based definition of a fair day's work; and a decentralized managerial structure allowing shop management to set and adjust production standards in accordance with this definition.

Part III traces the actual postwar history of the relationship between market and shop-floor developments in auto manufacturing, using the conjunctural types specified in chapter 5 as interpretive reference points. Chapters 6 and 7 trace developments through 1946–1952 and 1953–1958 respectively. They present evidence suggesting that the conjunctural theory does reasonably well in predicting shop-floor stability and militancy and in explaining the postwar emergence and breakdown of the hegemonic structure.

Chapter 6 begins by documenting the diversity existing in the industry at the onset of the postwar period. Through rich archival data drawn primarily from United Automobile Worker union sources, the authority structures governing relations in each auto firm are defined and illustrated. These systems are linked to market conditions and then correlated with wildcat frequencies. Those firms and divisions experiencing high levels of wildcat activity were those that failed to embrace quota-based authority. Those with quota-based authority in Sloanist-regulated market segments experienced lower levels of wildcat activity. The chapter also shows that the industry, as a whole, was moving toward the legitimation of quota-based authority by the end of the Korean War, when the market stabilized as the result of government intervention. The political and economic conditions supporting this limited form of regulation are examined in the conclusion to chapter 6. A key support of the structure was the federal government's commitment to industrial pluralism and to using antitrust laws as a means of preventing destructive price competition.[13]

Chapter 7—again drawing primarily from archival sources—develops a narrative account of the breakdown of Sloanist regulation as fiercely competitive conditions returned to the industry during the Eisenhower years. The chapter documents increased market instability and both managerial and worker's responses to the breakdown of Sloanist regulation. Those managements most affected by the new market conditions abandoned their commitment to quota-based authority and embraced the drive system. They attempted to increase production standards in their plants in line with those of the most efficient in the industry. Solidary workers—with experience in the quota-based authority systems that managements legitimated in the past—defined these assaults on time-honored production standards as illegitimate and reacted militantly to them. The plant-level conflicts spurred by these competing ideological frames are illustrated and documented. They are contrasted with the labor militancy initiated in the 1930s, and their impact on development is assessed. The chapter concludes with evidence suggesting that this militancy was spreading industry-wide.

How was this new wave of crisis and conflict resolved? Chapters 8 and 9 address this. Chapter 8 presents empirical evidence of post-1958 market developments suggesting that the industry's firms reembraced their commitments to Sloanist marketing strategies, and that this led to limited market stabilization. A major factor in reestablishing Sloanist regulation was the renewed pressure put on GM by the Antitrust Division of the Justice Department. This pressure forced GM to brake its expansionary designs. Rather than continue a policy of market expansion, it targeted the high-margin segments of the market and left the lower-margin segments for its competition. After experiencing hardship during the intensely competitive 1950s, GM's weaker competitors were willing to accept this. They had little choice but to do so.

However, the picture is complicated. The chapter shows that, while the auto firms did embrace Sloanist market prescriptions from 1959–1973, the extent to which they lessened shop-floor pressure was limited. For reasons specified in the chapter, profit margins were squeezed and real pressure for cost reduction persisted. Because of this, Sloanist market regulation did not trigger a return to quota-based authority industry-wide.

Chapter 9 argues that, after a failed experiment with deskilling and atomizing technologies, auto managements won labor peace by decoupling those occupational groups with capacities for militant collective action from those without such capacities, and by responding to each in different ways. The chapter suggests that, as a result, dual labor process trajectories developed: (1) a hegemonic trajectory within which a quota-based authority system reemerged to govern production practices and relationships; and (2) a despotic trajectory involving increased managerial dominance and speedups. The solidary work groups holding capacities for militant collective action in the body supplier plants—a minority of auto workers—experienced the hegemonic trajectory. Those atomized and structurally powerless in the final-assembly and automated plants experienced despotism. The final chapter summarizes the historical account and assesses its importance for understanding industrial development.

Method

The evidence used, both in constructing ideal types and in tracing this history, is primarily archival. It consists of data from United Automobile Workers records collected from the Archives of Labor and Urban Affairs at Wayne State University; news periodicals published by key UAW locals; biographical and autobiographical accounts of industry leaders; articles published in engineering journals—a good many of which were written by auto managers and engineers; newspaper and business periodicals; and secondary sources. In describing specific labor processes, technologies, and shop-floor authority systems, the work draws heavily from oral history and key informant interviews of auto workers. I interviewed ten workers from an auto stamping plant, who, for confidentiality reasons, must remain anonymous.

Two statistical data sets were constructed: the first on local auto strikes occurring from 1946 through 1973 from *Wall Street Journal* and *New York Times* reports; the second on divisional market performances from *Automotive Industries* and *Ward's Automotive Yearbook.*

This study is interpretive. Throughout, the ideal type constructs presented in Part I and II of the book are used to develop what I believe are reasonable and persuasive interpretations of the actual market and shop-floor developments of interest. I have triangulated the available data and have constructed accounts that do not appear to be contradicted by it. However, we cannot rule out the plausibility of alternative interpretations to the ones developed throughout, nor can I claim that my interpretations will not require revision with the mining of new evidence. In light of these limitations, my approach is to be as honest as possible. The evidence used throughout is cited extensively. I have attempted to demarcate the interpretive and the more speculative accounts from the factual data upon which they are derived.

Frankly, none of these scientific limitations bother me. For the most part, they are part and parcel of doing historical research. My aim is not to close the discourse on auto-industry development, but to open it. I create new theoretical constructions that will sharpen our understanding of one important case—the work challenges existing interpretations and tries to push the discourse on advanced capitalist industrialization to a richer level.

If this study inspires further analysis, refutation, and heated debate, so much the better. From my point of view, this is the best way to advance the field of industrial development.

Part I—
Sloanism as a System of Market and Shop-Floor Regulation

CHAPTER 1

Sloanist Market Regulation

The institution of monopoly capitalism has been linked to the U.S. economy's postwar recovery. This concept denotes a transition from a competitive and unregulated market environment to one that rationally regulates price competition among firms. "Monopoly capitalism" is the catchword denoting this rationally regulated environment. Its components are the Keynesian welfare/warfare state, which buffers—often half-heartedly—the effects of the business cycle with countercyclical fiscal policies,[1] and the modern firm, which regulates market competition through both vertical and horizontal integration and through collaborative price-fixing and market-sharing schemes.[2] Just how these structures work to buffer competitive dynamics, however, remains vague in most formulations. I sharpen this conceptual imagery here so as to better illuminate auto industry developments in the United States.

Historical Factors Selecting the Form of Market Regulation

A transition from a competitive and unregulated market environment to a rationally regulated one involves a shift in firm managers' action orientations. Within an unregulated market environment, managers act instrumentally and rationally, calculating their courses of action so as to achieve their desired ends, and choosing appropriate means for accomplishing these ends. Such actors relate to others in their action fields as objects to be manipulated in pursuit of these ends. They do not take into account the interests of these others when choosing their courses of action.

This rational, self-oriented pursuit of immediate interests creates an environment that threatens the long-term interests of all involved. As Marx and others have pointed out, this orientation leads to overproduction crises and depressions, once firms invest heavily in capital intensive production processes. During such crises, firms quickly stockpile inventories and face the prospects of tremendous loss. In turn, they slash prices, cut wages and increase worker exploitation to reduce production costs. Such actions, while rationally consistent with the firms' immediate interests, tend to damage their long-term prospects. Over the long haul, they reduce aggregate demand, drive the rate of profit down, and discourage investment.

Action orientations become more civic within a rationally regulated market environment. As in the unregulated environment, company managers calculate their courses of action rationally so as to achieve desired ends consistent with their interests. Unlike in the unregulated environment, however, they take the interest of competitors into account when doing so. They aim to pursue courses of action that will benefit their immediate self-interests without threatening competitors' opportunities. They steer toward courses of action that are calculated to reduce the threat of losses and reduced profits for the industry as a whole.

Firms may commit to courses of action consistent with this more civic orientation in a number of ways. This can occur, for example, when a firm's autonomous decision-making prerogatives are taken over by an external planning agent. In this case, the external agent—a state, a cartel, or a monopoly firm—regulates market competition by prescribing courses of action for subordinates to follow. Coercion—or its threat—is at the root of a company's compliance with these prescriptions.

Although the U.S. auto industry has experimented with it, this type of prescriptive regulation has proven to be incompatible with the political traditions legitimating the exercise of power in American society. Richard Hofstadter describes these traditions as "the sanctity of private property, the right of the individual to dispose of and invest it, the value of opportunity, and the natural evolution of self-interest and self-assertion."[3] In the auto industry, the opponents of external regulation have mobilized these traditions to delegitimate it.

The industry has experimented with at least two prescriptive regulatory structures in its history. The first was a trade association that acted as a cartel to control the actions of its members. It regulated entry, prescribed production quotas, and set standard prices. The earliest of these—and perhaps the only one to exert influence—was the Association of Licensed Automobile Manufacturers which acquired the rights to the Selden patent, a patent awarded in 1879 on an early motorized vehicle design. ALAM attempted to control the industry by extending the Selden patent's jurisdiction to all firms manufacturing motorized vehicles.[4] The second type of prescriptive regulation involved the state's active intervention in prescribing and planning firms' courses of action. Moves toward this regulatory form were made during the early 1930s under Roosevelt's National Recovery Administration, again in 1946 when the Office of Price Administration attempted to enforce price ceilings on auto sales, and once again during the Korean War when Truman's National Production Authority (and later his Office of Price Stabilization) controlled auto production with quotas and price schedules. The NRA represented the most comprehensive of these attempts. Under the NRA, the automobile firms were required to participate in a trade association holding the authority to regulate production, pricing, wages, and collective bargaining.[5]

External regulation in auto manufacturing failed miserably. The early trade associations proved incapable of forcing independent manufacturers to comply with their regulations. Renegade manufacturers mobilized support against these regulatory associations from other manufacturers and from the public at large.[6] Even the federal government had difficulties in forcing manufacturers' compliance. The NRA failed. The only agreement reached in the auto industry was to a minimum wage below what most firms were paying at the time.[7] Ford adamantly refused to participate in even this limited form of cooperation, and the federal government proved to be incapable of forcing Ford's compliance.[8] The OPA's 1946 attempt to control pricing was abandoned late in the year because of the agency's inability to force firms to comply. The production and price controls put into effect during the Korean War were also quickly abandoned for similar reasons.

There were a number of reasons for these failures. One was simply that the industry was too large and unstable in its early years for an external agent to control production schedules, pricing, wages, and other factors. Another was timing. Auto firms began to consolidate after the antitrust movement had gained political strength and influence. Another reason was that intransigent firms successfully mobilized popular support whenever they took a stand against external regulation. This ability may be explained by the hold of distinctive political traditions on the American public, such as the sanctity of private property, the freedom to use one's property as one sees fit, the freedom to take advantage of opportunities, and the freedom to pursue self-interested goals without external interference. These traditions may have functioned to limit the range of developmental courses open to the industry, thus blocking the path to external and prescriptive regulation.

Hegemonic Market Regulation and Its Sloanist Form

Firms may acquire the civic orientation necessary for rational market regulation in another way. Their managers may internalize such an orientation and willfully pursue courses of action that are consistent with it. This may take place when firm managers commit themselves to a strategy for manufacturing and marketing their products that is capable of coordinating the pursuit of their individual interests to the industry's collective interest. Following Gramsci,[9] such strategies are labeled *hegemonic.* Firm managers commit to such strategies because they believe that their interests will be better served by them than by other available alternatives.

When a hegemonic strategy is adopted by all of the major manufacturers competing within a given market, a market-regulating structure emerges. The coordinating mechanism of the structure is the hegemonic strategy or ideology. Such a hegemonic structure does not reproduce itself by relying on the coercive power of an external agent, nor does it encroach upon the decision-making autonomy of its firms. Rather, the hegemonic structure generates active consent from its constituent firms. Unlike the types of prescriptive structures already discussed, the functioning of such a structure is compatible with the values of American political culture.

Prior to World War II, two distinct hegemonic ideologies competed for dominance over the auto industry. Both Henry Ford, after 1908, and Alfred P. Sloan, after 1921, propagated distinct strategies for producing and marketing automobiles that took on the qualities of hegemonic programs.[10] Both Ford and Sloan attempted to persuade their competitors to adopt their respective business strategies as their own, arguing that their individual interests—and the interests of the industry as a whole—would best be served by doing so. Both Ford and Sloan believed that their respective strategies offered the industry an escape route from the destructive consequences of unregulated market competition. Ford's strategy—involving mass-production of a single product line, volume expansion through price cutting, constant productivity enhancing innovation, and high wage policies to stimulate demand—was discredited and abandoned by the end of World War II. Sloan's strategy triumphed and structured subsequent industrial developments with varying degrees of success.

At this point, I will define as an *ideal type* the essential features of Sloan's strategy which are its business goals, definition of the market situation, and defining characteristics. I will also examine how commitments to this strategy at the company level produces and reproduces a market-regulating industrial structure, specifying both the developments necessary for this structure to emerge and reproduce itself, as well as those tending to break it down.

The ideal type developed here is a heuristic concept for use in explaining complex historical development. The extent to which actual cases conform to its characteristics is an empirical question. The ideal type serves as a reference category in subsequent chapters for discerning when a Sloanist regulatory structure was in place, the extent to which it was in place, when it broke down, and what difference it made to labor process development.

The Sloanist Business Strategy

The term "Sloanism" designates the general business strategy which Alfred P. Sloan developed in the 1920s as GM's president. Sloanism reflects the concerns and cautions of a firm that experienced near disaster during economic crises in its formative years. It is a firm-level strategy for buffering the effects of the business cycle on profit margins, and it aims, above all else, to protect the investments of its capital investors. It aims to earn steady profit rates from such investments.

Sloanism begins with three sets of assumptions about the nature of the auto market. First, Sloanism anticipates the development of a society composed of a variety of differentiated market classes. Variations in income, tastes, and needs define these classes. These anticipated variations lead Sloanists to envision several markets for basic sources of transportation. Second, Sloanism anticipates an open and fluid social structure and a rising level of income.[11] These conditions create a market demand for products that reflect the rising aspirations and pretensions of a society "on the make." They enable a large number of buyers to afford and demand increased luxury, comfort and performance, even when these items significantly increase prices. Third—and given this definition of the market—Sloanism perceives the potential demand for any given auto line as limited and unstable. It sees little potential for stabilizing this demand over an extended period. The changes in tastes and desires afforded by a rising standard of living and upward mobility fuel this instability.

Given Sloanism's definition of the market situation, and its basic interest in assuring high rates of return on investment capital, the following strategies are quite rational. When auto firms adopt them, we consider them as being Sloanist.

First, acting in ways that maintain the price structures required to assure high rates of return on their investments, Sloanists avoid head-on price competition with their competitors. They segment the market into distinct classes that correspond to the differentiated market classes existing in society. They then selectively enter those segments that are not overcrowded, targeting only portions of those which they calculate to be safe.[12] They also compete in new markets—not with competitive pricing, but with styling and product innovations—attempting to create untapped niches from existing market segments. This minimizes the risk of price competition driving down their profit margins.

Second, Sloanists blanket the market, targeting a variety of market classes with multiple product lines. This buffers against the potential for market fluctuation to harm investment returns, protecting the firm from a product failure in a single segment—something perceived of as being likely within the Sloanist definition of the market situation. This strategy detaches the fate of the firm from the fate of any particular product line.

Third, Sloanists invest their creative energies in improving the autos they market. They assure demand for their products by changing them frequently and by improving their styling and surface appearances. This is rational behavior, given the definition of the market situation which such firms embrace.

Fourth, Sloanists are not profit maximizers. They do not continually invest in business expansion up to the point where they can only break even on an additional increment of investment. Rather, Sloanists desire to earn high rates of return on these investments. They will expand their businesses only if that expansion will not threaten these rates.[13] They will not sacrifice profit rates for expansion, even when expansion promises them higher aggregate profits.

Fifth, Sloanists are instrumentally rational within the firm. They regard all operations solely as a means of earning steady return rates on capital. Sloanists do not make unconditional commitments to maintaining wage and employment levels, to production schedules, or even to staying in the market. They are free to deploy, reorganize, and reinvest resources in ways that optimize return rates, regardless of the consequences for those whom they employ.

The Sloanist Managerial Organization

Sloanists organize investment decision making in the following manner. Before investment and production commitments, they calculate (1) anticipated costs, (2) the extent of the potential market for the proposed product at various price levels, and (3) the price and volume that will enable them to earn the desired return rates. If these calculations suggest that the market for the proposed product will sustain sales at the volume and price levels required to meet the desired rate of return, Sloanists invest in it. If not, they look for more favorable opportunities elsewhere.[14]

Sloanists organize their business practices so that they buffer the effects of risk upon their operations. They reduce the risk of fixed-cost investments by making investment decisions contingent upon the forecasting of long-term market conditions, and by employing a statistical estimate in their pricing calculations referred to as "standard volume." Standard volume estimates the proportion of the firm's production capacity that it will realize during the period in which its investments amortize. Sloanists buffer the risks of making inaccurate long-term forecasts by using very conservative estimates of standard volume. GM's estimate of standard volume in the early postwar period, for example, presumed no more than a 64 percent long-term utilization of production capacity.[15] This was the estimate employed to determine the price levels required to make the 20 percent return rate which GM targeted.[16]

In contrast to fixed-cost investment calculations, the time frame involved in variable-cost calculations is short. Auto firms build huge inventories in very short order, and production schedules geared to inaccurate forecasts can cause incredible losses.[17] Realizing that long-term market forecasts are at best speculative, Sloanists do not set their actual production schedules to such forecasts. Instead, they set production schedules to short-term forecasts that account for immediate production and market conditions.[18] This enables the general office to spot decreases in demand and to halt quickly the stockpiling of inventory.[19] In sum, Sloanists control fixed-cost and variable-cost risks by making investment decisions contingent upon the forecasting of long-term and short-term market demand, through buffering their operations from miscalculated forecasts with conservative standard volume estimates, and through developing information feedback loops that detect and correct miscalculations in such forecasts.

The Sloanist managerial organization involves a division of labor between two sets of critical managerial functions: (1) coordination, forecasting and monitoring; and (2) the making and selling of products.[20] The general office performs the first set of functions far removed from the point of production and sales. It determines and promulgates general policy, provides the forecasts used to guide the firm's operation and investment decisions, and monitors statistically the performance of its invested capital by calculating the rate of return which each unit earns.[21]

Within the statistical controls set by the general office, operations managements in Sloanist divisions hold far-reaching discretion and autonomy in accomplishing their objectives—the actual production and marketing of automobile lines. Aside from general policies and guidelines, the general office does not prescribe divisional managements' day-to-day practices or courses of action. It merely watches both market and inventory statistics closely for signs of depressed sales and operations' managements' rate-of-return-on-investment statistics. If these statistics indicate favorable markets and desired investment returns, the general office allows divisional managements to continue producing results with minimal interference. If these statistics indicate market slowdowns, it brakes production. If they indicate undesirable returns, it makes personnel changes.

The Sloanist managerial structure, then, is best thought of as hegemonic. It wins the active commitment of a variety of diversely skilled management personnel with potentially divergent interests and aims to a common end—a high rate of return on the firm's capital investments. The Sloanist structure does this by clearly defining and rewarding the types of goal-oriented performances which it requires, by generating a consensus on the objective indicators used to monitor and reward managerial performance, and by granting those with operational skills a wide-ranging discretion and autonomy in pursuing the desired ends.

This section has defined the business strategy and structure Alfred P. Sloan originally put into practice at GM in the 1920s as an ideal type. The extent to which a given firm conforms to it is the extent to which it will be considered as being Sloanist.

From Firm-Level Strategy to Systemic Regulation

We move now to a discussion of Sloanism as a mechanism for regulating interfirm competition. What happens to an industry when its dominant firms adopt Sloanism as their action-orienting definition of the market situation?

To illustrate this, consider the actions of four company managements in two distinct sets of market conditions. Two of the managements are Fordist, two Sloanist. One Fordist and one Sloanist management are dominant producers with superior production capacities. One Fordist and one Sloanist management are weaker competitors. The distinctive market conditions confronting the four firms are, on the one hand, market expansion and, on the other, market saturation and/or contraction. Each firm's management acts rationally in this illustration and in accordance with its respective definition of the market situation.

The Fordist firms' managements act the same way under both market conditions. They maintain commitment to the single product line for which they have invested considerably in fixed-cost plant and technology. Under periods of market expansion, both Fordist managements respond by increasing their production capacities on their particular product lines. They reinvest profits in these lines and expand accordingly. This growth is fueled by reduced prices for their automobiles. Such price decreases are made possible by cuts in production costs attained through increasing economies of scale and process innovations.

Under periods of saturation and/or contraction, Fordists firms continue to produce at the production schedules for which they have invested, dropping prices to whatever level it takes to clear inventories. Under these conditions, Fordist firms attempt to profit through cutting production costs to the level that enables them to employ the resources which they have committed to production. As production proficiency increases under the new conditions, profit margins are expected to improve gradually.[22] While wrenching in its consequence, this response is rational, given the Fordist assumption of a product-specific market.

In contrast, each Sloanist firm acts differently in each market situation. Under a condition of expansion, the dominant Sloanist firm's management attempts to predict, not only the degree of expansion, but the actions of its competitors. The dominant Sloanist management then positions its products in those segments of the market which are predicted to earn the highest return on investment. To reap the anticipated returns, the dominant Sloanist firm refrains from over-investment or from provoking competitors to take action that will spoil its markets. It picks the best market segments for itself, but leaves ample market opportunities for weaker competitors. This is rational behavior, given the Sloanist definition of the market situation already discussed. The goal of the dominant Sloanist firm's management is not to control the market, but to choose only those portions of it that will return high profits.

The weaker Sloanist competitor will also attempt to maintain high investment returns in this situation. However, its management watches the dominant producer closely and targets those segments which it leaves alone. Often, the weaker Sloanist firm will target a market segment untapped by the existing producers, or it will attempt to split off buyers from two adjacent segments with a novel or innovative product. This enables the weaker firm to avoid head-on price competition with the larger, stronger competitors and still earn an acceptable rate of return on investment. When the new market segment pays off handsomely—and the dominant producers enter in response—the weaker Sloanist firm will reposition its product lines in new, untapped segments. The weaker Sloanist management will also reinnovate in order to protect its earning rates.

Managements of both Sloanist firms act similarly under conditions of market saturation or contraction. When an existing market segment becomes saturated, rather than maintain their positions within the segment with price-cutting strategies, both dominant and weaker Sloanist firms respond by searching for new markets and classes of buyers. This avoids price competition and the lower return rates that inevitably follow.

When the total market declines or collapses, both dominant and weak Sloanist firms will act to protect their investments as well. If they are effective at forecasting future demand levels, they will retreat from the market in orderly fashion as it declines. They cancel fixed-cost investments, and, if need be, shut down production schedules completely. This enables them to avoid ruthless price competition and protect the profit rates earned on fixed investments.

Thus, by respecting established market shares—and by rationally and selectively pursuing business in market segments that support high profit margins for themselves—Sloanists respect and take account of the actions and interests of their competitors in making fundamental business calculations and decisions. When all adopt the Sloanist strategy, such rational accounting assures the industry of access to stable markets that can provide the rates of return desired. The Sloanist orientation leads firms collectively to avoid overcrowding market segments, thereby discouraging the price competition and reduced profit margins that follow from such overcrowding. The rational self-interested pursuit of Sloanist ends protect competitor's interests as well. When the major firms in a given industry embrace Sloanism, market competition becomes self-regulated without external prescription. Sloanist firms' managers accept the balance of competitive forces existing in the market arena, and their Sloanist strategies tend to balkanize the product markets which they target.

Of course, this self-regulating tendency is not as simple to establish in actual practice as is presented here. There are four primary threats to Sloanism's regulatory efficacy at the industry level: (1) overproduction/underconsumption crisis tendencies, (2) unstable field conditions, (3) what I refer to as the "champion's dilemma," and (4) interest group dynamics within a firm's managerial structure.

The first threat relates to the inability of Sloanism to stimulate depressed demand during downswings of the business cycle. Sloanists respond to depression conditions in ways that protect their capital investments. If this is impossible, they reduce losses by halting production schedules and investments until favorable conditions return. While these strategies prevent ruthless competition from driving profit margins down, they do nothing to stimulate demand and the return of prosperity.

Structures outside the firms emerged in the United States after World War II to mitigate this threat and regulate its manifestations. Although playing a more central regulatory role in Western Europe than in the United States, these structures were the Keynesian state, and the collective bargaining system patterned after the historic UAW-GM contract of 1948. This collective-bargaining system indexed wage levels systematically to annual increases in productivity levels. Others have dealt with this type of regulatory development,[23] and this will not be of central focus to our concerns. It must suffice to note that such macrolevel economic regulation is a requisite foundation for the types of developments on which we focus.

The second threat is an unstable field of action that precludes Sloanist firms from calculating and predicting accurately the effects of market conditions on their anticipated investment returns. Such a field threatens Sloanists firms' abilities to avoid courses of action that provoke destructive price competition and slash profit margins. When the industry is relatively new and unstable, supports a large fluctuating number of competing firms, and has yet to establish effective barriers to entry, it becomes difficult to forecast resulting market conditions with any precision. Miscalculation becomes the inevitable norm, and such miscalculation engenders overcrowded market segments and subsequent price competition.

To serve as a hegemonic industry-regulating force, then, Sloanism requires an environment in which the actions of firms in the industry are predictable. This functional requirement leads me to hypothesize that: (1) the number of firms operating in the industry must be restricted in order for Sloanism to regulate it effectively, and (2) Sloanism will be most effective in those cases in which a single Sloanist firm dominates and can influence the actions of its competitors. This dominant firm—the hegemon—must lead in establishing prices and in delimiting its market segments and shares.[24] Fearing unbridled competition with this hegemon, the less powerful firms in a given industry react accordingly. They accept the hegemon's price structures and established market segments and pursue those it leaves for them. They do this because they believe that their interests will be best served by doing so. This type of relationship developed in auto in the postwar period.[25] I will trace its development and consequences in subsequent chapters.

However, this relationship structure is inherently unstable. What is to prevent the industry's hegemon—dominant in size, market penetration, and productive forces—from invading its competitors' market, especially when such a firm could maintain high profit margins and undercut its competitors' prices without much sacrifice? Pursuing such a course would be instrumentally rational, especially in situations in which the dominant firm's production capacities are underutilized. It would, however, undermine the efficacy of Sloanism as a regulatory structure—but nothing welds such a firm's commitment to this structure indefinitely. Indeed, as argued later in this chapter, power dynamics within a firm's managerial structure may function to undermine such commitments.

This is the third threat to Sloanism as a market-regulating mechanism—the threat of the champion's dilemma. The power to mitigate this threat—the power to force or persuade the hegemon to steer a civic course of action when its self-interests might steer it away from such a course—will most likely lie outside of the industrial arena and in the hands of external agents capable of forcing firms' compliance with their mandates.

The state is the likely candidate to play this role. It intervenes to prohibit dominant firms from pursuing courses of action threatening to the balance of competitive forces established by Sloanist industrial regulation. In the U.S. context, this involved the state prohibiting disruptive action by industrial hegemons without prescribing their day-to-day practices or their alternatives courses of action. Following Fligstein's general treatment of this issue,[26] I argue that this limited intervention and its continued threat was critical in shaping the auto industry's regulatory structure in the post-World-War-II period.

The fourth threat comes from within the managerial structure of powerful firms within a Sloanist-regulated industry itself with two distinct managerial groups, motivated by quite different sets of interests, competing for power and policy influence.[27] The first group is involved directly in producing and selling the firms' products, and it defines its interests as linked to the particular products which it produces and sells. It aims to extend these products' influence.

The second interest group—finance—is detached from the material side of capital accumulation. It identifies with capital in its abstracted, reified form—that is, its money form. It views the local, national, or even international arenas within which it transacts business as an open market for its investment capital. It aims to invest in those ventures that can promise the highest rates of return. This finance management's commitment to a particular business venture is instrumental and contingent upon the rate of return which it earns. It does not see its interests as being linked unconditionally to any material medium—or business—through which capital develops.

The interests, goals, and definitional frameworks of these groups stand in perpetual conflict. Expansion serves the interests and aims of the product-centered management, and this management tends to steer firms toward expansionary policies. Sloanism's primary aim, however, is not business expansion per se, but producing high rates of return on investment. It attempts to create and stabilize market conditions that will provide a favorable climate for such returns, even at the expense of restricting expansion. Because of this, finance management tends to embrace Sloanism and champion its viability. When confident in its own abilities to make and sell its products, product-centered management tends to view such a strategy as overly restrictive and limiting in its potential influence.

While this interest conflict may be subordinated at times to a hegemonic organizational form—such as that developed by GM in the 1920s—it always threatens to surface and can lead, as we shall subsequently see, to the subordination of the interests of one faction to the other. The effectiveness of the decentralized managerial structure as a hegemonic organization uniting the interests of both factions has proven to be much more limited than Sloan anticipated, as subsequent chapters in this book will clearly show.

The critical point is that, when product-centered management wins the interest group struggle and dominates firm-level policy decisions, it tends to pursue expansionist policies that undermine Sloanism's regulatory capacities. For Sloanism to function effectively at the industry level, it may be necessary for finance management to gain dominance and put tight reigns on the product-centered faction. The outcomes of such factional struggles will take center stage in subsequent chapters of this book.

In sum, the establishment and maintenance of a Sloanist market-regulating structure is quite problematic. The macroeconomic, industry-level, and firm-level conditions previously specified must all materialize and stay in place in order for such a structure to work effectively. At the macroeconomic level, this involves, at a minimum, the establishment and maintenance of sufficient aggregate-level demand, effective national-level regulatory policy, as well as developing and legitimating institutions that police firm-level behavior in a nonprescriptive but effective way. At the industry level, this involves, at a minimum, oligopolistic closure by a relatively small number of firms, effective barriers to entry, the stabilization of market segments and shares, and industry-wide firm-level commitments to Sloanism. At the firm level, this involves the development of effective techniques for forecasting demand, monitoring operations with regard to the rates of return which they earn, and controlling expansionary impulses. It also involves balancing power between managerial interest-group factions in a way that wins their active consent to policies that may not serve their fundamental interests.

Given these difficult contingencies, one might question the prospect of Sloanist regulation ever manifesting itself in actual practice. Indeed, such regulation has been problematic, often short-lived, and mostly ineffective. However, I contend that such a regulatory structure did emerge by the end of World War II as a viable alternative to unbridled, free-market competition, and that the industry practiced it thereafter—off and on with varying degrees of success—until the mid-1970s oil crises triggered restructuring. In the next section of this chapter, the historical developments that catapulted Sloanism onto the industrial stage as a viable program of hegemonic regulation are discussed. In subsequent chapters, I use the Sloanist ideal type as a reference category for assessing actual market-level developments.

The Prehistory of Hegemonic Market Regulation

The period spanning 1929–1945 was critical in shaping the structure that emerged to regulate postwar competition in the auto industry. The Great Depression hit the industry hard. There were forty-four major auto firms at the Depression's onset. By 1945, there were only eight. All were forced to reshape their marketing policies and organizational structures during the catastrophic ordeal, and all but GM came out of it weakened.

By 1946, auto firms were willing to participate in an industrial structure offering protection from the ruthless rounds of competition which they had experienced during the Great Depression. All were willing to accept GM's role as the industry's price setter, and most were willing to respect one another's established market shares. After experiencing conditions that drove them to the brink of insolvency, they defined such courses of action as best serving their interests.

Oddly enough, the major obstacle to Sloanist regulation after the war was GM itself. GM had veered away from Sloanist marketing practices during the Depression, embracing instead competitive and expansionist policies. GM displaced Ford as the industry leader, and its size, cost, and power advantages grew substantially throughout the Great Depression ordeal.

By 1946, GM was in a position to pursue successfully either a competitive/expansionist or a Sloanist strategy. Had it desired to exploit its cost advantages through competitive pricing, GM would have caused its competitors grave hardships and might have propelled itself to a monopoly position. GM was in a position in 1946 to pursue the more civic Sloanist courses of action as well. If it chose to act as the industry's hegemon firm, it could have realized high profit margins and stabilized interfirm relations, and could have benefited the financiers holding controlling interest in GM's voting stock, as well as those heavily invested in all but one of the surviving auto firms, namely Ford.

The Depression ordeal had created the stability required for the effective functioning of Sloanist regulation. High concentration, prohibitive entry costs, and secure membership enabled accurate forecasting of market conditions and investment calculations. GM's power advantage would likely discourage its weaker competitors from pursuing disruptive courses of action that would encourage price competition and upset the emerging balance of power. GM also had uncontested access to the safest and most lucrative markets in the industry. Unable to challenge GM's market share or price leadership, competitors had little choice but to target those market segments which GM had left behind. This proclivity would protect the price levels that GM used in its investment calculations and assure it of anticipated profit margins.

To understand why GM reembraced Sloanist marketing policies, we must turn to a power outside of the industry—the Roosevelt administration. After 1936, and through antitrust enforcement, this administration prohibited firms from pursuing expansionary policies disruptive to the balance of competitive forces established in major industries.[28] More than any indigenous development, this welded GM's commitment to Sloanism.

Market Collapse and Transformation

Following the 1929 stock market crash, the demand for automobiles collapsed. Industry sales dropped in 1932 to one third of their 1929 level. Auto sales began to recover in 1933, and this recovery continued into 1937. The recovery halted in late 1937 and depression conditions returned in 1938 and 1939. The industry began to recover in 1940, and the World War II years offered much needed relief. Government contracts enabled those hardest hit to recover and prosper on protected margins. Civilian auto production was suspended from 1942–1945, as auto firms engaged in war production. This created a tremendous demand for automobiles after the war, for, by 1946, more than 50 percent of the cars on the road were older than seven years.[29] This seller's market provided the space needed for the remaining firms to survive and prosper. It even created room for two new entries—Kaiser-Frazer and Crosley.

GM's Responses

Armed with Sloanist forecasting techniques, GM's general office actually anticipated the industry's sales decline prior to the October 1929 crash. GM's general office immediately began to formulate its policies for responding to the ensuing Depression. It halted fixed-cost capital investments and began to adjust its production schedules. In this way it judiciously avoided overproduction throughout the worst Depression years. From 1929 to 1932, GM's sales declined by 72 percent. Throughout most of 1932, GM operated at only about 30 percent of its production capacity. Yet, even with this decline, GM protected its capital investments. It did not register a loss at the firm level during any Depression year.[30]

However, a simple policy of capital withdrawal and restraint was not an adequate strategy for attaining market success under the altered conditions. GM won success during the late 1920s in a market that supported its Sloanist upgraded-car policy. In 1926, for example, 48 percent of GM sales were in the higher priced market segment.[31] Unlike Ford, GM preferred this segment because it returned much higher margins.

However, Depression conditions collapsed this market segment. In response, GM was forced to downshift to the low-priced segment and restructure itself to compete there. Accordingly, GM placed the bulk of its lines in the lower priced segment, reduced its body shells to three, and centralized purchasing and manufacturing.[32] GM profited on its lower priced lines by increasing production economies. These economies were made possible through standardizing parts used by the divisions, sharing basic bodies, and renewing emphasis on productivity and labor exploitation.[33] The cost savings of this standardization were considerable, and GM gained competitive advantage.

The Auto Industry and Roosevelt's New Deal

To understand why GM abandoned its competitive/expansionist policies and reverted to Sloanism at the end of World War II, we must examine the relationship that developed between GM and Roosevelt's "New Deal" administration. It is common knowledge that Roosevelt responded to the Great Depression crises with two distinctive recovery programs. During his first term, Congress enacted Roosevelt's National Industrial Recovery Act. During his second term, Roosevelt embraced a strong antitrust policy.

The NIRA called for the establishment of institutions for regulating the business activities that many in the Roosevelt administration thought to be responsible for causing the severe depression—unregulated expansion, overproduction, cut-throat price competition, and wage slashing. The Act established the National Recovery Administration to oversee the establishment of trade associations in major U.S. industries. These associations were to set prescriptive codes for regulating firms' pricing, production, and labor relations practices. The NRA encouraged all firms in the designated industries to participate actively in the establishment of these codes. It granted the trade associations authority to enforce compliance.

Sidney Fine chronicles the auto industry's experience under the NRA.[34] He shows that the major auto firms railed against the NRA as a socialistic infringement on their rights and liberties. They participated reluctantly, if at all, in establishing the industry's meager regulatory codes. They pressured Roosevelt into promulgating labor regulations that allowed company unions. They also supported Roosevelt's Republican opponent in the 1936 election. This opposition created a hostile relationship between the major auto firms and the administration.

When the Supreme Court ruled the NRA to be unconstitutional, the Roosevelt administration's orientation to industrial regulation shifted. The administration abandoned its attempt to create a cooperative relationship between industry and government. Instead, it committed itself to employing punitive sanctions against firms pursuing destructive courses of action. It shifted to a mildly prounion policy.[35] Most importantly, Roosevelt's second recovery program involved a renewed commitment to enforcing the nation's existing antitrust laws. The Roosevelt administration was especially diligent in enforcing the antitrust violations of those that had opposed it.

By 1937, public sentiment had ripened in favor of such action. Industrial concentration increased notably during the Depression. The threat of monopolization undermined the beneficent, free-market cultural myth that had traditionally legitimated firms' autonomy and independence. Most importantly, the large oligopolistic corporations had failed to deliver what they had promised throughout the 1920s—that is, relatively stable employment, rising real wages, and improved standards of living.[36] As the large corporations proved incapable of leading the economy out of the Depression, the American public increasingly defined their self-interested responses as callous, and warmed to the idea of some form of government intervention and regulation.

The economic collapse of late 1937 started in the auto industry. GM responded by halting production and laying off workers. This strengthened the Roosevelt administration's resolve to take action. In May 1938, a federal grand jury indicted GM, Ford, and Chrysler on charges of monopolizing the financing of consumer automobile loans. Ford and Chrysler pleaded guilty and complied with the Justice Department's demands. GM fought the case in court and lost.[37] The details and immediate outcomes of the case are not as important as is the signal which it sent to the auto industry in general, and to GM in particular. According to Ed Cray, Sloan became convinced that GM was singled out by the Justice Department for prosecution because of his political opposition to New Deal policies and support for Roosevelt's opponent.[38] Sloan feared that Roosevelt's Justice Department might take action to hurt GM, especially if GM continued to increase its market share. To forestall such action, Sloan restricted GM's market share to 45 percent. Sloan's managers continued this cautious policy until the Eisenhower administration took office in 1953. This politically motivated policy was instrumental in shaping the early postwar regulatory structure.

A Sketch of the Emerging Regulatory Structure

The havoc reaped by the Great Depression left the U.S. auto industry ripe in 1946 for some form of hegemonic regulation. Two barriers blocking the industry-wide institutionalization of the Sloanist system in the past were eliminated. The first was the industry's demographic instability. Prior to the Great Depression, the number of firms operating in the industry remained rather large, with considerable numbers entering and exiting routinely. This made a hegemonic regulatory structure difficult to institutionalize, because it made accurate calculation of competitors' courses of action impossible. By 1946, the industry's demographic composition had stabilized. Only eight firms survived. Of these, GM was, by far, the largest and most powerful—almost twice as large as either Ford or Chrysler. Ford and Chrysler followed GM in size and power, while the independent firms were much smaller. Two tiny new firms—Crosley and Kaiser-Frazer—entered the industry in 1946. No domestic firms entered after that.

The second barrier was the viability of the Fordist alternative. Throughout the industry's history, the Ford Motor Company's successes and failures had served as the litmus test of its radical business strategies: mass-production of a single product line, volume expansion through price cutting, constant productivity-enhancing innovation, and high wage policies to stimulate demand. When Henry Ford prospered during the 1910s and early 1920s, his policies were taken seriously. They were an effective challenger to Sloanism's hegemony.

However, when the Ford Motor Company failed miserably throughout the Depression and World War II years, Ford's radical business policies were debunked and discredited—particularly his single-product and price-cutting policies.[39] Henry Ford II sealed the fate of such policies' influence in 1946 when he installed Sloanist marketing, pricing, and investment strategies at Ford, along with the Sloanist organizational structure. After 1946, Fordism was no longer a viable market-regulating ideology, and Sloanism faced no ideological competition.

Having its competitive/expansionist policies bridled by the federal government's renewed commitment to antitrust enforcement, GM was cast in the role of the industry's hegemon. GM used its power to establish stable and predictable relations between auto firms competing for market shares and segments. GM did this in two ways. First, it targeted for itself only 45 to 50 percent of the total auto market, leaving its competitors ample niches within which to compete and prosper. GM concentrated its sales efforts in the middle- and upper-middle segments of the pricing market, which reemerged in the early postwar period.

Second, GM served as the industry's postwar pricing leader. GM set prices on its own models on the bases of a priori rate of return calculations, and then publicly announced them to the press. The competition accepted GM's pricing announcements as their benchmark, and then set their own prices in accordance with them. In essence, GM's market forecasts and rate of return calculations served as the pricing guidelines for the industry. Because of their relative weakness, GM's competitors accepted its leadership. When effective, this steered the industry away from serious price competition and market instability.

Others adopted the Sloanist organizational structure as well. The Ford Motor Company literally restructured itself in GM's image with top management personnel drawn from GM. The new managers set up a general office that functioned similarly to GM's, redefining Ford's production operations as profit centers, setting up rates of return measures for each, and using these measures to make investment decisions.[40] They also developed long-range forecasting and planning capacities, and employed standard volume estimates in making investment decisions.[41] In the wake of a severe financial crisis in the 1950s, Chrysler reorganized further along GM's line, borrowing personnel familiar with Sloanist controls from both GM and Ford. AMC, formed by the merger of Nash and Hudson, did the same in the early 1960s, again borrowing key players involved in the earlier Sloanist reorganizations at Ford and Chrysler.[42]

Thus, the Sloanist market strategy and organizational structure was destined to become hegemonic during the early post-World-War-II period. The surviving firms perceived Sloanism as the most effective means of prospering in the auto market. By 1946, all auto firms were committed to the Sloanist goal of stable rates of return on investment. They were willing to adopt more civic orientations toward one another's market shares. These commitments provided a commonalty of interest and purpose compatible with Sloanist regulation. Alternatives were not contemplated seriously after the war.

This hegemonic structure began to emerge in major market segments during the period spanning the end of World War II to the Korean War. It broke down considerably after the 1954 recession, as the postwar sellers' market dissipated, and as Ford and GM began to pursue more expansionist strategies. This deterioration was arrested following the 1958 recession, after GM defeated Ford's assault on its dominant position, and after GM itself began to curb its expansionary designs in response to renewed antitrust threats against it. This brief outline will be developed more fully and linked to shop-floor developments in subsequent chapters of this book. We now turn to the postwar emergence of the labor relations structure that was functionally compatible with Sloanist market regulation.

CHAPTER 2

Sloanist Labor Regulation

Workers confronted auto managements during the crisis period spanning the Great Depression through World War II with unprecedented levels of shop-floor militancy. Such militancy was potentially disruptive to the emerging Sloanist structure, as it threatened functional requisites at both the firm and industry level. At the firm level, Sloanism requires that firms develop capacities for forecasting accurately all conditions affecting investment returns. This requires the ability to deliver production outcomes that can be quantified accurately in advance of production and realized dependably after planning decisions are made. Labor processes must deliver the goods anticipated in such forecasts without interference from unplanned and unanticipated contingencies.

Such predictability is also necessary for the effective functioning of Sloanism as an industry-level regulatory system. Timing and dependability become critical factors in firms' abilities to establish and hold markets in the Sloanist structure. When firms establish themselves in a particular market segment, their Sloanist competitors are not likely to invade their terrain because the probability of securing high profit rates from such invasions are slim. A failure of the established producers to service their markets, however, invites invasion and subsequent instability. Thus, a capacity to service markets dependably is vital to the success of Sloanist regulation.

Labor militancy poses a potential threat to firms' capacities to realize these demands. Chronic, unpredictable work stoppages might thwart managements' abilities to forecast outcomes and actualize anticipated profit rates. This, in turn, could create serious market instability because a strike-prone firm loses its capacities to service its markets dependably. In the postwar political environment, the instability precipitated by such militancy was also potentially threatening to the Sloanist hegemon firm. If the hegemon's market share increased as a result of this—as well it might—it could very well trigger punitive antitrust action.

This peculiar political threat united the interests of both strike-prone and hegemon firms in institutionalizing a labor-relations structure that would ensure firms of a capacity for delivering stable and predictable production outcomes. In the auto industry, GM took the civic lead in forging a stability-enhancing labor-relations structure that was functionally compatible with Sloanist market regulation. Formally, this structure enabled managements to use cost-benefit calculations in responding to labor demands. I will outline this structure's key components and define how it served the historically conditioned interests of the parties it regulated.

Features of the Labor-Relations Structure

The labor-relations structure that emerged in the postwar period was designed to provide the stable and predictable production outcomes which Sloanism required. This structure was hegemonic, serving the interests of the major parties involved. Yet, the historically conditioned and situationally contingent nature of this hegemony must be stressed. Under certain conditions a given party's interests could diverge radically from those served by this structure. When these conditions developed, the affected party could—and, at times, did—choose to act in ways leading to systemic disruptions.

For the sake of clarity, I begin by specifying the structure's general features, reifying it as a static, fully developed entity. For now, this structure's historical evolution is ignored, as is its variations among firms. These aspects will be taken up in subsequent chapters of this book. The general features specified in this chapter were institutionalized throughout the industry by the 1940s.

Collective Bargaining at the Firm Level

The Sloanist labor relations structure in operation from 1946–1973 was a dual structure. Labor demands and issues were negotiated at different organizational levels and by different parties representing the interests of both management and workers. Issues of general interest to all workers in the firm were negotiated by the United Automobile Workers International and corporate labor relations departments. The agreements they reached were codified as prescriptive law in the national contract, and they were legitimated formally by the majority vote of workers affected by them. These agreements were nonnegotiable during the length of the contract.

There were no formal restrictions placed upon the types of issues negotiated at this level. However, both parties tended to limit their concerns. The issues typically negotiated were wage increases, formulas for determining wage increases within contract periods, fringe benefit packages, and general procedural rules concerning matters such as discipline and firing, hiring, transfers, and grievance procedures. Demands concerning specific working conditions were generally ignored at this level. Instead, they were passed to local bargaining tables.

An informal, pattern-bargaining arrangement was instituted in the late 1940s. This arrangement worked as follows: The UAW chose a single firm as its strike target upon termination of its contract. It then negotiated exclusively with that firm before it began serious negotiations with other companies. This pressured the target firm to reach a contract agreement without a strike. After the UAW settled with the targeted firm, it began negotiating with the remaining firms in the industry. These firms typically conceded whatever gains were won from the initial strike target.

This informal arrangement spread the gains which the UAW won at the national level to all the workers whom it represented in the industry. This served to legitimate the UAW without disadvantaging a particular firm. It also served to stabilize wages across the industry, thereby removing them as a firm-level cost factor in market competition.

Collective Bargaining at the Local Level

UAW locals, representing workers in specific plants, and plant managements typically negotiated issues concerning specific working conditions. These representatives negotiated local contracts or supplements similar to those negotiated at the national level. The agreements reached at this level were codified as prescriptive law. These agreements were also legitimated by the majority vote of the rank and file represented. As with agreements in the national contract, these other terms were nonnegotiable during the length of the contract, and the locals agreed not to strike over them. Many aspects were typically negotiated in these contracts, ranging from agreements over procedures for policing production standards to procedures for alleviating traffic congestion during shift changes.

Local contracts did not restrict job outcomes as much as we might believe. The local contract—as did the national one—tended to prescribe procedures. Specific job outcomes—such as output quotas, use of a given type of machinery, line speeds, and manpower allocations—were seldom specified at the local level.

Indeed, the industry's labor contracts during the period in question granted each party leverage for changing production outcomes. These contracts typically granted managements the right to set and change production standards during the contract period. They also preserved the right of union locals to dispute these changes, bargain collectively over these disputes, and strike during the contract period if these negotiations failed to produce acceptable results. UAW locals struck plants legally during contract periods to force concessions on production standards, health and safety conditions, and wage rates on new jobs.

While granting its locals the right to strike, the UAW International demanded that they pursue such action through bureaucratic channels. Locals were required first to exhaust the grievance machinery before they pursued strike action. This involved filing grievances against management, and then processing these grievances through several stages.

If negotiations through the grievance procedure ultimately failed, the local typically passed the grievance on to an impartial umpire. Some categories of grievances—such as issues concerning production standards, health and safety, and wage rates on new jobs—did not go to the umpire, however. In these cases, after the final grievance stage, UAW locals could strike to force a resolution to these issues.

However, before the strike, the local was required to exhaust another set of procedures. It first petitioned the International for approval to take a strike vote among its members, and then took the vote. If the strike won a majority vote, the local then posted a strike deadline and awaited final authorization from the International. Typically, the UAW International negotiated with the company to avoid the strike. If these final negotiations failed, the local strike occured.

While the local was exhausting these procedures, aggravated workers had to remain on the job and tolerate the conditions that they were attempting to change. It usually took several months—and, at times, years—for the union to process the grievance through all of its subsequent stages, and the UAW International could refuse the local's final request for authorization after the effort was expended.

The Structure's Hegemonic Foundations

Management, the UAW, and workers defined this formal labor relations structure as best serving their immediate interests, given the alternatives open to them in the early postwar period. They participated actively in this structure's institutionalization. This chapter section specifies how this structure served the historically conditioned interests of each party.

The Structural Foundation of Managements' Consent

Managements legitimated this structure because doing so served their historically conditioned interests. Yet, it is safe to say that, if they had another viable option, they would have taken it. A high-ranking Chrysler official admitted as much at the onset of the postwar period. In an infamous speech, he insinuated that Chrysler was only tolerating the UAW until public opinion shifted. Then, Chrysler would rid itself of union interference.[1] This official was not alone in these sentiments. Why, then, did auto managements agree to legitimate the structure previously defined, as well as the UAW's secure position within it?

From World War I to the Great Depression, auto managements' domination over their production processes was never seriously challenged by auto workers. A combination of coercion and beneficence secured this system of domination. While its coercive features have become legend, its more beneficent ones are not often recognized. Auto managements ran up against limits in imposing their will on their labor forces prior to the Great Depression. The labor market offered workers mobility options, and they often exercised such options to protest managerial impositions. Tight labor markets encouraged employers to institute more positive incentives in winning workers' commitments to staying with them.

Prior to the Great Depression, the industry was a bastion of paternalism, or welfare capitalism. We should follow Brody in taking seriously the efficacy of this system.[2] Virtually all major auto firms practiced variants of it. Welfare capitalist programs provided workers with unprecedented standards of living and financial security. Workers placed their faith in their employers' abilities to provide for their families, sacrificing much in the workplace in exchange for this security. It makes sense to link these beneficent programs to managements' successes, both in thwarting unionization and in preserving their labor-process domination.

However, this paternalistic system crumbled as the Great Depression deepened, and workers began to challenge managerial authority. As Edsforth suggests, there were a number of factors contributing to this.[3] First, workers' faith in managements' abilities to "deliver the goods" was shaken profoundly. Materially, auto workers paid a stiff price for the Depression. Fine reports that hourly wages dropped by 16 percent from 1928 to 1932, and real income fell by as much as 43 percent because of reduced working hours.[4] For the first time, auto workers' standards of living appeared to be in a state of steady decline.[5] Second, auto managements instituted brutal speedups throughout the industry during the crisis period. As the lower priced market began to improve, they drove workers hard to attain the productivity levels needed to prosper on lower margins. This speedup created industrywide discontent and dissatisfaction.[6] Third, dissatisfied workers' employment options narrowed or closed during the ordeal. This locked workers into their employment situations, forcing them either to tolerate conditions, or fight them at that level. Fourth, the demographic composition of plant labor forces stabilized as well. Lacking viable alternatives, "stuck" workers began to form informal, primary group relations on the shop floor.[7] Finally, Roosevelt and the majority in Congress possibly contributed somewhat to workers' withdrawal of consent. While always somewhat ambivalent toward union militancy, government policy slowly shifted in unions' favor, sponsoring legislation protecting the rights of unions and strikers. This encouraged organization and mobilization.

Thus, as Edsforth demonstrates, auto workers drew upon their experiences in the welfare capitalist systems of the 1920s to interpret and evaluate the wrenching changes they experienced during the Depression. Managements' more paternal and beneficent orientation to their workers' interests in the pre-Depression era became the standard with which workers critiqued Depression-induced changes, as well as the ideological foundation for mobilizing collective action against managerial assaults.[8] The closing of the tight labor markets of the pre-Depression era forced workers to react to the indignation fueled by this ideological frame directly on the shop floor. Also, Roosevelt's administration and the majority in Congress seemed, at times, to condone such responses. This conjuncture provided the cultural and structural foundation for industrial workers to organize and fight managements' shop-floor dominance on an unprecedented scale.

Strike activity increased considerably in the 1930s, as managements' hegemony began to deteriorate.[9] Managements fought to preserve their labor-process dominance by breaking strikes ruthlessly, destroying unions with spies and private armies, and replacing striking workers with the unemployed.[10] Auto managements also generally refused government mediation and disobeyed the rulings of the National Labor Relations Board.

Yet, management's success proved to be temporary, as the UAW organized workers, forced managerial concessions, and mobilized support from the community at large. Its most effective tactic was, of course, the sitdown, a strike form enabling small bands of unionists in strategically located plants to shut down highly interdependent production systems. The sitdown checked managements' capacities for replacing strikers with the unemployed.

The most famous sitdown was the 1937 Flint strike. In occupying the Flint plants making the bulk of GM's body stampings, local UAW militants shut down GM. The UAW International sanctioned this strike and mobilized support from the local community and the larger society, forcing GM to recognize the UAW as its workers' bargaining agent.[11] After its success in organizing GM, the UAW struggled to organize workers throughout the industry. By the end of 1941, and after a long bitter struggle, the UAW had finally won representation in all major auto firms.

Yet, managements did not consent to the institutionalization of this labor-relations structure merely because of UAW strength. This is much too simple. The real threat came after the recognition strikes—not from the UAW, but from the shop floor.

After collective-bargaining agreements were signed with the major auto firms, workers began to seek immediate resolutions to their demands through localized work stoppages. In doing so, they shut down highly interdependent production lines and threatened production schedules. They expropriated the weapons used to win recognition for their own purposes in order to force foremen to comply with their particularistic demands. For a time, it appeared as if managements would lose shop-floor control. It was also unclear whether the UAW had the power at the national level to control and regulate such behavior.

William Knudsen, GM's president during the 1930s, claims that more than two hundred wildcat strikes occurred in GM plants *after* the Flint agreement was reached, and that these strikes threatened GM's ability to return to full production.[12] Edsforth reports that more than thirty wildcats occurred in the Flint plants alone immediately after the 1937 agreement was signed.[13] He reports that informal steward systems were developing throughout the complex, and that workers were striking over the specific issues affecting them. In taking matters into their own hands, such workers were not beholden to the UAW International for their gains, nor were they willing to subordinate their demands to its prescriptions.

These independent, shop-floor-centered organizations were a force in the industry during the late 1930s and 1940s. Accounts from those participating in them are most insightful. The following account is from a Chrysler unionist describing local union practices at Dodge Main during the period:

> Once we got our first contract, we set about improving the working conditions. First, we had to cut down the size of those hard-boiled foremen. . . . We told them that the contract called for a fair day's work and a fair day's pay, and, by God, a fair day's work was all they were going to get. . . . We told them that if they wanted extra work turned out, they should hire extra workers. At first they ignored us. So every time [the foremen] turned out work, we simply turned out less work. Sometimes the foremen would jerk up the automatic conveyor a couple of notches and speed up the line. We cured them of that practice; we simply let jobs go by half finished. Make no mistake about it; in those days we had power.[14]

The following account is from a unionist working in the Motor Building at Ford River Rouge:

> The workers chose as their committeeman a man who had done an outstanding job as picket captain during the strike. When he was elected committeeman, he walked over to the foreman, pointed to his shining committeeman's button, and exclaimed: "Do you see this?" The foreman replied: "Ah, yes, you are the new committeeman, congratulations." The committeeman snapped, "Congratulations, hell. I'm running this department now, you scram the hell out of here."[15]

A unionist working at GM's Fisher Body plant in Atlanta recalled:

> I think, following the settlement of the strike we had some of the most effective collective bargaining in the plant that I think we ever had, because of the way we handled it. . . .

> What we did, in the departments, one employee had a problem, we all had a problem, and so we would all go down to the office to discuss our problem with them. Now that shut the whole plant down, because they had to settle the department's problem before they could get the plant to operate.[16]

Summing up management's perspective, Alfred P. Sloan, wrote:

> What made the prospect [of unionization] seem especially grim in those early years was the persistent union attempt to invade basic management prerogatives. Our rights to determine production schedules, to set work standards, and to discipline workers were all suddenly called into question. Add to this the recurrent tendency of the union to inject itself into pricing policy, and it is easy to understand why it seemed, to some corporate officials, as though the union might one day be virtually in control of our operations.[17]

As illustrated, these informal shop-floor-centered organizations were threatening managements' control over production. The institutionalization of the formal grievance procedure can be interpreted as an attempt by both auto managements and the UAW International to establish an alternative means of resolving worker grievances—one that did not shut down production in an unpredictable fashion, and one that did not threaten firms' abilities to plan and actualize production schedules.

Edsforth's history of labor relations at GM Flint illustrates the process involved in institutionalizing the formal labor-relations structure.[18] Edsforth reports that GM and the UAW International established the grievance procedure at Flint as a direct response to wildcat activity.[19] Increasingly under pressure from federal arbitrators and the Roosevelt administration, the UAW moved to delegitimate spontaneous shop-floor-led work stoppages, clamping down on local stewards, and redirecting grievances through the formal procedural channels.[20] By 1940, the UAW had stripped the shop steward system of its legitimacy at Flint. By 1945, Edsforth claims it had lost effectiveness.[21]

With the complicity of Roosevelt's National War Labor

Board and top UAW officials, Big Three managements attempted to delegitimate these independent sources of shop-floor authority and win workers' commitment to the formal structure during World War II.[22] The UAW agreed to a no-strike pledge and disciplined militant local leaders breaching the agreement.[23] This allowed the Big Three to retain formally their right to set production standards in their shops.[24] However, the extent to which this formal control could be translated into shop-floor practice varied considerably, and this variation is specified in subsequent chapters. Strong militant steward organizations did survive into the 1950s in the smaller, independent firms,[25] and in some of the Big Three plants as well.

Given the alternatives confronting them, auto managements' postwar participation in institutionalizing the labor-relations structure is understandable. The functioning of this structure proved compatible with their interests in pursuing Sloanist courses of business action. At the local level, the bargaining table displaced the shop floor as the arena within which management and labor resolved conflicts.[26] The grievance procedure prevented local conflicts from disrupting production schedules by legitimating peaceful step-by-step mechanisms for resolving disputes. It placed the responsibility for conflict resolution in the hands of negotiators removed from the shop floor. The direct actors in the dispute continued to perform their vital routines while their grievances were being processed.

These step-by-step procedures also signaled to managements when and where labor conflicts would occur, the likely severity of these conflicts, and the date when these conflicts would materialize into actual work stoppages. This signaling mechanism provided managements with time for planning responses to conflicts. It also enabled them to make cost-benefit calculations concerning the effect of factors such as potential strikes and concessions to union demands upon rate-of-return and market projections. This system provided management with leverage for controlling the timing of the strike, and for preventing it from occurring if it so desired. Such signaling delivered the stability necessary for the functioning of the Sloanist business strategy. It also enabled managements to live with the threat of work stoppages by stripping them of their disruptive and unpredictable qualities.

At the national level, the collective-bargaining contract locked in wage rates and fringe benefit costs for extended periods and forbade labor from striking over them. This enabled managements to calculate production costs with precision and to engage in long-range planning. The national contract also established parameters at the local level concerning what was negotiable and what was not during the course of the contract. This reduced the scope of labor demands voiced from the shop floor and fostered stability. Prior to the labor-relations structure's legitimation, this scope was unlimited.

Finally, the institution of pattern bargaining at the national level functioned to stabilize interfirm relationships in the product market by mitigating the competitive effect of wage and benefit differentials upon market outcomes. Pattern bargaining helped to standardize wage and benefit concessions across the industry,[27] reducing individual firms' leverage in using wage cuts as a means of reducing prices and expanding markets, and thereby stabilizing the market environment.

The Labor Relations Structure and the Union

Understanding labor's commitment to this system is more problematic. We must draw a sharp distinction between the interests of individual workers and those authorized to represent them. We begin with the representatives' interests.

Why did the UAW International attempt to delegitimate the militant steward organizations that emerged during the union mobilization of the late 1930s? Why did it attempt to displace these organizations with a bureaucratic grievance procedure compatible with managerial aims?

A common response is to interpret this type of action as a sellout by opportunistic labor leaders who were indifferent to workers' fundamental interests and interested primarily in furthering their own personal career goals. Yet, focusing as it does upon the individual proclivities of union leaders, the sellout explanation is inadequate for understanding this behavior.

Why do union leaders, in general, tend to sellout workers' local struggles and subordinate spontaneous action to bureaucratic procedure? To answer this, we must explore the structural dilemmas confronting union organizations as they attempt to mobilize support from workers in capitalist-dominated organizations. Offe and Wiesenthal develop an excellent theoretical account of these structural dilemmas.[28] Let us summarize their arguments and apply them to the auto industry.

Offe and Wiesenthal's theory. According to Offe and Wiesenthal,[29] union organizations confront considerable obstacles in organizing workers against capitalist domination. First, unions organize a constituency already organized by capital in alienated and atomized work relationships. The structural alienation and atomization experienced everyday on the job impedes the development of collective consciousness and capacities for militant collective action. Second, labor organizations must represent a plethora of worker demands and needs that vary from work group to work group.[30] Why should workers in a firm or a plant necessarily have an interest in one another's particularistic struggles? A strike by a particular work group over a particular demand threatens the employment prospects and benefits of other groups employed in the plant or firm who may not have a vested interest in its outcome. The nonaffected workers lose wages during the strike, without winning tangible gains from it. This pits the particularistic interests of work groups against each other, tending to break down solidary commitments. The diverse—but interdependent—production processes in industries such as auto manufacturing tend to fragment workers' interests and struggles.

For which set of demands should the union mobilize support? The plethora of worker demands in a given industrial setting cannot be quantified easily. Unlike those organized by Sloanist managements, these interests cannot be plugged into a cost-benefit formula nor can they be related to one another as exchange value equivalents. There are few common denominators with which unions can optimize their interests.[31]

This dilemma places union leaders in a double bind. Their failures to mobilize support for particularistic demands threaten their legitimacy. Yet, pursuing strike action for the particularistic interests of a given work group will cause considerable hardships for those shut down by the action but not immediately affected by the issues for which the union strikes. This, too, can threaten legitimacy.

The solution is for unions to mobilize widespread support for hegemonic programs that unite varied worker interests. Yet, this is much easier said than done. The union must create consensual support for its demands from a constituency that may not have an immediate structural foundation for such a consensus. In mobilizing this constituency, there is always the risk that the consensus will break down, and that workers will use the organization so mobilized to pursue their own more localized and particularistic demands. This tendency toward fragmentation could lead to delegitimation.

For these structural reasons, Offe and Wiesenthal see unions as becoming increasingly committed to opportunism and business unionism.[32] They propose a stage theory of union development. In their model, unions initially mobilize workers support by establishing binding obligations to nonutilitarian norms.[33] Such nonrational binding creates the solidarity and commitment required for pursuing high-risk militant action that is initially necessary for winning union recognition.

After recognition, unions take action to delegitimate unpredictable shop-floor-centered action, and to dismantle the structural foundations enabling it. In doing so, they make the survival of the union as independent of members' "willingness to act" as possible. This is necessary for the union to protect itself from the mobilization dilemmas already discussed. However, in doing this, unions threaten their legitimacy by undermining their support base. They make themselves vulnerable to capitalist offensives. This, Offe and Wiesenthal speculate,[34] could lead to the delegitimation of established unions in times of crisis, or to new progressive forms of mobilization.

The interests of the union representatives. Offe and Wiesenthal's structural explanation of union opportunism goes a long way toward explaining the developments in the late 1930s and 1940s that led to the institution of the auto industry's postwar labor-relations structure. The type of breakdown anticipated in their model seems to have occurred. The

UAW International's move to displace militant steward systems with bureaucratic grievance procedures can be interpreted as an attempt by the International to maintain its legitimacy. The structures it instituted mitigated the threat of particularistic labor demands to its leadership.

Both components of the dualistic labor-relations structure previously defined served the leadership's interests. First, the national-level collective-bargaining structure allowed the leadership to establish monopolistic closure over the negotiation of hegemonic issues—that is, those issues concerning the interests of all workers in a given firm or industry, such as wages, fringe benefits, and general procedural rules. For the most part, all auto workers had an interest in these issues, and victories here could be communicated as collective victories. To some extent, the UAW International set aside the general issues that could be quantified, posited as exchange-value equivalents, and used to generate widespread rank-and-file support as its exclusive bargaining domain.

Second, as we have seen, the grievance procedure mechanisms established in the national contract to handle local labor disputes functioned to disconnect such disputes from one another and to minimize the effect of particularistic demands on production processes. While serving managements' interests in maintaining its planned production schedules, this structure also served the majority of workers' interests not immediately affected by the dispute.

In fact, this structure sacrificed the aggravated workers' immediate interests for those of the majority who were unaffected by their particular disputes. The unaffected continued working and earning hourly wages, while the aggravated workers' disputes were processed through the grievance procedure. The majority was not required to make sacrifices for the aggravated's struggles against conditions that did not affect them. When grievances led to a strike vote, the unaffected majority held veto power over whether or not the strike would proceed. This system thus subordinated strike action to the tyranny of the unaffected majority. In doing so, it protected the position of the union leadership in two ways.

First and foremost, UAW union leaders were dependent upon the votes of this unaffected majority to stay in power at both local and national levels. Second, at least since the days of the Roosevelt adminstration's National War Labor Board, union leaders have been under considerable pressure from the state to use their influence to stop spontaneous wildcat work stoppages. Taft-Hartley outlawed wildcat strikes and made unions liable for the damages caused by them. In providing a legal alternative to unpredictable and unruly wildcat strikes, bureaucratic strike procedures protected union leaders from legal liability and state interference.

This leads us to our final question. How did this labor-relations structure serve the interests of the aggravated who, under normal conditions, stood as a small minority in relation to the unaffected majority, but who had an immediate interest in taking action to resolve their grievances?

The interests of the aggravated. The labor-relations structure was most vulnerable in how it related to the interests of workers seeking resolution of a grievance. Why would workers choose to submit to a grievance procedure that was cumbersome and lengthy, required them to experience aggravating conditions until their grievance was resolved, placed the grievance in the hands of union officials who handled it as but one of many grievances to process, and who were likely to treat it as an exchange-value equivalent to gain concessions from management calculated to best serve their political interests, and could not guarantee that management would honor the agreement after it was reached?

My answer is simply that workers consented to the procedures stipulated in this bureaucratic structure only when they saw no other viable alternatives immediately available on the shop floor for resolving their disputes. When such direct-action alternatives existed, workers were likely to pursue them. My critical focus becomes these alternative options. Did they exist, and how do we explain them?

The data. My central focus is on wildcat strikes and managements' reactions to them. I argue that understanding both is vital to understanding the industry's stabilization in the post–World-War-II period. Wildcat strikes occurring from 1946–1973 typically took place outside of the formal procedural mechanisms enabling managements to use rational, cost-benefit calculations in determining their responses to workers' demands. They inserted an unpredictability into labor relations that was threatening to the Sloanist, market-regulating structure.[35]

In contrast, the procedural mechanisms built into the labor-relations structure buffered somewhat the threat of authorized strikes on firms' operations and functions. In following the specified procedures, strikers allowed managements to assess the effects of possible strike outcomes on their production operations in rational cost-benefit calculations. Strikers pursuing the authorized local strike option allowed management to use such assessments in deciding their courses of action with regard to strikes. Finally, authorized strikers gave managements some leverage in determining whether, when, and for how long strikes would occur. When these authorized strikes did occur, they did so with managements' forewarned knowledge and consent.

Because of this, the common abstracted variables used in more traditional strike analyses—variables such as "strike duration" and "person hours lost to strikes"—are poor indicators of labor militancy and/or worker power in labor-relations structures similar to those established in the auto industry. In such structures, long, costly strikes are as likely to signify managements' advanced calculations of their power in negotiation with unions as they are to signify labor militancy. As decontextualized variables, they tell us little about the impact of strike activity on industrial development.

The way in which both managements and the UAW International reacted to wildcat strikes support my position. While signing contracts with authorized local strike provisions, both managements and the UAW defined wildcats as contractually illegal, and mobilized their resources to crush them.

This is not to say that the types of mobilizations involved in plant-level authorized strikes are unimportant, or that the solidarity involved in them is insignificant to industrial development. Unlike in wildcat strikes—which were often occupationally specific—the types of solidarity mobilized in authorized plant strikes involved diverse constituencies agreeing to work stoppages through democratic means. Authorized plant strikes required these diverse constituencies to maintain strong collective commitment to the collective action throughout its course.

The critical difference is the nature of the threats involved in each type of local strike to the functioning of the

Sloanist system. Sloanists defined the authorized strike option as acceptable because it signaled to managements the possibility of a work stoppage long before the actual event. If managements wished to stop the strike, it also gave them the option of making critical concessions to the demands which workers made prior to the stoppage.

Second, authorized local strikes were relatively rare events during the critical period spanning 1946 to the middle 1950s. The type of strike activity providing management and the UAW International with their biggest headaches was the unauthorized wildcat strike. How was this threat contained? This is the particular question addressed in this book. A full understanding of the mobilization dynamics involved in authorized plant-level strikes and an understanding of changes in their frequencies over time requires separate treatment.

Another significant type of militant action taking place outside the procedural mechanisms built into the automotive collective bargaining system was the production slowdown. As in wildcat strikes, workers engaging in slowdowns took direct collective action on the shop floor to force management or the union to resolve their grievances. Unfortunately, these types of protest actions did not leave the types of documentation required for systematic analysis. They were not likely to be noted in publicly available sources, unless they ended in work stoppages. Because of this, we shall focus primarily on wildcat strikes.

I have aggregated strike data on local, plant-level strikes occurring from 1946-1973. These strike data were collected primarily from two sources—*Wall Street Journal* and *New York Times* reports. Additional information was added from other local newspapers, such as the *Chicago Tribune*; from business journals, such as *Business Week* and *Fortune*; from the UAW files available at the Archives of Labor and Urban Affairs at Wayne State University; from *Voice of Local 212*, the newspaper of the Amalgamated Briggs/Chrysler UAW local; and from *Ford Facts*, the newspaper of the Ford River Rouge UAW local.

This data set represents a good approximation of the total population of local strikes which closed down major auto lines. However, it more likely underrepresents: (1) strikes occurring in supplier plants that did not immediately affect the production output of major firms; (2) brief wildcats usually lasting less than a shift and that were resolved quickly on the spot; and (3) strike votes that did not culminate in strikes. Because we are concerned with the impact of wildcats on the industry's development, these shortcomings do not pose major problems.

Postwar wildcat activity. If it is correct to link the decline in the number of wildcats to the establishment of the formal labor-relations structure already defined, the strike data should show a decrease shortly after it was instituted. Since bureaucratic grievance procedures were established in the auto plants by 1945, we should see evidence of this decline throughout the late 1940s and 1950s. However, the data fail to show this.

Table 2.1 reports the number of local strikes occurring in the post–World-War-II period by strike type and year. The frequencies show that wildcat activity did not wane in the 1950s. There was more activity in the late 1950s than in the

Table 2.1
Local Strikes in the U.S. Automobile Industry 1946–1973

Year	Wildcat Strikes	Authorized Strikes[a]	Year	Wildcat Strikes	Authorized Strikes[a]
1946	25	10	1960	6	12
1947	39	5	1961	14	13
1948	31	9	1962	1	7
1949	57	5	1963	6	20
1950	34	5	1964	6	17
1951	31	4	1965	3	6
1952	12	5	1966	2	6
1953	14	6	1967	15	26
1954	7	3	1968	6	34
1955	60	15	1969	6	9
1956	14	9	1970	4	3
1957	12	16	1971	3	2
1958	80	23	1972	3	25
1959	5	1	1973	8	9

[a]Authorized strikes include strike votes taken in the local that were resolved prior to the actual walkout.

Sources: New York Times and *Wall Street Journal*, various years.

late 1940s, and it was not until 1959, that we begin to see a significant decrease in wildcat numbers.

This suggests that automotive wildcat activity was not tamed by the labor-relations structure on which we have focused. Peak wildcat years were 1955 and 1958. These wildcats took place more than a decade after the labor-relations structure already discussed was institutionalized. Workers continually chose alternatives to the legitimated means of grievance resolution with a frequency that was alarming to both managements and union officials.

Part II— Ideal Types Linking Noninstitutionalized Militancy, Work Organization, and Systems of Market Regulation

CHAPTER 3

Work Organization and Work-Group Solidarity

Our examination of the auto industry's formal labor-relations structure left interesting, unanswered questions. What enabled workers to pursue resolution to their disputes directly on the factory floor, ignoring the grievance procedure? Given the formal structure's hostility toward it, why did outlawed wildcat activity persist well into the late 1950s?

This chapter addresses these critical questions. Drawing heavily from previous work, this chapter specifies both the structural conditions enabling workers to initiate collective factory-centered protests in an antagonistic institutional environment and those structural conditions tending to reduce workers' capacities for doing so.

Alternative Theories

This section begins with a brief discussion of alternative responses to the questions posed in the previous paragraphs. These alternatives have located the sources of shop-floor militancy in (1) the larger institutional environment within which the affected labor process is embedded; (2) workers' residential communities; and (3) deskilled production processes that employ extreme divisions of labor, transfer control of work pace from workers to managers, and subject workers to degrading working conditions.

The Institutional Environment and Resource Mobilization

The resource mobilization perspective is one of the most popular approaches to the study of labor militancy and industrial unrest. This perspective defines strike activity as a social movement, and explains it in terms of its sponsoring organizations' capacities for mobilizing resources and support from the larger society.[1]

Yet, for all of its popularity, the resource mobilization perspective is of limited use in explaining wildcat activity in the postwar auto industry. Postwar wildcats tended to be localized disruptions initiated by small groups of workers seeking immediate, tangible gains on the factory floor. The organizations initiating these strikes were not well-connected with their external environments or to one another. These organizations had local, particularistic aims, ambitions, and orientations that seldom extended beyond the horizons of the immediate shop floor.

A social movement organization with a capacity and resolve for organizing these unconnected wildcat rebellions into a strategically coordinated campaign never developed, although some coordinated activity did occur during the 1955, 1958, and 1961 contract negotiations, and also during the period of racial strife spanning the late 1960s and early 1970s. While the resource mobilization perspective may be useful in explaining why these local rebellions did not develop into a social movement, it cannot explain why they persisted well into the late 1950s without institutional support.

Mobilizing Commitment from within the Work Group

However, the resource-mobilization conceptualization is useful in developing an explanation for this activity. Individual workers took considerable risks when participating in wildcat strikes. The United Automobile Workers International left wildcatters without contractual protection, conceding to managements the right to discipline and fire them. The state also prohibited wildcat activity, and wildcatters were served with court injunctions ordering them to halt their strike and return to work. Some were jailed for violating these court orders. In engaging in wildcat activity during the postwar period, auto workers knowingly and willingly broke the law in order to resolve their grievances on the shop floor, and, in doing so, they risked their employment status. In the face of this formidable threat, what encouraged and enabled them to initiate this outlawed activity?

Workers' capacities for acting collectively and autonomously as a solidary group in the face of tremendous institutional pressure was the backbone of these strikes. When initiating wildcats, workers had to trust that their fellow workers would honor their strikes, staying off the job until their disputes were resolved favorably. A breakdown in individual wildcatters' commitments to these actions jeopardized their possibility of success. Such breakdowns allowed managements to have their way in the dispute, and they threatened the jobs of those committing themselves to wildcats. Without the firm commitment and support of other strikers, individual commitments to wildcat action were foolhardy and dangerous.

Lippert describes the types of concerns that preoccupied individuals participating in wildcat strikes.[2] Lippert joined a wildcat at GM's Fleetwood plant during the mid-1970s. He describes his own thoughts and concerns while awaiting the moment of the strike call. Questions of doubt seemed to preoccupy him. Thoughts of the consequences of walking out without the support of other workers stood to inhibit his willingness to act, as did questions of his workmates' resolve to follow through with their commitments.

Pursuing wildcat activity in an institutional environment which is openly hostile to such action requires high levels of trust and solidarity among strikers. These are the resources that must be mobilized for the act to occur. In pursuing resolutions to their grievances on the shop floor, wildcatters must believe that their workmates will stand up and support their actions in the face of tremendous hostility from the formally legitimated authority centers. They must believe that their immediate work group holds the power and resolve to force its will on management independently of external resources. Following others,[3] I contend that auto workers mobilized the support and resources required to initiate this outlawed activity from within the everyday work groups which they formed in the factory. The strong levels of solidarity experienced in these work groups made commitments to wildcat action appear to workers as viable avenues for resolving shop-floor grievances.

What types of relationships tended to spawn this high level of trust and solidarity among workers? What types of experiences produced and reproduced the group orientation and consciousness required of those initiating militant wildcat action? Where were these relationships within the postwar auto industry?

The Residential Community and Militant Solidarity

Kerr and Siegel have located one of the sources of industrial worker militancy in residential communities isolated from the larger society.[4] Friedlander's more recent study of union mobilization in an auto supplier plant also stresses the importance of solidary communities for mobilization.[5] While I accept the possibility of workers developing solidary commitments through such out-of-plant associations, I do not define them as their primary sources, because postwar demographic changes in residency patterns had weakened the impact of community ties on in-plant relationships.

It is common knowledge that postwar suburbanization, spurred by federal housing and transportation policies, weakened the class composition of residential neighborhoods. Factory workers are no longer concentrated exclusively or even typically in working-class communities surrounding their immediate factories. The geographic dispersion of a given plant's workforce has grown considerably since World War II.[6] As a result, workers are far less likely than they once were to interact in their residential communities with folks from their work groups. I contend that these demographic shifts have decreased the potential for the out-of-plant community to serve as the spawning grounds for militant worker solidarity.

Auto managements have also used their labor recruitment policies to weaken the effect of residential solidarity on workers' factory relationships. A local UAW official made this clear in an interview. He states that:

> The plant manager at the time [1950s] was paranoid of the [city's] labor force. He went to the South and recruited

> Southerners into the plant. That retarded our [union's] efforts. They didn't just recruit from places like Kentucky and Tennessee. They went into the deep South—Georgia, southern Mississippi, and Alabama. They had more people from certain rural counties in these states working in the body plant than men over 21 in these counties.

This account illustrates managements' potential for controlling the effect of residential solidarity by recruiting workers from outside of it. Auto managements have a long history of engaging in this practice. They have drawn their labor forces from populations that were regionally, ethnically, and racially diverse, as well as newcomers to the residential communities surrounding their plants. Whether intentional or unintentional, this practice has tended to weaken plant-community linkages. It has weakened the residential community's potential for serving as a spawning grounds for the intense worker solidarity needed for generating militant collective action in the factory. For these reasons, I do not locate the primary source of workers' shop-floor militancy within the residential communities.

In-Plant Homogenization and Militant Solidarity

Neo-Marxist labor scholars have drawn heavily from Marx's homogenization thesis in explaining labor militancy. They link increases in militancy to the detailed division of labor; the concentration of unskilled, undifferentiated workers in the factory; and the combining of formerly segmented and independent operations into an integrated, centrally coordinated production process.[7]

I contend that this militant homogenization thesis must be refined considerably before it can serve as a valid explanation for the incidence of noninstitutionalized labor militancy in the auto industry. In making this assertion, I accept much of Lukács's critique of this type of argument. Lukács challenges the deterministic linkage that many Marxists make among revolution, class consciousness, and the structures of everyday life created by capitalist development.[8] Lukács does not see capitalist factory developments—such as proletarianization and deskilling—as automatically spawning an increasingly militant proletariat. Rather Lukács sees capitalist domination as being most pervasive in the factory. This domination tends to strip workers of their capacities for initiating independent, collective courses of protest action, even when it is in their best interests to do so. Lukács supports his position with two arguments.

First, while Lukács sees workers as becoming increasingly integrated into highly interdependent production systems within capitalism, he does not see them as this process' active agents. Adumbrating Braverman's central thesis,[9] Lukács sees managements achieving this integration by alienating workers from the conceptual functions involved in production.[10] Workers themselves do not organize their everyday socialized activities in the factory. They merely carry out managements' detailed prescriptions. Thus, workers' activities become increasingly reified as quantifiable exchange values that managements direct and manipulate. Such activities become stripped of their subjective content, and workers do not gain a sense of authorship from engaging in them. For Lukács, this alienation has profound consequences for workers' consciousness. Their reified experiences in the factory as the objects of capitalist manipulation do not prepare them adequately for pursuing independent and collective courses of militant action against their employers.

Second, Lukács views capitalist managements as actively structuring everyday factory relationships to serve their interests in maintaining domination. For Lukács, managements control the types of relationships that workers develop with one another in the factory, subjecting them to intense surveillance. As a result, workers do not necessarily experience class solidarity through such relationships. For Lukács, total domination in the factory has as much potential for passive atomization as it does for militant homogenization.

While I argue that Lukács and his followers push the total-objectification thesis a bit too far in reference to factory workers' consciousness and managements' potential to control it,[11] his major points must be taken seriously. Concentrating masses of unskilled factory workers into interdependent production processes does not automatically spawn worker consciousness and labor militancy, even with increases in exploitation. In individuating and atomizing job functions—and in organizing and monitoring in-plant interactions so that workers work in structural isolation from one another—managements have leverage for mitigating solidary worker commitments on the job. As typically formulated, the homogenization thesis fails to account for this leverage. The theory I specify next will do so.

Labor Process Distinctions

I locate the source of the worker solidarity required to initiate militant collective action in the organization of particular types of labor processes employed in the postwar auto industry. The theory begins with the recognition of three basic facts: (1) many types of production processes exist in the industry; (2) these processes are organized differently; and (3) these organizational differences create very different working conditions. Some tend to spawn worker solidarity on the shop floor, while others do not. This section of the chapter defines ideal typically the general labor process conditions that both impede and facilitate worker solidarity. The concrete labor processes in the auto industry that conform to each ideal type are also specified. The characteristics of the particular labor processes described next held throughout the 1946–1973 period of interest, unless a more restrictive periodization is noted.

Atomizing Labor Processes

Atomizing labor processes inhibit the development of worker solidarity on the job, as well as the development of collective capacities for militant action independent of the legitimated authority structure, such as worker-initiated slowdowns and wildcat strikes. Such labor processes transfer the control over work pace from workers to machines; reduce the scope of workers' responsibilities to that of carrying out individually a few prescribed functions; and, most importantly, impede the formation of primary, functional work groups through the detailed specialization and atomization of operations. Such labor processes create work milieux that alienate workers from their production operations, from the products they produce, and from relationships of solidarity with their workmates.[12]

I hypothesize that atomizing labor processes do not generate much wildcat activity because they do not provide a structural foundation for developing high levels of worker solidarity independent of the official bureaucratic authority structure.[13] While I accept the jump from a shop-floor condition of worker isolation and atomization to one of fever-pitched solidarity as possible, I hold it to be improbable. Instead, I hypothesize that atomized auto workers typically seek either individualistic resolutions to their disputes—such as quitting, absenteeism, isolated acts of sabotage,[14] or exhaust the grievance procedure and submit to official union mediation when such avenues are available.

Some industry analysts have typified the auto labor process as displaying the characteristics of this ideal type.[15] This characterization may indeed capture a good part of the reality of many jobs in the industry. Actual jobs conforming in varying degrees to the characteristics of the atomizing ideal type can be found on the machine-paced chassis and final-assembly lines; on automated machine-paced subassembly processes, such as those employed in the machining and assembly of engines and transmissions after the mid-1950s; and on solitary subassembly operations in which operators work on their tasks in isolation from one another.

Jobs on the machine-paced chassis line conformed closely to the ideal type during the period of interest. In chassis assembly, assemblers worked in structural isolation from one another. They typically worked alone in pits below the machine-paced conveyor lines, fastening components to moving chassis as they passed over their work stations.

This environment obviously did not encourage the formation of strong solidary worker relationships. On the chassis line, workers' capacities for interacting with one another were extremely limited. They could not converse with one another easily, because of the isolation and the noise from their tools. Working in pits beneath the line, they could not even see one another easily (lest they risk getting hit in the head by moving chassis).

However, the working conditions experienced by assemblers along the chassis lines were the extreme case. Polishing jobs on the final-body line were more typical during the period of interest.[16] Here workers polished a finished auto body as it moved down the machine-paced line. An individual worker walked along the line polishing his or her assigned body section. When finished, he or she walked back up the line to begin another.

While several workers polished a given body at the same time, they did not form task-oriented work groups. Body polishers' operations were not integrated with one another. The operations of other polishers did not affect the quality of an individual polishers' work, nor the time it took him or her to finish the task.

This structural environment provided more opportunities for workers to establish relationships than that of the chassis assemblers. Workers could see one another and at least converse. However, we should not overplay the significance of these opportunities. Walker and Guest show that the scope of interaction between operators was restricted to the few workers in immediate proximity. Also, because these workers did not work together on given task assignments, and because they worked with noisy tools, their interactions were likely to be brief, and the substance casual. Without minimizing the importance of these relationships, I hypothesize that they were not the relationships through which workers sacrificed their jobs to resolve grievances favorably through noninstitutionalized collective action. Structurally, this work environment did not facilitate the levels of trust and solidarity required.

After they were automated in the 1950s, jobs on machining operations for engines and transmissions also conformed to the atomizing ideal type. Faunce documents the effects of in-line transfer machines on work in an engine plant in the late 1950s.[17] These machines transferred control over machining operations from workers to electronic devices, completely removing operators from the manufacturing process. Operators simply monitored the control modules pacing operations there.

Faunce found that this new technology had profound effects on workers' interactions. Those working in the automated plant were recruited from older engine plants employing the labor-intensive technology replaced by the in-line transfer machines. In the older plants, conveyor lines linked machine operators together and transported engine blocks from workstation to workstation. However, workers collectively gained some control over the pace of production by controlling machine loading, activation, and unloading. Faunce found that in the old plants: (1) less than 10 feet typically separated work stations; (2) strong work groups formed among operators working on the lines; and (3) their social interaction was quite frequent.

In contrast, Faunce found that the automated technology impeded frequent worker interaction and the formation of solidary relationships. Workers had less control over the pace of the lines they monitored, for they did not activate these processes. As distance between workers increased, interaction decreased, and so did workers' feelings of team solidarity.

The type of automatic in-line transfer technology employed in engine manufacturing and assembly was extended to the manufacture of other automotive components, such as stamped metal casings, transmissions, body hardware, and smaller component parts in the middle and late 1950s. This technology was employed successfully during this period in the manufacture of parts with long production runs. It has not been employed successfully in the manufacture of parts with shorter runs, such as body parts.

Finally, individual subassembly jobs off-line conformed to two of the atomizing conditions. They tended to reduce the scope of workers' operations to a few prescribed tasks, and they did not create task-oriented work groups. However, these jobs did provide workers with much more opportunities for controlling work pace than did those on machine-paced lines.[18]

Solidarity-Generating Labor Processes

Functional work groups and work-group consciousness were created by solidarity-generating labor processes. Workers in these processes did not experience profound alienation in their factory activities and relationships. These workers engaged in shop-floor confrontations—not because their factory experiences left them degraded, desperate, and with nothing to lose, but because these experiences provided them with rewards worth protecting, as well as resources for protecting them.[19]

Ideal-type definition. Solidarity-generating labor processes encouraged workers to form primary, functional work groups in the factory in order to accomplish their work tasks.[20] They provided workers with collective control over their workpace,[21] and some leverage for redefining the ends to which they directed their workplace activities as their own.

This labor process actually homogenized workers into solidary communal groups with a collective consciousness. It linked the everyday interests of those involved in it to the pursuit of a collective work goal. It forced workers to coordinate their activities consciously, often on a moment-by-moment basis, to accomplish this goal. Most importantly, this goal—as defined in the collective consciousness of those participating in its pursuit—lay outside of managements' sphere of domination and control. This labor process mobilized in-group solidarity between workers, day in and day out, and prior to the initiation of the wildcat action. I contend that this a priori mobilization was a necessary condition enabling workers to initiate noninstitutionalized protests within factory settings pervaded by structures of domination and surveillance.

The eyebrow-raising aspect of this theory is its implicit assumption that such labor processes played a prominent role in the postwar auto industry. Until quite recently, dominant theories of industrialization have not generally recognized this labor process' importance.[22] Such theories have predicted that, as industries develop, managements continually reduce their reliance upon workers' discretion and control by increasing the division of labor, mechanizing production processes, and instituting ever more pervasive control systems. The conception of workers themselves taking collective initiative in organizing and controlling even a part of their work activities stands as an anomaly to the predicted tendency.

Those labor processes spawning noninstitutionalized militancy in the auto industry did not follow the path predicted by dominant theories. Auto firms have employed these alternatives throughout the industry's history, and they will likely do so in the future. Such labor processes are often more efficient and cost-effective than are the alternatives. Automotive jobs which had solidarity-generating characteristics were located on stamping and welding-press subassembly lines, cushion-building subassembly, body-framing operations prior to the mid-1950s, and interior trim.

These solidarity-generating labor processes have been identified from a variety of sources, including (1) technical reports of plant layouts and technologies published in trade journals, such as *Automotive Industries* and *American Machinist*, (2) archival information obtained from UAW records; (3) information reported in *Voice of Local 212*, the official newspaper of the union representing workers at the Briggs/Plymouth Body complex, and *Ford Facts*, the newspaper of the union representing workers at the Ford River Rouge complex; (4) key informant interviews with ten experienced stamping-plant workers and local union officials; (5) information provided in newspaper coverage of strikes; as well as (6) secondary sources.

The operator-paced, subassembly lines. Auto stamping-press, welding-press, and cushion-building operations typically employed a similar technological organization from 1946–1973. Workers performed high-speed, manual operations at stationary settings. On the presses, they loaded parts into machines, activated and unloaded them. On cushion building, they manually stuffed, tacked, or sewed together seats, back cushions, and upholstery components.[23]

The spatial layout of these operations spawned the solidary workgroup characteristics of interest in this study. For efficiency, managements grouped work stations together along subassembly lines. Parts flowed down the lines to stations along conveyors in sequential order. Lead workers set the pace parts flowed down the lines as they finished their own operations. Subsequent workers grabbed them off the conveyor and worked them up manually in their stations or in machines that they loaded and activated. They then placed them back on the conveyor for transport to the next station. There, workers did the same. At the end of the lines, finished parts were stacked and transported to final assembly.

While parts travelled along moving conveyors, operators controlled line pace by altering the time involved in either manually working up their workpieces or in loading and activating their presses. Lead workers initially set the pace, but workers down line had the power to slow them. They could prevent work from flowing to those behind them, as subsequent operators had to wait for their finished parts in order to perform their own operations. They could force those in front to coordinate their work pace in concert with theirs as well. If the lead workers refused and continued working at the faster speeds, parts piled up or bypassed needed operations, causing chaos and serious production bottlenecks.

In order to run efficiently, all operators along the subassembly line had to coordinate their work speeds with one another. Standardized production quota incentives were used to encourage them to do so.[24] This technology necessitated tightly coordinated teams, putting a collective stamp on the control that individual operators had over pacing. Managements encouraged team formation in order to get parts out efficiently.

The collective aspect of workers' moment-by-moment task performances on these operations distinguished them sharply from those found on the final-assembly lines portrayed so vividly in the literature. This collective coordination of moment-by-moment activities conditioned such workers to act as a group both in consent with and in opposition to managements' aims.

This group consciousness and commitment was structurally generated by the worker-paced, subassembly-line technology, and the quota-based, incentive-reward scheme managements employed to monitor output. Similar systems governed these activities throughout the postwar industry. Descriptions of stamping, welding-press, and cushion-building operations found in archival sources support the generalizability of these conditions.[25] While managements attempted to atomize these work groups with automation in the 1950s, such attempts generally failed. Technical efficiency requirements forced managements to live with them and their consequences into the 1970s.

Fabric trim installation. Interior trim installation was organized differently. Workers installed cloth and component materials in bodies moving along machine driven lines. They therefore could not control line speeds or build inventory banks, as could, say, the seat-cushion builders feeding them materials.

However, trim jobs were quite distinct from those typically found on final assembly. Trimmers cut cloth to proper size, stretched it across body surfaces, and set it in place with tacks or glue without wrinkles or damage. Unlike the one-minute final-assembly job,[26] trim installation frequently required up to twenty minutes or more per body.[27] Jobs here were labor intensive, involving experiential knowledge and skill.

Trim installation gave rise to solidary teams. Trim panels were typically too large for one person to handle alone. The precise stretching and placing of the material across large panel surfaces demanded that workers work together on the task in small groups. For example, four-person teams worked on interior trim installation on the Lincoln line in the late 1940s.[28] Lichtenstein notes that four- to five-person teams were the typical industry pattern in the early postwar period.[29]

Trimmers' job performances were directly dependent upon the others holding tension in the cloth with which they worked. The conscious, moment-by-moment coordination of effort involved here was even more intense than that taking place on the high speed subassembly lines discussed previously. Most everything that trimmers did on the job was dependent on the actions of their fellow workers. Finishing jobs within allotted standards required that teams race together, coordinating their activities in concert. Interior trim operations also took place inside of the moving body, outside of managements' view. This gave trimmers autonomous space within which to organize their activities, as well as freedom from managerial surveillance and control.[30]

Finally, until the middle 1950s, body framing typically required workers to coordinate their moment-by-moment activities with one another. Body framing was the operation within which the major body subassemblies were welded together. Until the introduction and spread of gate-line systems, welders performed this operation in massive, stationary welding bucks that held the major subassemblies in place. On this operation, body framers placed the subassemblies into the buck, secured them with clamps, welded them together and unloaded them with power tools. After framing, the body was placed on the machine-paced final body line for subsequent metal finishing, painting, and trimming operations.

Again production quotas typically paced these manually activated operations. Workers worked together as a team to perform their tasks. The number of workers working together in these welding bucks has varied throughout the industry. In

1957, for example, six workers worked in each of the framing bucks used in the Lincoln plant.[31]

Thus, the technological organization in stamping and welding-press operating, cushion and back building, interior trimming, and frame building spawned solidary work groups. Such organization demanded that workers closely coordinate their moment-by-moment activities with one another in order to accomplish what management demanded of them.

The preexisting patterns of intensive interaction and group coordination that these workers experienced everyday enabled them to mobilize support for their grievances quickly and to act decisively as a collective unit. The requirement that workers coordinate their actions with one another on job-specific tasks distinguishes these jobs from the atomized jobs described earlier.

Worker-Defined Work Goals

I now address workers' behavioral incentives and motivations, examining how workers were able to redefine the ends to which they directed their work activities as their own. In the theory developed here, such a redefinition was critical for it provided workers with a collective identity independent of that which managements assigned to them in their official job definitions.

Earlier Studies

Industrial analysts, working within various traditions, have developed numerous theoretical explanations of workers' work motivations. Industrial field researchers who have conducted intensive, ethnographic studies of workers in industrial settings have tended to define workers' motivations in reference to the actual production-reward structures existing in the workplace. The piece-rate system has been studied most extensively. Roy's study of a piece-rate factory during the 1940s,[32] and Burawoy's study of the same factory thirty years later provide us with some of the richest accounts.[33] In both the 1940s and mid-1970s, workers' motivation for performing their tasks was similar. They worked to "make out" on their particular jobs. "Making out" consisted of meeting, but not exceeding by a wide margin, a production quota that earned them the most wages possible without encouraging management to increase the rate.

Workers honored and encouraged one another to respect quota ceilings. These ceilings did not dissuade workers from working hard and fast. Rather, they encouraged workers to race to meet the quota as fast as possible and then spend the rest of the day in the factory in nonproduction pursuits. Burawoy suggests that those operators most adept at doing this won status honor from their peers. In addition to purely economic pursuits, the pursuit of status honor appears to have played a big role in motivating workers.[34]

What is the significance of such behavior? For many of the industrial sociologists of the 1940s and 1950s, the types of workers' cultures that developed around the pursuit of "making out" represented informal behavioral systems beyond managements' sphere of domination.[35] These analysts saw industrial workers as essentially sabotaging piece-rate systems to pursue nonproduction goals that management never intended them to serve. Piece-workers manipulated these systems collectively to enhance their freedom and control over their activities. These researchers found that this freedom and control often became the focal point of industrial conflicts. These informal systems were even thought to represent a limited or embryonic form of class consciousness.[36]

Burawoy views these "making out" cultures as having similar motivational significance than what the early postwar researchers imputed to them. He sees such cultures as granting workers limited forms of control over their everyday work activities, thus motivating them to work hard on the job. However, Burawoy did not find the persistent management-worker conflicts and struggles noted earlier, and he directs much effort explaining this apparent decline. He argues that political economic developments in the postwar period enabled firms to co-opt these "making out" cultures in the service of management's historically conditioned interests.

"Running for Time" in Auto Manufacturing

Similar work goals motivated the behavior of postwar auto workers, and shop-floor game cultures akin to those described by Roy and Burawoy developed in auto plants as well. These cultures redefined work activities into a "making-out" game that absorbed workers' commitment and energy. Instead of making out, the end motivating work activities is referred to, in this instance, as "earning time," and the shop cultures developing from its pursuit are referred to as "running-for-time" cultures. However, the incentive system giving rise to such shop cultures was not typically a piece-rate system.[37] Typically, auto workers were not paid by the piece, but were paid categorically by the hour. Their wages were not directly tied to their individual task effort. This gave them no incentive to produce more than what was typically demanded by managements' job definition.

In cases when production processes have been manually activated, managements have regulated jobs by setting production standards, or quotas, per operation. Once workers met their standards within the allotted times, their production obligations ended. They earned time. What they were allowed to do with this earned time has varied historically from firm to firm and even from plant to plant within firms.

I argue that these shop cultures did not universally tend to generate the possessive individualism which Burawoy notes in his shop. Rather, in solidarity-generating labor processes, earning time was pursued collectively by work groups. This intensified rather than muted work-group solidarity.

I also contend that the pursuit of this end was somewhat independent of managements' domination and control, and that this fostered the development of independent collective identities. Managers did not create this end intentionally, nor could they fully control workers' pursuit of it.[38] Under certain conditions specified in chapter 5, such pursuit was acceptable to managements' interests, while under other conditions it was not.

Work motivations on stamping and welding-press lines. In the stamping plant where my informants worked, the pursuit of earned time motivated workers' activities and interactions. This pursuit absorbed their energies. It generated an interest and a stake in the output of all workers on a particular line. Indeed, the informants whom I interviewed suggested that workers played key roles in setting and maintaining line speeds.

> *Zetka*: "Who controls the pacing of the line?"
>
> *Worker*: "Usually, the first man is on a punch press, and he can see down and tell what to run."
>
> *Zetka*: "He sets the speed?"
>
> *Worker*: "Yeah. "I don't want to cover you up, and you don't want to cover me up," you know? And if everybody works together, you don't really bust your balls. You keep busy. . . . If you so happen to get on a good line, you can get through an hour, hour and a half early. . . . A lot of people, they don't want to go fast. A lot of people like to take their time and get through about a half hour [early]. Then, other guys they like to get through early, and they try to go together. They go real fast so they can get done."

They also suggested that workers pressured others to keep pace.

> There's the psychological thing that, if you're the slow one on the line and everybody else wants to run fast and get done, they make you feel bad if you're not running as fast as they are.

A union official described the end to which these workers directed such activities as "earned time." "Running for time" was used to describe its pursuit. Running for time involved racing ahead of managements' production standards and banking the excess production in order to earn time off the line. Such activity was protected in the collective bargaining agreement. Once workers met their preset rates, management could not demand more production.

To workers on the shop floor, earned time meant time free from the subassembly lines, from production requirements, and from managerial surveillance. Once workers met their standards, they shut down their lines and left their immediate workstations. They used earned time for conversation, sleep in the locker room, or for playing cards or dominoes in the cafeteria.

"Running for time" and beating managements' production standards gave operators a sense of control over their working environment, as well as a badge of status honor for their ingenuity in beating the industrial engineers' production rates. While to an outsider unaccustomed to the rigors of factory life this end may seem trivial, to those forced to labor in such an environment day in and day out, it made an oppressive everyday worklife bearable. I will show that workers have defined the freedoms made possible within this work organization as freedoms worth fighting for, even when this fight had to be carried on outside of the parameters legitimated in the labor contract.

The prospects of winning earned time drove workers to run fast, to organize, and to regulate the flow of work down the lines. It made group cohesion, commitment, and consciousness even tighter. In this technical organization of work, earned time was a collective goal. To earn it, every worker had to coordinate their moment-by-moment activities with others on the line. They had to be willing and capable of running faster than managements' pace. Other workers expected—even demanded—that they do so.

My contention is that this "running-for-time" shop culture typically operated industry wide, as it was structurally generated by worker-paced subassembly technologies and noneconomic, quota-based incentive-reward systems. This generalization is supported in descriptions of stamping operations found in the departmental reports in *Voice of Local 212*, the official newsletter of the Briggs/Chrysler Plymouth Body local; in *Ford Facts*, the official newsletter of the Ford River Rouge local; and in the strike reports published in *The Wall Street Journal* and *The New York Times*.

Work motivations in machine-paced team processes. On machine-paced assembly-line operations, the work technology itself precluded the emergence of the type of game cultures forming on worker-paced subassemblies. Here, workers did not enjoy the freedom to manipulate the pace at which workpieces moved down the line. They could not bank work. They could not do, say, eight hours work in six, working faster in the morning, slower in the afternoon, and so on.

However, these limitations did not necessarily rivet workers to the job every minute of the working day. On certain operations, workers could and did "run for time" in ways comparable to those on worker-paced subassemblies. Lippert's description of the Kotan top builders in the Cadillac body plant provides an informative glimpse of the leverage available to trimmers for earning time on machine-paced lines.[39]

The Kotan workers worked in pairs securing vinyl tops to Cadillac bodies moving down a machine-paced conveyor. At the time of Lippert's report, seventy-two cars moved down the line per hour. Thirty-five teams of two worked in rotation while the line was moving. These teams worked for twenty minutes or more per body, cutting, placing, stretching, and gluing the vinyl into place.

Lippert suggests that the Kotan workers enjoyed a considerable amount of free time per hour.[40] Under the most favorable conditions—when teams were able to make the twenty-minute rate per car—each Kotan team finished three cars per hour. The thirty-five teams held a maximum capacity for finishing 105 cars per hour. Working under favorable conditions at the seventy-two-car-per-hour pace, the thirty-five teams would accumulate 660 total minutes of earned time, amounting to about nineteen minutes of earned time per team per hour. This earned time did not include lunch, break, and relief time allowances.

Lippert's descriptions of the down time activities of the Kotan workers were similar to those reported by my stamping informants. Specific activities included informal group conversations, pitching quarters, and playing miniature paper basketball. The point is that the Kotan workers used this earned time to pursue activities they defined as their own, activities lying outside the realm of management's sphere of authorized domination.

Another way in which workers typically attempted to earn time on machine-paced lines was "doubling up." Interior trim operations were especially conducive to this, because workers performed their operations inside the car body. Managers could not readily see who was inside the car, or what each worker did there. On such operations, a four-person team might agree that three operators would perform all of the prescribed operations in order to allow one teammate down time. They would then rotate positions so that each take a turn. On a very good team, the four person operation might be done in a two-on, two-off arrangement.[41]

Again, my assumption is that jobs organized as team processes on machine-paced lines throughout the auto industry encouraged the development of these types of informal arrangements. Sayles reports that trimmers' capacities for asserting such informal control over their work organization, and for carving out a generous realm of freedom for themselves on the job, were recognized throughout the industry by both management and union officials.[42]

Work motivations in atomizing labor processes. Following Goffman's classic analysis of "making out" in total institutions,[43] I question the extent to which even the most prescriptive, atomizing labor process strips workers of a capacity for asserting some subjective control over their everyday work activities. I assert that the Lukácsian, or the Bravermanian, notion of total objectification—that is, the idea that work in advanced capitalist society has become degraded to the point that workers become mere automatons passively responding to managerial prescriptions—is a myth obscuring what actually takes place on the shop floor.[44] Following Burawoy, I hypothesize that, even in the most atomizing labor processes, workers create, pursue, and partially actualize work goals that are beyond managements' sphere of domination.

To illustrate, I use Lippert's account of his own work motivations and behavior.[45] Lippert's job on the body assembly line conformed to the characteristics of the atomizing ideal type. It involved installing components on door exteriors as bodies moved down the machine-paced line. Lippert's tasks were privatized in that they did not require group coordination. For the most part, Lippert worked alone, isolated from others.

Yet, Lippert claims to have protected his identity from the imprint of managerial domination by finding ways to beat his job's time-studied prescriptions. Through his own ingenuity, Lippert discovered shortcuts enabling him to work faster than the specified rate and he used these shortcuts to earn time on the job. Lippert reports that most workers at Fleetwood Body discovered and used such shortcuts to earn time.

Lippert transformed his job into a game that worked like this: Lippert used his ingenuity to work up the line a couple of jobs, gaining twenty seconds or so on his production standard. He used these seconds for reading, while walking back down the line. He then returned to the job and began to work rapidly back up the line to gain more reading time. Because Lippert's job could be performed without much thought or attention, he focused his mind during production on what he was reading. The end motivating Lippert's activities was earned time for reading.[46]

Thus, Lippert's personal example illustrates how workers can manage to turn very routinized and atomizing jobs on the moving conveyor into winnable games. Learning shortcuts and using them to earn time appears to be quite common on moving-belt assembly systems.[47] The ability to pursue this type of worker-defined, identity-preserving end enables workers to turn a hard job that they have to perform day in and day out into a bearable one. Redefining the job as a game allows workers to assert some subjective mastery over their work situations. I assume that this type of redefinition occurs everywhere on machine-paced lines.

Work Goal Redefinition and Militant Capacities

I argue that this work goal redefinition enhances work group solidarity for noninstitutionalized collective action only on the solidarity-generating labor processes, not the atomized ones. A brief comparison and contrast will make my reasoning transparent. For workers in both types of labor processes, these line-beating activities require extra exertion, initiative, and cunning. They represent a moment of freedom from perhaps an otherwise oppressive experience. However, these workers experience such activities quite differently.

For the atomized, working up the line is experienced as a privatized game—a game not requiring group consensus, coordination, or solidarity. Pursuing earned time in this instance does not bind workers into a task-oriented community of fate because other workers are not typically a part of a given worker's private game. They do not benefit directly when he or she wins, and an individual's game can be defined as a threat. Lippert, for example, reports that one of his workmates became angry with him for reading, fearing that this open display of idleness would provoke management to add to the job. Because of their privatized nature, such pursuits do not tend to generate or strengthen relational ties that can serve as a springboard for future collective action.

In contrast, teamworkers, even on machine-paced lines, must coordinate consciously their moment-by-moment activities intensely as a group in pursuit of such ends. In order to earn time, everyone has to race ahead as a team. If one member refuses, or is incapable of running faster, no one earns time. This extra managerial end is pursued collectively. Its booty is shared collectively. It is won or lost by the group, acting as a collective entity. Such pursuits—when successful—strengthen relational bonds of trust and collective commitment. Most importantly, they detach them from managerial direction and control.

There is an exception to this dichotomization, however. The privatized ends which workers typically pursue in atomizing labor processes may be transformed into collective ends by deals between workers and managers. Such a transformation occurred on the paint spray operations at the Dodge truck and Studebaker plants during the early postwar period.[48] Technically, these lines were organized like atomizing labor processes. Paint sprayers individually sprayed a demarcated section of each of the car bodies passing them on the line. They did not coordinate their moment-by-moment work activities with one another.

However, deals were made at both plants to run a forty-minute-on/twenty-minute-off schedule. After the deal, sprayers performed their hourly production schedules in forty minutes. They then shut down the line for twenty minutes, leaving their booths for more hospitable confines. In entering into this agreement, paint sprayers committed themselves to running faster than the original rate. In order to make this agreement work, everyone on the line had to make a commitment to the deal.[49] In doing so, they all shared the end gained from it collectively. This created a community of fate and a collective consciousness in a labor process that was technically atomized.

Summary

What are the structural conditions that enabled auto workers to initiate noninstitutionalized protests on the shop floor in an industrial environment which was openly hostile to such protests? These structural conditions were located in a labor process that (1) encouraged workers to form task-oriented work groups, (2) gave workers collective control over their work pace, and (3) provided them leverage for redefining the ends to which they directed their activities as their own ends. Actual jobs holding these characteristics were found on stamping and welding-press subassembly lines, on cushion-building subassembly lines, on body-building operations in stationary bucks, and on machine-paced, trim assembly lines.

This solidarity-generating labor process was contrasted with one that transfers control over workers' work pace to machines and atomizes workers' relationships with one another. Jobs having the latter characteristics were found on the machine-paced chassis and final-assembly lines, on automated engine-machining operations, and on subassembly operations performed by solitary workers.

Finally, I predicted that the former labor process spawned more wildcat activity than did the latter, because it encouraged the development of close relationships that could be mobilized quickly for noninstitutionalized collective action in shop-floor disputes. In contrast, the latter discouraged such development, leaving workers without relational support for independent collective action on the shop floor outside of the legitimated authority structure.

CHAPTER 4

Evidence Supporting the Solidary Work-Group Thesis

This chapter aims to establish empirically that workers in solidarity-generating labor processes initiated more wildcat activity than did those in atomizing and other labor processes. It is hypothesized that such workers tended to favor shop-floor militancy as a means of resolving their disputes with management. I test this hypothesis against popular competitors with plant-level data compiled from newspaper sources.

The purpose of the quantitative analyses presented here is primarily heuristic. The quantitative results are employed as guides for steering the interpretive historical analyses down fruitful paths. This approach is consistent with the aims of Weberian case-based analyses.[1]

On empirical grounds, I want to justify treating the workers experiencing solidarity-generating and atomizing labor processes as separate and distinct categories—categories having differential impacts on the development of the postwar auto industry. The results presented here are used to support an argument that auto labor processes developed along dual trajectories in the postwar period. The first trajectory involved increased managerial domination and atomization on the shop floor, while the second involved quite a different development—the legitimation of a quota-based form of shop-floor authority within which past practice became accepted by both management and workers as the reference for assessing the validity of work expectations. I argue that wildcatters in solidarity-generating labor processes forced managements' acceptance of this trajectory.

This is quite a contentious argument, challenging common interpretations of postwar labor-process development in the auto industry. My claim is that, by focusing exclusively on the atomizing features of final assembly work, and ignoring the significant labor process variation within the industry, analysts have overlooked the latter trajectory. I contend that an understanding of this trajectory—which I label hegemonic—must be at the core of a valid explanation of how auto management resolved its labor crises in the postwar period.

In this chapter, I lay the foundation for such an argument. I begin by reviewing some fairly recent historical research employing theoretical categories similar, but not identical, to mine. This literature develops revisionist accounts of the strike waves occurring in the U.S. auto industry from 1937 to the early postwar period. I turn next to quantitative analyses testing the strength of the association between a variety of labor process types and wildcat frequencies. These analyses support the solidary work-group thesis presented in chapter 3.

Occupational Foundations of Militancy, 1937–1945

Lichtenstein and Friedlander have each developed provocative revisionist interpretations of the rise of auto-worker militancy in the late 1930s and 1940s.[2] The structural theory of direct-action militancy specified in chapter 3 draws heavily from each scholar's keen insights. Both refuse to depict the rise of auto-worker militancy as a mass-initiated movement of alienated, atomized, and powerless assembly line workers. In doing so, they have abandoned, for the most part, the Marxist notion of class as an explanatory category. Lichtenstein locates the source of this militancy in the everyday work experiences of distinct occupational groups in the industry. Friedlander locates the source of this militancy in traditional ethnic communities.

Lichtenstein's Structural Theory

Lichtenstein begins his analysis by making a conceptual distinction between the everyday factory experiences of assembly line workers and that of off-line, semiskilled workers similar to that presented in chapter 3. Lichtenstein claims that the latter workers initiated the lion's share of the militant activity that shook the industry in the late 1930s to 1955. Lichtenstein attributes the militancy of the latter workers to both their relative autonomy and control over their work activities and their occupationally centered consciousness and solidarity. Trimmers, body builders, torch welders, and metal finishers make up Lichtenstein's militant-worker category. In Lichtenstein's formulation, two factors distinguish them from other workers: (1) operator pacing; and (2) skill levels thought to be higher than those of assembly line workers.

According to Lichtenstein, these auto workers' shop-floor rebellions were spurred by: (1) a decline in their wage levels vis-a-vis other workers because of managerial manipulation and exploitation of piece- and group-rate systems during a loose labor market; (2) managerial assaults against their job control; and (3) managerial assaults against their privileged occupational status in the factory. These workers managed to turn their strategic positions in the production process into weapons against managements' assaults on them. The close knit webs of factory relationships experienced by these relatively privileged production workers provided a ready-made base of support for their militant shop-floor activities.

The strongest support for Lichtenstein's theory comes from oral history interviews of active United Automobile Worker militants available in the Archives of Labor and Urban Affairs at Wayne State University. These oral histories suggest that the commitments of trimmers, body builders, and metal finishers' to their occupational associations—or their crafts—transcended their firm commitments. Prior to the lean years of the Depression, workers in these occupations tended to change jobs frequently, moving from plant to plant with relative ease. This mobility encouraged the formation of extended webs of cross-plant relationships between workers, as well as the transmission of industrywide occupational traditions and norms.

Lichtenstein documents the militant actions of these occupational groups throughout the 1930s and 1940s. He suggests that by the end of the war they had developed strong steward systems, and that these organizations were developing along a trajectory similar to that taken by labor in Great Britain—that is, toward the development of a system in which power was anchored on the shop floor in steward organizations.

Why then did this budding steward's movement fail to take institutional root in the U.S. automobile industry? In his explanation, Lichtenstein points to three developments. The first was the consolidation and centralization of power at the apex of the UAW, a development that did not bode well for the position of local labor militants. The second factor was the institutionalization of formal bureaucratic procedures aiming to remove the resolution of labor disputes from the factory floor. This was sponsored by the UAW International, and served as an alternative to the confrontational tactics favored by shop-floor militants. The acceptance of this system was inversely related to the decline of the shop-floor militants' power. The third, and most important, factor was automation and the elimination of many worker-paced operations in auto factories—a development which eroded the relational foundations of the semiskilled workers' militant solidarity.

Lichtenstein's work on early auto-worker militancy has influenced greatly the theoretical formulations presented in chapter 3. As did Lichtenstein, I locate the source of noninstitutionalized militancy in workers' everyday shop-floor experiences. I also employ the distinction between final assemblers and workers controlling aspects of their own work pace. However, my conceptualization does differ at critical points from Lichtenstein's.

First, operator-paced operations, collective experiences, and distinct levels of skill are all factors that Lichtenstein links to workers' capacities for militancy. In contrast, my conceptualization links only operator-paced operations involving group coordination to such capacities. I do not predict high levels of militancy from those performing individual bench-work jobs, for example.

Second, while I am aware of the role that skilled workers played in initially organizing union locals in the 1930s,[3] I do not link a notion of "skill" to workers' collective capacities for initiating noninstitutionalized militancy, once unions and collective bargaining systems were established and legitimated. My rationale for ignoring this is simply that many of the most militant workers in the postwar period never experienced the craft orientation and craft communities of the early trimmers, metal finishers, and body builders of the 1930s. Some of the most militant of them worked in newer stamping plants built after World War II. The production workers at these plants were not skilled and did not experience craft traditions. They did, however, experience operator-paced progressive subassembly lines that were conducive to the formation of solidary work teams.

Third—and most important—I reject Lichtenstein's explanation of the decline of shop-floor militancy in the postwar period. I have suggested that the incidence of wildcat activity did not wane with the institution of bureaucratic grievance procedures nor with the consolidation of power at the UAW International. I will also show that, on critical operations, managements' capacities for eliminating operator control over pacing was much more restricted than we have assumed. Because of this, managements were forced to deal with these militants in other ways (specified in chapter 9).

But my differences with Lichtenstein's account are minor, stemming more from adjustments to the different periods involved than from any major theoretical difference. Lichtenstein's work is brilliant and well-documented, and I have drawn considerably from it. His findings concerning strike activity in the late 1930s and 1940s are consistent with theoretical expectations. Subsequently, we will explore the extent to which the patterns that Lichtenstein found continued into the postwar era.

Friedlander's Cultural Theory

Friedlander's key theoretical category is not occupation, but cultural subgroupings among workers. Through oral-history interviewing of a local labor leader, Friedlander studied the emergence of a UAW local in a Michigan supplier plant. Friedlander linked workers' participation in the development of this local to their relationships to union activists outside the plant in local ethnic communities and neighborhood gangs.[4]

However, it is interesting to note that the background of these participants conform strikingly well to those specified in the structural theory that Lichtenstein develops. Those workers joining the union at the supplier plant tended to join in small groups that—according to Friedlander's informant—represented operator-controlled work teams employed on press-line subassemblies. These work groups tended to initiate wildcat actions after the contract was signed in order to resolve their specific grievances with foremen. Friedlander links these spontaneous outbursts to gang community solidarity that existed prior to these workers' employment with the firm.

Another interesting part of Friedlander's work is his generalization from this case to broader labor developments during the formative period of the UAW.[5] Drawing from oral histories held at the Archives of Labor and Urban Affairs, Friedlander correlates shop-floor militancy and workers' left-wing political orientations with distinct occupational and ethnocultural groups in certain plants. Friedlander's militants work on operations identical to those which Lichtenstein specifies. They are trimmers at the Flint plant, metal finishers at Briggs, frame builders at Studebaker, trimmers and cushion builders at Dodge Main, and metal finishers at Hudson and Packard. Occupationally, these workers were semiskilled and more highly paid than were others. They also tended to hail from Catholic and Eastern European backgrounds which was a key factor in Friedlander's theoretical scheme.

Friedlander suggests that shop-floor quiescence, commitment to formalistic grievance actions, support for business unionism, and support for right-wing political causes were all attributes of unskilled, final-assembly workers that were ethnically and culturally distinct from the more militant activists. These workers tended to be Protestant, native-born, and mostly from the South. Many had ties to conservative organizations—such as the Masons and the Knights of Columbus, or to blatantly racist organizations—such as the Black Legion and the Ku Klux Klan. The linkages that Friedlander makes among labor-process conditions, ethnic origins, and workers' political orientations are provocative and deserve further systematic study.

The key point is that Friedlander's work can be used to

support either a cultural or a structural interpretation of the rise of auto-worker militancy in the 1930s. As Lichtenstein notes, the key cultural categories appear to be confounded greatly with the types of structural factors favored in both Lichtenstein's and my own frameworks.

So, the oral history data concerning the differential participation of various occupational groups in militant union activities during the late 1930s and early 1940s appear to conform to theoretical expectations. The groups initiating the militancy of this period experienced working conditions quite similar to those specified in the solidarity-generating ideal type. The groups that tended not to participate experienced atomizing conditions. To what extent did this pattern continue into the postwar period?

Operationalization, Data, and Measurement

The thesis developed in chapter 3 defines a solidarity-generating labor process as a necessary structural foundation for facilitating high levels of wildcat activity. It predicts that such labor processes generate more wildcat activity than do others, while atomizing processes generate less. This thesis is tested here as a predictor of militancy against a homogenization, strategic location, militant craftworker, and homogenized community thesis.[6] These tests establish that the labor process distinctions made in chapter 3 are vital to an understanding of the determinants of wildcat activity and should serve as the foundation for further theoretical development.

Occupational data on wildcat activity are required to test this solidary workgroup thesis. I have compiled such data from the *Wall Street Journal* and *New York Times* reports.[7] The production sites included in the target population are stamping, final-assembly, and body-building plants, as well as large multioperation complexes.[8] Of all wildcat strikes reported, 78 percent occurred in these sites.

Together the *Journal* and *Times* provide sufficient information for specifying the occupation initiating wildcat strikes for 60 percent of all wildcats reported in these sites. Of course, newspaper reports are subject to pressures over which researchers have no control. However, there is no sensible reason to suspect that newspaper reporters and/or editors would systematically choose to report more of one occupation's wildcats than others. Because both papers regularly reported auto production outputs, it is reasonable to assume that wildcats shutting down major lines were reported. Even a single day of lost production would show up as considerable losses in these production statistics. Finally, while the wildcat frequencies presented here are lower than auto strikes reported by others using different sources, yearly frequencies vary consistently among data sets.[9] This provides some evidence for the face validity of the data.

Table 4.1 reports aggregated, occupationally specific wildcat frequencies. Occupationally specific strikes involve a distinctive occupational group mobilizing itself on the shop floor independently of outside organization. For preliminary analysis, wildcat strikes are grouped according to the primary characteristic of the occupation of those initiating them. The categories used here are (1) solidary occupations, such as trimmers, trim-component assemblers, and operators working in team-paced progressive subassembly processes; (2) atomized occupations, such as chassis and final assemblers; (3) craft occupations, such as skilled trades workers; (4) strategic occupations, such as truckers, stock, shipping and receiving workers; and (5) other occupations, such as on-line welders, metal finishers, inspectors, and repair workers.[10] An expected value for each occupational category's contribution to the wildcat total (column 2) can be crudely estimated from the distribution of the occupations studied over the target population (column 1).[11]

The results lend some preliminary support to the solidary work-group thesis. Solidary workers initiated many more wildcat strikes than expected. Atomized and other workers initiated less than expected. Strategic workers initiated wildcat strike frequencies closer to the expected values. However, craft workers also initiated many more wildcats than expected. While the solidary work-group thesis does not predict this result, it is consistent with the expectations of the militant craftworker thesis developed by those studying earlier periods of labor militancy.[12]

Multivariate analyses with more fine-grained occupational distinctions and controls are in order to test the viability of these competing theories. The unit of analysis for the multivariate models is an occupational grouping of workers in a col-

Table 4.1
Distribution of Wildcat Strikes by Type of Occupation Initiating the Action, 1946–1963

	Wildcat Strikes		*Estimated Percent of All Workers in Sample*		
Type of Occupation	Number	Percent of Distribution	Percent of Distribution	Confidence Interval	*z*-Score
Solidarity-generating	108	51	16	16–26[a]	8.33*
Craft	35	17	9	4–14	4.00*
Strategic	22	10	12	7–17	-1.00
Isolated	14	7	34	29–39	-9.00*
Other	32	15	29	23–34	-4.67*
Totals	211[b]	100	100		

*p<.001.

[a]I suspect that the percent distribution reported for the solidarity-generating group may underestimate the group's size. To guard against this, I used the population estimate of 16 percent as the lower range of the confidence interval, and I used 26 percent as the population estimate in the z-score calculation.

[b]Total includes multiple strikes at the same plant. The 211 wildcat strikes shown in this table are fewer than the more than four hundred automotive wildcat strikes for which I found information in newspaper reports. Of the total, 22 percent occurred in types of plants not included in these analyses. Information concerning the agent initiating the strike was not included for about 40 percent of the strikes in the targeted plant types. Of those with agent information, twenty-six were led by the local union, eleven by a plant-level or an external organization (such as militant retiree groups, black-power militants, and so on). These strikes were excluded from the analyses because they were not occupation-specific, and they likely had different mobilization dynamics and constraints than did those specified in the work-group-solidarity thesis.

Sources: Wall Street Journal and *New York Times*, various issues.

lective bargaining/production site during one of four periods: 1946–1950, 1951–1955, 1956–1959, 1960–1963. Table 4.2 lists the 16 possible occupational groupings included. There were a total of eighty-eight plants in the sample, but many contained only some of the sixteen occupational groups, and some opened or closed during the period analyzed. When the occupational group was not represented in the plant/bargaining unit, it was not listed as part of the sample.

Coded in this way, wildcat activity occurred in only 159 (5.5 percent) of the 2,904 possible cases. In those cases with wildcat activity, the frequencies range from one wildcat strike during the period (79 percent) to a high of seven separate wildcat strikes. Given this skew, the models tested predict only the dichotomy of whether or not any wildcat activity at all was waged by the occupational group during the period.

Serial and within-plant correlation pose more serious problems. Wildcat activity—in a given occupational unit and in a given period—may well affect subsequent activity there, as would activity from other occupational units in the given plant from which the occupational observations are drawn. To help control for these effects, I have calculated models on data from 1951–1963 (periods two through four) that include measures of the effects of wildcat activity in the preceding period on current period activity. These include a dummy variable indicating whether the occupational group in question initiated wildcat activity in the preceding period, as well as a variable measuring the general level of strike activity occurring in the plant in the preceding period (coded as 0 for no activity; 1 for a low level of one to three wildcat strikes; and 2 for a high level of four or more wildcat strikes). I have also controlled for systematic plant-level effects by including variables that capture firm, plant-size, plant-type, and community-type influences.[13] Finally, I have included a variable that controls for the effect of authorized plant strikes on workers' propensity to wildcat in a given period.

The periodization employed serves primarily as a control on the occupation/wildcat relationship of interest. Moreover, it enabled me, through archival sources, to account for when plants entered and exited the industry, when occupational groups entered and exited plants, and when occupations' work organization were radically altered by automation.[14]

For these analyses, I rank each occupation along dimensions of three distinct variables: (1) the degree to which the occupational grouping's work organization forced workers to coordinate their activities as a solidary group; (2) the degree to which the occupational grouping enjoyed craft status; and

(3) the degree to which the occupational grouping was strategically located in the production process in the plant. Table 4.2 reports each occupation's rank along these dimensions.

The solidary work-group variable is coded as a dummy variable differentiating those whose labor process forced them to coordinate their work activities in pursuit of common work ends from those that did not.

The craft status variable serves as a more refined test of the militant craftworker thesis. It has three ordinal categories that differentiate among unskilled workers (coded as 1); more skilled but nonapprenticed production workers (coded as 2); and apprenticed craft occupations (coded as 3).

Throughout the period of interest, the industry recognized the distinction between skilled (apprenticed) and nonskilled workers in its collective bargaining contracts, and this distinction is not problematic. While recognized as nonskilled, the workers in category 2 required more knowledge of the materials, tools, and methods employed in their jobs, and have been recognized by industry officials and scholars as being more skilled. This is reflected in higher earnings and longer training periods.[15]

The strategically located variable has three ordinal categories that differentiate among those—such as inspectors and car repair workers—whose work was not immediately linked to major production lines and whose work stoppages would not cause an immediate shutdown (coded as 1); those production workers whose work was immediately linked to a major line and whose work stoppages would cause an immediate shutdown (coded as 2); and those—such as stock suppliers and truckers—whose work was vitally linked to multiple lines in the plant and whose work stoppages would cause multiple line shutdowns (coded as 3).

The analyses employ measures for four additional independent variables. The first is a dummy indicator for small, nonurban, racially homogeneous, working-class communities. This crudely tests the Kerr-Siegel hypothesis locating the source of worker militancy in solidary, occupationally homogeneous communities isolated from urban influences.[16] The second is a dummy indicator denoting whether the plant is a supplier of multiple plants. This measures the effect of strategic location at the plant level. The third is a measure of the interactional effect between solidary workgroup formation

Table 4.2
Occupation Codes and Plant Types for Occupation Groups

	Occupation Code in Each Time Period				*Plant Type*			
Occupation Group	1946–1950	1951–1955	1956–1959	1960–1963	S	FA	BB	FBB[a]
Solidarity-generating occupations								
Trim department	122	122	122	—[c]	—	—	+	+
Body builders	122	122	122	—[c]	—	—	+	+
On-line Groups[b]	112	112	112	—[c]	—	—	+	+
Progressive manufacturing lines	112	112	112	112	+	—	—	—
Motor line	112	112	012[d]	012	—	—	—	—
Non-solidarity generating occupations								
Maintenance	033	033	033	033	+	+	+	+
Tool builders	031	031	031	031	+	—	—	—
Cranes, transport	023	023	023	023	+	+	+	+
Metal finishers	022	022	022	022	—	—	+	+
On-line welders	022	022	022	022	—	—	+	+
Paint department	022	022	022	022	—	—	+	+
Material suppliers	013	013	013	013	+	+	+	+
Final assembly line	012	012	012	012	—	+	—	+
Chassis line	012	012	012	012	—	+	—	+
Final body line	012	012	012	012	—	—	+	+
Auxiliary workers[e]	011	011	011	011	+	+	+	+

[a]S = stamping plant; FA = final-assembly plant; BB = body-building plant; FBB = final-assembly plant with body-building facilities. + denotes the presence of the occupation group.

[b]Prior to automation, these occupations typically handled large subassemblies, such as hanging doors on the body lines.

[c]During the 1960–1963 period these occupations were partially automated and/or transferred to centralized supplier plants.

[d]This change in the occupation code represents changes brought about by automation.

[e]These occupations typically provided services which were not vital to immediate production outcomes of a major line, for example, inspectors, repair workers, and janitors.

and supplier plants. The fourth is a categorical variable for firms.

Results

Logistic regression models were estimated to predict the (log) odds of a given occupational group initiating occupationally specific wildcat activity in a production/bargaining site during a period. Equations were generated for a general model for 1946–1963, employing the finer period distinctions as dummy controls. Ford was used as the reference category for the firm coefficients; 1960–1963 was used for the period coefficients. The bivariate correlations suggest low levels of collinearity among the independent variables.

Table 4.3 reports the results of the general model equations. Equation one reports the results of the basic model. Equation two adds an interaction between supplier plants and solidary work groups. Equation three reports the results for 1951–1963 introducing the preceding period controls.

The findings strongly support the predictions of the solidary-work-group thesis. Controlling for firm, period, community, and plant-level effects, workers in labor processes requiring solidary-work-group formation were much more likely to initiate wildcat activity than those who were not. They were more than four times as likely to do so in equation one. This effect was still significant when controlling for the interaction between supplier plants and solidary-work-group formation in equations two and three. This finding supports the theoretical contention that labor processes requiring solidarity-work-group formation structurally facilitated wildcat action.

While generally weaker, the craft status variable also increased the likelihood that an occupational group would initiate wildcat activity. The two variables operationalizing variants of strategic location theory did not do as well, however. The measure for strategic location at the occupational level was insignificant in all of the models. The plant-level measure (supplier plant) was both positive and significant in equation one, but washed-out with the introduction of the interaction effect of supplier plant and solidary-work-group formation in equations two and three.

This finding suggests that, while the strategic location of a plant potentially enhances workers' capacity to act collectively in pursuit of common interests, strong relational foundations are necessary for actualizing that capacity. Those occupational groups that were both strategically located at the plant level and solidary were more than seven times as likely to initiate wildcat strikes as those who were not (equation two), and about ten times as likely to do so when controlling for preceding-period effects (equation three).

Thus, the results support the hypothesized effects of solidary working conditions on the likelihood of workers wildcatting. Solidary work groups were behind the lion's share of the militancy waged in the early postwar period. Because of this, it makes sense to explain militancy declines in reference to the postwar experiences of these groups.

However, the independent measure of skilled status also had a positive effect on workers' propensities to initiate wildcat strikes during the period in question. In addition, many of these workers did not experience the type of solidary work organization defined in chapter 3. This leads me to suspect that the structural impediments to collective action specified in chapter 3 might not have been as debilitating for skilled workers as for those experiencing truly atomizing conditions—that is, those who were structurally isolated and driven by a machine-paced line throughout the day. Perhaps because of their mobility and relative control over their moment-by-moment activities, these skilled workers seemed to be able to overcome their isolation, generate group awareness of their strategic power, and act collectively to maximize their gains. The question of how these skilled status groups were incorporated into the postwar industrial order requires separate treatment. This important question will not be addressed here.

The workers experiencing solidary work-organization in production will take center stage in subsequent discussions. I will document how these groups were incorporated into the hegemonic order that began to emerge in the U.S. automobile industry after World War II.

Table 4.3
Logistic Coefficients for Regression of Wildcat-Strike Activity on Selected Independent Variables, 1946–1963

Independent Variable	Model 1	Model 2	Model 3
Work-group solidarity	1.42*** (.20)	1.11*** (.21)	.95** (.35)
Craft status	.45*** (.13)	.61*** (.14)	.88*** (.22)
Strategic location	0.01 (.15)	-.03 (.16)	.27 (.25)
Supplier plant	1.09*** (.26)	.40 (.34)	.55 (.50)
Plant size (log)	.78*** (.12)	.78*** (.12)	.33* (.18)
Community solidarity	.38 (.26)	.36 (.26)	.63 (.43)
Work-group solidarity x supplier plant	—	1.96*** (.50)	2.28*** (.71)
Authorized plant strikes	.30 (.29)	.33 (.29)	.63 (.43)
Firm			
General Motors	-.63* (.35)	-.69* (.35)	-.06 (.49)
Chrysler	1.60*** (.26)	1.62*** (.26)	1.02** (.42)
Independent	1.04*** (.28)	1.08*** (.29)	.48 (.46)
Period			
1946–1950	2.09*** (.40)	2.24*** (.41)	—
1951–1955	1.22** (.42)	1.36*** (.43)	1.44** (.49)
1956–1959	1.18** (.41)	1.31*** (.41)	1.26** (.46)

Table 4.3 (continued)

Independent Variable	Model 1	Model 2	Model 3
Wildcat strike in prior period	—	—	.72* (.34)
Level of prior strike activity	—	—	.82*** (.25)
Constant	-5.80***	-5.91***	-7.72***
-2 log likelihood	910.2	894.6	423.8
X^2	322.7***	338.3***	162.4***
Number of cases	2,904	2,904	1,991

*p<.05

**p<.01

***p<.001 (one-tailed)

Note: Numbers in parenthesis are standard errors. Reference categories are Ford for the firm variable, and 1960–1963 for the time-period variable.

CHAPTER 5

The Market/Shop-Floor Conjunctures

The theory of noninstitutionalized militancy developed in chapter 3 and tested in chapter 4 specified only the structural conditions providing auto workers with capacities for initiating collective action independently of the legitimated labor-relations structure. A distinction must be drawn between those conditions enabling such action and those precipitating or provoking it. I ignored the precipitating conditions in chapter 3, arguing only that the prior existence of a solidarity-generating labor process greatly increased the likelihood of wildcat strikes. Such a labor process enabled workers to overcome the isolation and atomization that tends to impede collective action in modern work settings.

In this chapter, I address the conditions triggering the courses of action which solidary workers pursue on the shop floor: those that lead them to honor managements' shop-floor expectations when they are not wildcatting; and those leading them to define their working conditions—or managements' expectations of them—as illegitimate. The first set of conditions creates consent to structures of managerial dominance; the second provokes workers in solidarity-generating labor processes to initiate militant collective action outside of the legitimated collective-bargaining structure.

The Definition of Legitimate Shop-Floor Experiences

The theory developed here borrows from Burawoy's explanation of postwar declines in worker-management conflict.[1] Burawoy links such declines to three developments: (1) structural labor-process developments; (2) developments in shop-floor-authority relations; and (3) developments in the structure of interfirm market relations.

Labor process developments playing a critical role in Burawoy's thesis involve the rise of both internal labor markets and internal states. Internal labor markets create in-plant status hierarchies and rationally regulate mobility within them. Such hierarchies generate possessive individualism and competition for higher status jobs, which, in turn, decrease class consciousness and commitment.

Internal states are collective bargaining systems that specify work rules to which both management and labor consent. They institutionalize a formal grievance procedure for resolving disputes off the factory floor without disrupting production schedules. In providing workers with legitimated avenues of grievance resolution independent of work-group solidarity, internal states atomize industrial conflict. They also generate commitment and participation to the system.

My account of auto industry development downplays the significance of both structures. Steep, multigrade occupational hierarchies were simply not present to a notable extent in postwar auto manufacturing, and, as we have seen, the institutionalization of an internal state did not produce an immediate decline in the incidence of wildcat activity. Consequently, I locate the source of the decline of shop-floor militancy elsewhere.

However, Burawoy's arguments linking the development of shop-floor authority systems and oligopolistic market arrangements to declines in factory conflict are very relevant to the auto industry. Burawoy notes a fundamental change in managements' orientation to the shop floor. Comparing his field experience at Allied's engine shop in 1974 to Roy's experience thirty years earlier, Burawoy notes a slackening of the more coercive features of managerial domination and surveillance. At Burawoy's shop, managers literally backed off the shop floor, allowing the piece-rate system to self-regulate. They allowed workers to take control over task organization and transform their activities into a game. With such control, workers "made out"—working at fever-pitched pace until they met their informal quota ceilings, then quitting for the rest of their shifts. When "making out" occurred, managers seldom looked for loose rates, nor did they retime jobs or pressure workers for more production. Because of management's tacit acceptance of this practice, Burawoy found little evidence that "making out" generated class consciousness or class conflict, as it had in Roy's day.

Burawoy explains this managerial orientation in reference to market developments. For him, the postwar shift from competitive to monopoly capitalism had partially arrested the competitive dynamics that compelled past managements to drive workers and increase productivity. This market development made "making out" compatible with managements' interests. Freed from competitive dynamics, managements were not continuously compelled to disrupt shop-floor relationships. Their interests rested in stable, predictable production outcomes. In allowing workers to "make out," managements could meet their production schedules. Both sets of interests were achieved within this market context.

My explanation for the decline of wildcat activity in postwar auto manufacturing follows closely Burawoy's argument. I equate "running for time" to "making out," and treat the shop-floor cultures generating the practice similar to the way in which Burawoy treats the "making-out" game culture.

I also equate the concept of Sloanism, as defined in chapter 1, to Burawoy's notion of monopoly capitalism, and argue that Sloanist market regulation provided managements with the shop-floor leverage required for instituting authority structures legitimating "running-for-time" shop cultures. I argue, as did Burawoy, that such legitimation served managements' historically conditioned interests. My contention is that, when effective, Sloanist regulation provided a structural foundation for realizing both managements' and solidary workers' immediate interests.

Manufacturing Rebellions among Solidary Workers

To specify the set of conditions provoking solidary workers to withdraw their consent from managerial authority, we must ask "What happens to the type of shop-floor hegemony which Burawoy specifies when the market environment supporting it collapses?" It is unclear whether workers' interests would follow managements' in the event that "making out" became incompatible with them. It is not clear what would happen on Burawoy's shop floor if, say, management took up the more despotic practices it employed prior to World War II—retiming jobs, tightening loose rates, requiring workers to work all day at their jobs, and more. Such actions could provoke collective-action protests. However, as Burawoy suggests in a subsequent article, structures such as the internal labor market and the internal state might inhibit such developments and encourage acquiescence and consent.[2]

These issues must be addressed in explaining wildcat activity in the postwar auto industry. I hypothesize that managerial assaults on production rates enabling workers to win "earned time" on the job would be defined as illegitimate by those accustomed to doing so routinely, especially when managements accepted such behavior in the past. This simple hypothesis assumes that the practice of "running for time"—if tolerated and sanctioned by management—would become perceived of as a *right* by workers engaging in it because it was legitimated through past custom and precedent. Workers would define the withdrawal of such a traditionally sanctioned right as an arbitrary action and a breach of a tacit, but binding, agreement.[3] I hypothesize, further, that such a breach would provoke a normative reaction from workers,[4] and that such a reaction would express itself as militant collective action whenever workers had a structural capacity for initiating it.

On the other hand, in those situations in which managements do not accept "earned time" as a legitimate worker right—or where the definition of a "fair day's work" is defined as managements' exclusive prerogative to determine at will—solidary workers are not as likely to perceive "earned time" as their legitimate right. While I argue that workers on collectively paced operations would still have a technical inducement to "run for time" in these systems, they would have to do so in covert ways and judiciously guard whatever earned time they made on their production schedules from foremen and time-study observers antagonistic to the practice. In these cases, I hypothesize that managerial assaults on this extralegal booty are not as likely to produce militant collective action, even when workers have a structural capacity for it. The reason is that it is unlikely that such assaults would be perceived as norm violations, and workers' reactions to them would not tend to be fueled by moral outrage. Because of the extraordinary risks involved in wildcatting, feelings of moral outrage function to spur workers to initiate wildcat strikes much more often than does a less emotional, more strategic rational orientation.

I argue that, entering into the postwar era, auto managements had accepted two very distinctive types of shop-floor authority systems. I label the first as the *drive system*. The definition of a fair day's work legitimated in this system is whatever management commands its workers to do. In this case, all labor time purchased by the firm is conceived as time that should be expended in productive activities. Management, in this definitional frame, has the right to use its purchased labor power as it sees fit. This definition is antagonistic to any conception of earned time on the job, and this authority system is therefore antagonistic to "running-for-time" shop cultures.

I label the second type of shop-floor authority a *quota-based authority system*. The definition of a fair day's work legitimated in the quota-based system is conceived as a routinized production standard or quota. The quota itself—rather than managements' arbitrary command—is accepted as the legitimate output expectation which determines workers' activities, and becomes the appropriate gauge for assessing the legitimacy of shop-floor demands and expectations. The logic of the definition of a fair day's work legitimated in this system is alien to the utilitarian, instrumental logic often thought to characterize modern industrial organization. When this definition of the situation is legitimated, it serves as a check on managements' abilities to impose its arbitrary will on shop-floor routines. These systems legitimate earned time as a worker's right and are functionally compatible with the institution of "running-for-time" shop cultures.

From the Shop Floor to the Market Arena

We must also recognize that shop-floor practices, and the authority systems governing them, are affected by conditions in the product market. Our question becomes "What types of market conditions are compatible with 'running-for-time' shop cultures and the quota-based authority systems legitimating them?" Conversely: "What types of market conditions are incompatible with them, leading managements to adopt the drive system?" These questions force us to return to the issues addressed in chapter 1—issues concerning interfirm competition and cooperation in the market arena.

Competition and the Exchange-Value-Equivalency Orientation

Fierce competition in unregulated markets creates an incompatible environment for the routinization of output expectations that is necessary for legitimating quota-based authority systems. Fierce market competition compels managements to cut production costs continually in order to reap either competitive advantage or survive in a market where their competitors are doing so. A failure to cut production costs could jeopardize a firm's survival in this type of market environment.

Thus, managements tend to adopt instrumental and reified orientations to shop-floor relationships and to the effort which workers expend there. They are not inclined to accept these relationships as being grounded in normative expectations, nor are they inclined to accept as legitimate output quotas established through past custom and precedent.

Operating within this environment, managements tend to conceive the efforts that workers expend on the shop floor as being quantifiable exchange-value equivalents, and as production costs universally comparable to and exchangeable with costs of other factors of production, or with costs of labor expended elsewhere. Operating within this definitional frame, managements tend to expect and demand that its labor costs on comparable operations reach and maintain parity with that of their competitors, regardless of what the translation of this demand entails for shop-floor activities and relationships. This equivalency demand is understandable, given the pressures placed upon managements' attempt to survive in a fiercely competitive market environment. It is functionally compatible with the drive system and its definition of a fair day's work as whatever management commands. Therefore, I hypothesize that as firms' product markets become fiercely competitive, their managements will drive workers and increase production standards arbitrarily in their plants.

Sloanist Regulation and Quota-Based Authority

The institutionalization of "running-for-time" shop cultures and the quota-based authority systems legitimating them requires that industries develop institutions for regulating serious competition between firms. As Burawoy notes, these market-regulating institutions allow managements the leverage to insulate their technical cores from the effects of competitive dynamics.[5] They enable firms to routinize production quotas and stabilize shop-floor relationships. This allows managements to attain stable production outcomes and to avoid disruptions in production.

Labor-process analysts have located this market stabilizing institution in the general shift from competitive to monopoly capitalism. In chapter 1, I developed a more industry-specific ideal-type of Sloanist regulation. My contention is that Sloanist regulation is functionally compatible with the institutionalization and reproduction of "running-for-time" cultures and the quota-based authority systems legitimating them. This structure allows firms to avoid the types of market competition that would force them to disrupt shop-floor expectations and relationships. By balkanizing product markets, this structure enables firms to profit without constantly revolutionizing their production processes. This structure also demands that firms develop production processes that will consistently produce and reproduce stable outcomes that enable managements to predict, in advance of production, their per-unit costs, the production volume attainable in the market at predetermined profit margins, and their rate of return on investment per operation. The routinized production standards that are required for institutionalizing "running-for-time" shop cultures are also functional for the type of production planning demanded by firms operating successfully in Sloanist-regulated market environments.

I hypothesize that, as a given firm's market segments become stabilized as a result of effective Sloanist regulation, "running-for-time" shop cultures tend to become institutionalized, and that shop managements tend to avoid disrupting shop-floor activities and relationships. I correlate this acceptance with declines in militant wildcat activity. The reasoning behind these hypotheses is twofold. First, managements are not constantly driven under these particular market circumstances to increase productivity in order to earn profits on the market. Second, an unpredictable disruption in a firm's production schedule might harm both a given firm's profitability and market position in this type of structure. Consequently, in a rational cost-benefit analysis, the risks of disrupting shop-floor activities and relationships outweigh the gains from doing so. I predict that managements will tend to avoid the possibility of such disruptions.

Market Shifts and Shop-Floor Consequences

What happens on the shop floor when the market environment supporting a particular authority system changes? What happens when Sloanist regulation fails to control interfirm competition in market segments, and firms experience market invasions? How do managements legitimating quota-based authority systems respond to this type of breakdown? Conversely, what happens on the shop floor when fiercely competitive markets stabilize?

The Market-Driven Transition

In the transition from a regulated to a fiercely competitive market environment, I hypothesize that managements respond instrumentally and in strategically rational ways. Under the new market pressures, managements are forced to forsake their shop-floor commitments to traditionally legitimated production standards and procedures. They are driven to cut production costs, and more.

In this shift, the market is theorized to be a sufficient condition for forcing management to change its shop-floor orientation. It also prevents them from continuing their more accommodative shop-floor policies, regardless of their proclivities. A refusal to respond to these conditions with a driving shop-floor orientation could have serious consequences for the firm's continued survival.

From the viewpoint of workers with notions of legitimacy spawned in quota-based authority systems, such management responses are illegitimate. Workers conceive of their assaults on established production standards as violations from the norm and fight to restore those norms through collective action. Because they believe their responses to these assaults are justified, they go to war with management over production standards and undergo considerable sacrifice and hardship to redress their grievances. In this situation, the two definitions of a fair day's work already discussed enter into a life-and-death struggle to establish hegemony over the shop floor.

The Transition from Drive to Quota-Based Authority

In the transition from an unregulated, fiercely competitive market environment to a Sloanist regulated one, I hypothesize that, over time, managements tend to accept the quota-based definition of a fair day's work. One reason for this is simply that the newly regulated environment provides managements with leverage for doing so. It also weakens the imperative to cut production costs.

In this shift, market stabilization is theorized to be a necessary but not a sufficient condition for changing management's shop-floor orientation. The regulated-market environment allows a driving management the opportunity to back off the shop floor and stabilize production relations there. However, such a management is not forced to do so. Nothing in the market environment dictates this choice as a necessity. Indeed, it would seem reasonable to expect that a management maintaining a driving orientation to production would be rewarded for doing so in a Sloanist-regulated environment as well. Their profit margins should be higher than that of those who accept the legitimacy of quota-based authority.

Managerial Levels and Shop-Floor Proclivities

Why, then, would a rational manager choose to accept a definition of a fair day's work bounded by past custom and precedent, even in those situations in which he or she has the option of doing so? My answer is that such a definition is quite effective at meeting production schedules in solidarity-generating labor processes because it harnesses workers' experiential knowledge and skill to production ends which serve the interests of both workers and managers. "Running-for-time" shop-floor cultures tend to be self-regulating or worker-regulating systems—as long as management does not establish production standards which workers believe are exploitative. They encourage workers to perform managerial functions in order to achieve their valued ends. This is expressed in the following account from a stamping-press operator whom I interviewed:

> Quite a few of us as a group got sent over to second shift when there was a slowdown in the work they were doing on a changeover and, believe it or not, they put us with a foreman who was known as a real wimp. You could just run all over this guy if you wanted to. And I had kinda gotten spoiled to finishing early every day. And we had enough people there. We had a nucleus of the group that we had had before. And I went around and I organized this line, because the guy wasn't capable. . . . And I went around and organized this line. I found out where the weak points on the line were, and I said to him: "Will you get this guy out and get this girl back here? We'll be able to make rate." And I was going around and helping everybody doing their job, while I was doing my own job and getting ahead and helping other people. We made rate the second day I was on second shift. So we didn't need him. . . . But you need management to get everything organized. After things are organized, everything pretty much runs itself.

As illustrated in this account, "running-for-time" shop cultures encourage workers to commit themselves to production outcomes because they can collect some of the benefits of that commitment. On worker-activated production processes, those who are "running for time" have a vested interest in "making rate." They tend to use their experientially acquired knowledge and skills to resolve production bottlenecks, organize production smoothly, and discipline one another in pursuit of the production ends which they value.[6]

It is easy to see why this type of worker commitment to production goals might be compatible with shop-managements' interests. Such a commitment enables this level of management to enlist the support of an experientially rooted knowledge of production operations in performing managerial functions that it might not hold. Such a commitment reduces a given production process' reliance upon management's knowledge and skill. The point here is that this experiential production knowledge might very well be valuable—if not indispensable—to getting the product out and in organizing the production process. Legitimating a definition of a fair day's work to be compatible with the institution of "running-for-time" shop cultures might allow management to co-opt this knowledge base.

I hypothesize that, when those in the layers of management closest to actual production—such as line foremen or departmental superintendents—hold the authority to make decisions concerning production operations, they are more likely to recognize workers' contributions to production and work within the parameters of the quota-based authority system. They do this in order to secure access to this worker contribution. Such access aids them in meeting their primary responsibility, which is making their production schedules. Some evidence suggests a tendency for this layer of management to accommodate workers' proclivities to restrict output.[7] Recent studies of radical innovations introduced in functioning production processes also suggest that levels of management closest to the shop floor are as resistant of these types of changes as are the workers affected by them.[8] The argument here is that both resistance to radical technological change and accommodation to worker demands have a rational foundation in these managers' structural positions.

Given the tendency for both labor and business historians to depict the foreman as the historical agent driving workers for more production, this argument might appear to be counterintuitive and wrong-headed.[9] And, being the level of management directly interacting with workers on the shop floor, this is the agent workers experience whenever management at any level decides to speed-up production and increase productivity, whether they are acting on their own initiative in doing so or not. It is likely that, during periods when relations between shop foremen and workers were most volatile, foremen were under intense pressure to increase productivity. The argument here is simply that, when this type of pressure eases, this level of management will favor a more accommodative stance toward workers' shop cultures. When such a management takes charge of the setting and adjusting of production standards, it will most likely honor past expectations.

It is further hypothesized that, when levels of management far-removed from the immediate shop floor—such as, corporate-level production engineers or a centralized labor-relations management—has authority to set and manipulate production standards, they are less likely to recognize this worker contribution, and they are also less likely to co-opt workers' commitment to production ends. In failing to do this, it is hypothesized that they are more likely to produce both worker revolts and shop-floor chaos.

Thus, another variable is introduced into the market—shop-floor linkage—the level of management empowered to make decisions regarding production practices. In market environments demanding predictable, stable production outcomes, I hypothesize that corporate managements have incentives to cede to shop management this decision-making prerogative because they are the most capable of producing the desired results. In market environments demanding increased productivity and reduced production costs, I hypothesize that corporate management expropriates this decision-making prerogative from its shop management in order to implement the radical shop floor changes it defines as necessary for competing successfully in the market.

Summary

I can demonstrate the existence of two conjunctures, each consisting of four sets of factors. The first conjuncture produces noninstitutionalized militancy and contains: competitive and unstable market conditions; shop-floor systems within which managements assault production standards arbitrarily; and centralized managerial structures within which corporate-level managements, far-removed from the shop floor, determine shop practices and production standards.

The second conjuncture produces low levels of noninstitutionalized militancy and contains: a stable, Sloanist-regulated market environment; shop-floor expectations legitimated within the quota-based definition of a fair day's work; and a managerial authority structure allowing shop-level management to set and adjust production standards.

In the militancy-producing conjuncture, I have specified the fiercely competitive market environment as the sufficient condition for triggering the other developments. Pressures emanating from the market arena force managements to adopt the drive system and to centralize production decisions in the hands of a management attuned to its demands. These factors are thought to be tightly coupled. They should materialize rather quickly, once a regulated market environment begins to break down.

The linkages in the stabilizing conjuncture are different. When Sloanist-regulated markets, the legitimation of quota-based shop-floor authority, a management structure granting shop management the authority to set and adjust production standards come together, then low levels of noninstitutionalized militancy should result. If it does not, the theoretical model washes out.

However, the linkages among the factors in the stabilizing conjuncture are not tightly coupled in the theory. That is to say, the Sloanist-regulated market environment does not, of necessity, drive managements to adopt specific policies or structures, as does the competitive environment. Instead, Sloanist-regulation provides a foundation enabling managements to stabilize the shop floor, as well as some tangible gains for doing so. However, this is not required. The more benign market environment may allow firms to prosper with conflictual labor relations that result in high levels of work stoppages, so long as those stoppages do not unduly threaten the ability to serve market segments.

Predictions concerning this conjuncture are less deterministic than in the first one. Over time, firm managements should move toward the more accommodative labor position, and pass authority to set and adjust production standards to shop management. There are real incentives for doing so. If firms refuse this alternative, we must draw upon factors outside of the model to explain this recalcitrance, whether they be political, cultural, personal, or historically contingent. While strictly subordinated to market dictation in the first conjuncture, such extraneous factors have more room to influence outcomes in the regulated-market environment.

The chapters in Part III use these ideal-type conjunctures to examine and interpret the postwar development of the market and shop-floor relationships in the U.S. automobile industry. The efficacy of these theoretical linkages lies in their utility in illuminating this history.

Part III—
The History of Market and Shop-Floor Regulation in the Postwar Automobile Industry

CHAPTER 6

The Skittish Emergence of a Hegemonic Order, 1946–1952

This chapter reviews shop-floor and market-level data from 1946 to 1952. The evidence suggests that a Sloanist hegemonic order had begun to regulate major market segments by the end of the period. The ideal types developed in chapter 5 are employed to define the parameters of this regulatory structure and to specify the foundations enabling and constricting its functioning.

Dual Definitions of a Fair Day's Work

Here, I discuss the extent to which auto firms' shop-floor authority systems conformed to either the drive or quota-based ideal types as defined in chapter 5. The evidence suggests that, at the onset of the period, Studebaker, the independents, and GM embraced quota-based authority. Ford embraced the drive system. Chrysler and Briggs waffled between the two.

The Independents' Quota-Based Authority Systems

Studebaker's industrial-relations system represented the extreme case of tradition-bound, quota-based authority. Once set, Studebaker's collective bargaining contract placed severe restrictions on management's ability to change production standards. Section 3 of an early postwar agreement states restrictive conditions for such changes.[1] This agreement restricted management's contractual right to change standards to only those cases in which it corrected an arithmetic error in the standard calculation, readjusted rates upward after a technical change in the job made faster rates possible, or readjusted rates downward after a technical change in the job required operators to spend more time or effort on it.

Paragraph 3d went so far as to codify earned time as a worker's legitimate right in stating that "An employee's ingenuity or incentive shall not be considered as a method change and shall not constitute a valid reason for changing the production standard." This paragraph denied management the right to appropriate, for its purposes, the earned time that workers won through their own ingenuity and incentive, even when workers used it to run eight hours production in five, which was a typical practice in the Studebaker stamping plant.[2] Once a standard was set, all management could demand—until it altered the technological foundations of the job—was the production quota determined by custom and past precedent.[3] The independents appeared to have followed Studebaker,[4] accepting this tradition-bound authority system in order to take advantage of the immediate postwar sellers' market. Some—such as Nash—were using their local unions to police production-standard compliance,[5] and to assist them in job allocations.[6] It is likely that these union officials honored workers' quota-based expectations because they had to win their continued support for reelection.

General Motors' Authority System

In much of the postwar period, General Motors was noted for having the fastest work pace in the industry. During World War II, GM held its grip on production standards in its plants. GM used the CIO's no-strike pledge to curb the strength of its United Automobile Workers locals, replacing its militant shop-steward systems with the more formally bureaucratic and less responsive committee systems. Unlike its competitors, GM never ceded to its unions any control or voice in setting or policing production standards.[7] For this reason, the GM shop-floor authority system is typically thought of as conforming to the characteristics of the drive system as previously defined. Yet, I argue that, while GM management held the exclusive authority to establish and enforce production standards in its plants, it chose to use this authority in ways that were compatible with the legitimation of a quota-based authority.

In understanding GM's industrial-relations policy, we must keep in mind that GM's market supremacy was uncontested in the early postwar years. This gave GM leverage in dealing with labor that was not open to others. GM was in a position, for example, to accept a national strike for 113 days in 1946 so as to set favorable precedents for future contract negotiations. It was able to shut down completely from January to May, and still turn a profit at the end of the year.

In general, GM was concerned with using this leverage to structure a labor-relations system that was compatible with its interests in securing predictable production outcomes. GM pioneered the labor agreements that established the formal labor-relations structure defined in chapter 2. GM took action in the immediate postwar years to assure that its unions would process their demands through the channels specified in the collective-bargaining contract. GM acted swiftly and punitively against wildcatters, attempting to delegitimate unauthorized work stoppages as effective means of voicing and winning worker demands. While I argue that GM was successful at this, I explain this success in terms of the courses of action which GM managers took on the shop floor to create predictable, unambiguous role expectations that were legitimated in past custom and precedent.

The most significant GM response to wildcat strikes was its reacton to the April 1947 wildcat. The UAW International called this strike to protest the Taft-Hartley Act. Thirteen thousand GM workers walked out of several plants to demonstrate at Cadillac Square. In order to set an example, GM reacted to this walkout by firing 15 UAW local officials, placing 25 others on disciplinary suspension, and doling out 401 additional penalties. The affected included four local presidents, six shop committeemen, and twenty-two shop and district committeemen. GM refused to rescind these penalties, demonstrating early on that it was prepared to stick to its policy regardless of the consequences. GM agreed on 8 May 1947 to reduce the firings to long-term layoffs in exchange for a signed "Memorandum of Understanding" that proclaimed all such actions as being contract violations.[8] To my knowledge, the UAW International never again openly led a coordinated wildcat strike against GM.

GM stuck to its policy of harshly disciplining wildcatters throughout the late 1940s and 1950s. George B. Norris, a GM labor relations official stated:

> General Motors' record of disciplining the leaders of unauthorized work stoppages and disciplining the participants is well-known among union ranks and among arbitrators. Our consistent adherence to this policy puts the union leaders in a position where they can bring responsible leadership within their ranks.[9]

Labor relations scholars, such as MacDonald,[10] have viewed GM's firm treatment of those leading wildcat strikes as a decisive factor in discouraging them. It would be hard to argue to the contrary. I accept this policy as one—but only one—of the factors responsible for relatively peaceful labor relations at GM during the early postwar period.

Not enough detailed information concerning GM's shop practices in the early postwar years is available for making definitive statements about them. However, evidence does suggest that there was much more behind GM's peaceful labor record than effective coercion. In a UAW interdepartmental memo to Douglas Fraser dated 6 August 1954, Arthur Hughes, a UAW Chrysler Department official, compares Chrysler and GM's procedures concerning production standards.[11] This memo gives us valuable insight into GM's production standard policies and practices.

In the memo, Hughes criticizes the time-study methods that Chrysler management was using to readjust rates at the Dodge Main plant. He criticizes these methods for involving opinion and "guess-timation," arbitrary rate adjustments, and a blatant disregard for the validity of previous standards. Hughes then contrasts the Chrysler methods with those routinely practiced at GM plants. Hughes claims that GM managements did not typically change a set standard unless it changed the job in question or the method employed on the job. Once time studies set the standard, GM management honored this standard as legitimate and allowed it to pace production. Management accepted this rate as the standard for a fair day's work, according to Hughes, and did not adjust rates to make up lost production. We can assume that Hughes's description of GM policies and practices reflect the experiences of the UAW International staff negotiating with GM over production standards. Elmer Yenney, a local UAW official at GM's Janesville, Wisconsin, plant, confirms this interpretation. He claims that his local did not begin to experience serious production standards problems until after the Korean War.[12]

Hughes also claims that GM's policy was to negotiate production-standards disputes with its locals, rather than to force the unconditional acceptance of its managerial prerogative. Once grievances moved up to the final stages or once a strike vote was set in motion, GM plant managements would typically make concessions to union demands. Unlike Chrysler or Briggs, GM had developed a reputation with the UAW for honoring its negotiated grievance settlements—at least during the period spanning the end of World War II to the end of the Korean War.

I argue that GM's policy on production standards gave rise to a definition of a fair day's work that was closer to Studebaker's position than typically acknowledged. By honoring the production quota specified in its time-studied standard, GM legitimated the standard rather than the arbitrary command. Once set, a fair day's work was the output quota specified in the standard. This, in essence, was the definition accepted by Studebaker management.

The primary difference between these systems was that GM held onto its prerogative to set the initial standard on the basis of its own methods. GM's shop management never allowed its stewards to perform managerial functions as had Studebaker, Nash, and Hudson during World War II. GM never accepted union interference in policing standards or in disciplining those failing to meet them. This allowed GM to set and insist upon tight standards and, once set, to legitimate them by past custom and precedent.

GM's shop managements appear to have been competent enough to work with such a definition of a fair day's work until the end of the Korean War. GM managers were capable of meeting their production schedules without having to resort to daily manipulations of line speeds or of production quotas. A factor enhancing GM's ability to do this was that it employed many more subassembly lines dedicated to the production of single parts than did its smaller competitors. GM ran long production runs without constantly changing tools and fixtures. This practice was compatible with production standard routinization.

However, GM's definition of earned time appears to have been much more restrictive than the definition which Studebaker accepted. H. G. Riggs, an official from GM Delco-Remy, stated GM's official position on earned time succinctly in an article published in the *Society of Automotive Engineering Journal.*

> In nonincentive plants the supervision insists on a fair day's work. The operator must stay at his workplace and continue his job for the entire shift, even if he has made his standard production for the day sometime prior to the close of the shift. He may clean up his work area or do other work until quitting time but he must do a fair day's work for a fair day's pay.[13]

As expressed in Riggs's account, GM's definition of a fair day's work required operators to remain on the shop floor engaged in work activities, even when they made rate prior to quitting time. Unlike at Studebaker, earned time could not be used legitimately for nonwork purposes. GM management made claims on all work time for which it paid. However, workers were not required to continue with their production once their rates were met. Beating the rate, even within a system abiding by this restricted conception of earned time, still allowed workers a break from the tensions and strains of running on the line or on the machine. Workers would still define earned time for leisurely paced sweeping or for performing auxiliary functions as a valuable gain. I argue that, in acknowledging the probability of earning time and in defining parameters restricting workers' use of it once gained, GM policy legitimated and probably encouraged it. Since GM management did not often change rates once set, beating the rate in a nonflagrant manner was not likely to be a provocation for a speedup.

In the early postwar period, GM shop management had

considerable leverage in meeting its role expectations—much more so than either Ford's or Chrysler's.[14] GM's labor-relations system was much more decentralized, and the GM foremen were empowered to negotiate grievance disputes on the shop floor. MacDonald reports that, in 1953, about 92 percent of the grievances filed in GM plants were settled in the first or second stage of the grievance process compared to 77 percent of those filed in Ford plants.[15] He reports that only 1 percent of the GM grievances went to outside arbitrators compared to 6 percent of the Ford grievances.

Thus, the GM system encouraged those directly involved in the dispute to take the initiative required to resolve it on the spot. It placed less strain on the bureaucratic structure, freeing corporate and divisional-level labor relations officers—as well as their union counterparts at UAW's Solidarity House—for long-range planning functions. It also made grievance resolution the business of that level of management most likely to recognize the exigencies involved in production, and who were most likely, I argue, to be sympathetic to the merits of "running-for-time" shop cultures.

GM was much slower than others to embrace automation at this time. GM left decision-making prerogatives regarding the use of technologies largely to its division and plant managers. Operating under tight rate-of-return-on-investment constraints—but given considerable decision-making leverage to operate their plants—these managers were less likely to take risks on new technologies. They were cautious and quite skeptical of the claims of the vendors selling automated equipment.[16] Before the Korean War, GM shop managements had developed considerable organizational competence at managing labor. The prospect of replacing reliable labor with automatic machinery without a demonstrable track record was not appealing.

Chrysler's and Briggs's Authority Systems

Chrysler's relationship with the UAW in the early postwar period has become legend—a legend of bad faith, brinkmanship negotiations, and mutual disgust. Chrysler management did not accept the UAW's legitimacy, and K. T. Keller, Chrysler's president, refused to negotiate directly with the union. Chrysler was well-known for reneging on its labor agreements, and it refused to abide by the rulings of outside arbitrators in settling disputes.

Chrysler's highly centralized labor-relations structure stripped foremen of formal negotiating power in settling labor disputes. Disputes were passed up the formal chain of command for resolution, and this delayed reaction time. Workers often took direct action on the shop floor to force management's compliance to their demands.[17]

Chrysler tended to capitulate to workers' most militant demands whenever they halted production schedules and threatened to hurt sales. As Jefferys points out,[18] Chrysler's rigid labor-relations system and its inconsistent policies encouraged the development of strong militant traditions in all of its plants. While Chrysler's official corporate-level definition of a fair day's work was the drive definition, I argue, following Jefferys, that it could not establish the validity of this definition with either workers or line foremen on its shop floors.

Briggs's management's reputation for honoring its agreements with its UAW locals was as poor as Chrysler's. Its rank and file realized that their shop-floor gains had to be preserved continually with direct action or with its threat. What complicated the picture was Briggs's management's relationship with Chrysler. Briggs's labor-relations policy was, for the most part, dictated by Chrysler as its largest customer. Chrysler bought out Briggs in 1953, and Briggs Plymouth Body became Chrysler Automotive Body Division.

What type of shop-floor authority systems developed at Chrysler and Briggs during the early postwar period? Jefferys provides the most comprehensive and insightful answer to this question.[19] Jefferys argues that Chrysler's rigid corporate labor-relations structures created a power vacuum that was filled on the shop floor by sectional bargaining. Chrysler foremen routinely negotiated production standards with shop stewards in order to win worker acceptance of the negotiated rate and to avoid the cumbersome, unpredictable formal structure. While these unofficial negotiations appear to have honored past custom and precedent as legitimate benchmarks for setting rates, and while they appear to have allowed ample space for workers to win earned time on the job, they were not sanctioned officially in the formal structure, and this left them vulnerable to assault from the central office.

Thus, dual definitions of a fair day's work competed within the management structures at Chrysler and Briggs. The first defined a fair day's work as management's prerogative to establish, a definition which was unfettered by custom and precedent. This was most likely accepted by Chrysler's and Briggs's corporate-level managements. The second definition was the quota-based definition which was compatible with solidary workers' desire for earned time on the job. This was most likely accepted by line foremen. However, neither definition was hegemonic.

Accounts from Chrysler workers support this contention. They suggest that "running for time" was accepted practice on the early postwar shop floor.[20] Patricia Cayo Sexton worked at Dodge Main in the late 1940s on the trim line. She describes the standards there as involving "no pressure, little fatigue, and enough time for relaxed kibitzing." She states:

> In my time, we were lucky to have inherited standards set by the reportedly most militant workers in the plant, the trimmers, the tack spitters, the men (no women) who tacked up the upholstery trim inside the car. . . . These experienced men, white and predominantly Polish, were always ready to walk off the job when standards were threatened. . . . These trimmers pretty much set, and held, the standards for the rest of us.[21]

Following Jefferys, I contend that shop management, pressured to get the product out in a postwar sellers' market, negotiated with shop stewards to set rates consistent with workers' quota-based definitions of a fair day's work. Shop management used past precedent as a guide for establishing rates, even when these precedents were slack enough for workers to win generous allotments of earned time during the course of a work day. This definition, I argue, was most likely to prevail on Chrysler's shop floors until its divisions began to experience market losses. However, the "rightness" of these shop-floor practices was never fully accepted by all levels of Chrysler management, and this inconsistency made for some volatile local labor relations and a considerable number of wildcats.

The situation at Briggs is best illustrated in management's response to the 1946 strike threat waged by UAW Local 212. This case represents a successful attempt by a local union to force Briggs's management to honor formally a quota-based definition of a "fair day's work."

On 3 May 1946, following a production standard dispute, numerous disciplinary discharges, and a wildcat strike, UAW Local 212 filed a strike notice with Briggs, threatening Plymouth and much of Packard production. This shutdown would jeopardize the gains made by both firms during the long GM strike, as Briggs supplied both with finished bodies.

The major grievance provoking the strike was an alleged speedup. Tom Clampitt, UAW Local 212's newly elected president, charged that Briggs was violating the labor contract by increasing production standards arbitrarily and by docking pay from workers not making the new rates. The Briggs stamping plants were at the center of the controversy. However, Clampitt and his administration played on workers' fears that Briggs's management would extend this speedup throughout the plant complex.[22] They mobilized substantial support for the strike action.

The demands that the union local made in its negotiations were militant and bold. The local demanded that management accept and honor the 1941 production standards as the legitimate standards in pacing production. The union attempted to force management to commit itself formally to these standards. It was willing to accept management's prerogative to readjust a standard only when it changed the technology of the operation, and only *after* management won its case through the grievance procedure. The union demanded that, while production standards disputes were being negotiated, management honor the old 1941 standards. The local also demanded that management rescind its practice of deducting pay from workers failing to meet the contested production rates and that it reinstate with back pay workers discharged in the dispute.[23]

Undoubtedly under pressure from Chrysler to settle the dispute at all costs without a production stoppage, Briggs's management capitulated to most of Local 212's militant demands. The agreement legitimated the 1941 production standards as those pacing production on the 1947 models. It committed management to honoring these standards unless it changed the tools and equipment employed on its operations.

Briggs's management made other concessions as well. Briggs agreed to make available to union officials all pre-World-War-II production records so that the local could police the agreement. It committed itself to a speedier grievance procedure, agreed to add operators on contested lines, granted back pay to workers docked during the dispute, and restored seniority to those it had discharged.[24]

The 1946 strike outcome represented a clear union victory. Management succumbed to this position and formally accepted the 1941 standards on the production of its 1947 models. Management was not bound to this agreement beyond the 1947 model year, however, and it did not view this agreement as a permanent feature of its labor relations policies. The Briggs shop stewards could not count on managements' resolve to honor its agreements, and they had to defend the standards won against arbitrary managerial assault. This situation—which I attribute to contradictions between corporate and shop level management orientations—distinguished the Briggs authority systems from those which became legitimated at Studebaker and Nash, where both shop and corporate-level managements appear to have accepted the quota-based definition of a fair day's work.

However, the Briggs managers' assaults on production standards do not appear to have been as intense or as frequent as those occurring elsewhere during the period, or as those occurring at Plymouth Body itself in the later 1950s. The speedup issue did not appear to dominate the concerns and politics of UAW Local 212 after 1946. In a 1949 "President's Column," Ken Morris claimed that the speedup was not a major problem at Briggs during the late 1940s.[25] He links management's relative indifference to increasing production standards both to his local being ready and willing to fight and to the sellers' market that existed through the Korean War. While, as we shall see, the Briggs workers wildcatted frequently in comparison to workers in other plants in the early postwar period, production-standard issues do not appear to have been the major factor spurring these actions.

Ford's Early Postwar Authority System

Ford's future in the industry was more uncertain than the other established firms entering the postwar period. Harry Bennett's terroristic management methods, coupled with the senior Henry Ford's growing senility, produced such chaos at Ford during the 1930s and early 1940s that it was rumored that the Defense Department was planning to seize control over the River Rouge plant during the war. While Henry Ford II managed to defeat Bennett in a bitter power struggle at the onset of the postwar period, his ability to maintain control over the giant Ford production system was in serious doubt. While other firms prospered, Ford management was unable to turn a profit on the price controls set by the government during the postwar conversion. Ford's new management even lacked a firm conceptual grasp of the labor time it required to plan production efficiently. Labor costs stipulated in its initial postwar budgets were off by 65 percent.[26]

Largely because it lacked the background knowledge required to plan production efficiency, Ford management's position on production standards during the late 1940s conformed closely to that found in the drive authority system defined in chapter 5. Ford refused to accept any given production standard on its operations as binding and fought for a managerial prerogative to set production standards as it saw fit and change them whenever and however it saw fit. The only fetter to this right that it accepted was a health-and-safety provision. Unless management's shop-floor demands reasonably threatened their health and safety, workers at Ford were obligated to honor them unless and until they won relief through the grievance procedure. Such a definition granted Ford's management the right to any free time which workers managed to earn. The Ford position is summed up clearly in a 1948 communique sent to all foremen from John Bugas, Ford's industrial relations manager.

> The company has the right to set production standards by any means it desires. Employees need not be concerned unless they are disciplined unfairly for failure to meet standards which threaten their health and safety. Experience elsewhere with standards based on the same normal pace as our 100 percent shows that qualified men, with incentive pay and without limiting conditions, can work at 125 percent or more without endangering their health.[27]

In this communique, Bugas defines production standards as high as 25 percent above the established standards as legitimate production targets. Ford management wanted all it could get out of its workers during the workday, and it defined this expectation as its legitimate right. This definition rejected custom and precedent as a valid standard for establishing legitimate production rates.

Ford management defended its managerial prerogative against two co-ordinated local strikes in May 1949. These strikes were led by UAW Local 600, the local representing River Rouge workers, and UAW Local 900, the local representing Detroit Lincoln workers. These strikes represented attempts by UAW locals to force Ford's management to honor a quota-based definition of a fair day's work. Ford management resisted these local assaults and fought hard to preserve its formal prerogatives.

After exhausting the grievance procedure and after winning reluctant strike approval from the International UAW-Ford Department, UAW Locals 600 and 900 struck the Ford and Lincoln plant complexes from 5 May to 30 May 1949. In each plant complex, management had increased the speed of the machine-paced conveyors on the final-assembly, final-body-assembly, and motor-assembly lines by three percent over the established standards. Management claimed that it had a right to do so, and that the increases were needed to make up production lost to routine breakdowns and bottlenecks.[28]

The speedups on these lines are interesting. They came after the local unions and managements in question agreed to lock several rheostats pacing line speeds.[29] At the Rouge, Tommy Thompson had won reelection to an unprecedented fourth term as Local 600's president with a program promising to fight speedups. Winning agreement to lock line speeds was communicated as a union victory. That the company honored the union request with a 3 percent speedup was an embarrassment to Thompson.

The outcome of these strikes were mixed. The locals did win agreements assuring them of constant line speeds, properly balanced job assignments, and management's commitment to review and retime tight jobs. This agreement would prevent management from speeding up assembly lines arbitrarily during any given work day. It placed limits on the Ford management's prerogative to set and change production standards at will.[30]

However, the issue concerning the 3 percent speedup—

which set the rate higher than the time-studied rate in order to make up time for anticipated losses during the work day—went to impartial arbitrators.[31] In a split vote, the arbitrators reaffirmed Ford's management's right to set line speeds unilaterally at the start of the workday, but stipulated that management had to compensate workers who were forced to do more work than was stipulated in the time-study standard, either through frequent relief or other appropriate solutions.[32] This ruling upheld management's right to run its line speeds in excess of established production standards, unless it significantly harmed the welfare of the worker.[33] While certainly conditioning this managerial prerogative, and while establishing a foundation for further negotiations on production standard relief, the outcome of the strike was consistent with the managerial-prerogative definition of a fair day's work for which Ford's management fought.

The position on production standards that the Ford management defended in the 1949 local strikes did not legitimate earned time on the job as a worker's right, nor did it provide a favorable environment for the "running-for-time" shop cultures described in chapter 3 to flourish openly. Workers "running for time" in the Ford system during the late 1940s stood to have their production standards retimed and tightened. This constant threat made Local 600's representatives quite leery of "running-for-time" practices. They preferred their members to pace themselves so as to protect standards.

The drive system which Ford's management favored was functionally compatible with its approach to modernizing its production processes in the late 1940s. Realizing that GM would likely shift its production schedules to the higher margin market segments, Ford targeted the lower priced segment. However, long before World War II, Chevrolet had established market-share dominance in this sector,[34] and Ford's management had to reach parity with GM's production costs in order to establish a strong presence. In early 1946, Ford's production costs were so high that it lost money on each car it sold.[35] Ford's solution to this problem involved turning to the engineering sciences for direction in reorganizing production. In April 1947, Ford established the Ford Automation Department whose mission was to devise ways to increase productivity and decrease production costs.[36]

Ford granted FAD free reign in devising new production

techniques and in establishing production standards governing work activities. Unlike at Studebaker, Nash, or Hudson, Ford's time studies were not determined jointly by union and management, and FAD engineers were not constrained by shop stewards monitoring their activities or methods. The only contractual fetters placed on these engineers were the prospects of causing harm to the health and safety of the operators involved, a condition difficult for the union to prove in dispute negotiations. Throughout the 1940s, Ford management appears to have assaulted established production standards in the Ford plants with determination and vigor. Local union leaders cried speedup continuously on the pages of *Ford Facts* during this period, and production-standard issues appear to have been a major concern of local politics.[37]

Characterizations of the Firm-Level Authority Systems

The evidence suggests that, at the onset of the postwar period, the Ford authority system conformed most closely to the drive system, while the Studebaker system, the systems in operation in other independent firms, and the GM system conformed to the ideal type definition of quota-based authority. If variation in the type of authority legitimated makes a difference in determining shop-floor militancy, the number of wildcat strikes occurring in the Ford plants should differ markedly from those occurring in the independent and GM plants.

Chrysler's and Briggs's authority systems could not be categorized as either drive or quota-based systems. Their corporate managements did not appear to accept past precedent and custom as legitimate benchmarks for assessing the legitimacy of production expectations. Yet, they were not powerful or competent enough to impose their will on the shop floor. This situation led to confusion, to the decoupling of formal policy from practice, and to shop-floor practices that were put in place more by force than by commonly held beliefs in legitimate authority.

Finally, I must state that these characterizations are merely to serve as the starting points of the empirical analyses that follow. These were the authority systems with which the various auto firms began the period of interest. They were not rigid or closed systems, however, and they changed in systematic and measurable ways in reaction to forces yet to be specified in this chapter. I argue that, by the end of the period, all auto managements operating in Sloanist regulated segments had begun to embrace quota-based authority in their plants.

Evidence of Partial Sloanist Regulation

Table 6.1 reports the total annual unit sales for the industry; the percentage of change from the previous year's unit sales; and the annual market share for GM, Ford, Chrysler, and the Independents. The numbers in parentheses below the firms' annual market-share percentages show the absolute market share gained or lost by the firm from the previous year.

The evidence in total units and annual volume percentages show that the total market expanded rapidly from 1946–1950. In 1946, unit sales were stunted by the long GM strike and by numerous supplier strikes. From 1947 to 1950 sales increased. The federal government acted to depress sales in 1951 and 1952 in order to conserve resources for the Korean War.

Market-shares for the four manufacturing firms evince considerable market-share stability, even in the face of the 1947–1950 market expansion and the Korean War contractions. From 1947 to 1952, GM gained only 0.3 percent market share, Ford gained 1.8 percent, and Chrysler lost 0.3 percent. While the independents lost 1.9 percent overall, their 12.6 percent share in 1952 was still considerably higher than during the Depression. All in all, the industry's market-share stability was impressive.

In all prior periods of the industry's development, the dominant firm increased market share at the expense of its weak competitors. From 1947 to 1950, the dominant firm expanded in close step with its weaker mates. The reason for this pattern, I argue, is that the Sloanist regulatory ideology had become hegemonic and was beginning to operate effectively in major market segments. The stability which Sloanism created provided space, with the aid of a tremendous sellers' market, for all to expand and profit.

Table 6.1
Firm-Level Market-Share Data

			Market-Share Percentages			
Year	Total Units*	Percentage of Change in Unit Sales	GM	Ford	Chrysler	Independents
1946	1,812	—	37.9	22.1	25.8	14.3
1947	3,143	+74	42.2	21.4	22.0	14.5
			(+4.3)**	(-0.7)	(-3.8)	(+0.2)
1948	3,451	+10	41.1	19.1	21.7	18.2
			(-1.1)	(-2.3)	(-0.3)	(+3.7)
1949	4,796	+40	43.3	21.6	21.2	14.0
			(+2.2)	(+2.5)	(-0.5)	(-4.2)
1950	6,274	+31	45.8	24.3	17.8	13.2
			(+2.5)	(+2.7)	(-3.4)	(-0.8)
1951	5,011	-20	43.3	22.5	22.0	12.3
			(-2.5)	(-1.8)	(+4.2)	(-0.9)
1952	4,087	-18	42.5	23.2	21.7	12.6
			(-0.8)	(+0.8)	(-0.3)	(+0.3)
(1947–1952) Totals	—	—	+0.3	+1.8	-0.3	-1.9

*In thousands.

**Absolute values of market-share changes from the previous year are in parentheses. Market-share changes greater than 2 percent are underlined.

Source: Automotive Industries, various years.

Hegemonic Regulation in the Lower and Lower-Middle Segments

I have partitioned the auto market into four segments by price: the lower, lower-middle, upper-middle, and upper segments. Chevrolet, Ford, Plymouth, Studebaker, Kaiser-Frazer's Henry J, and Crosley were the competitors in the lower segment. Pontiac, Mercury, Dodge, Nash, and Kaiser-Frazer's Kaiser model were the competitors in the lower-middle segment. Oldsmobile, Buick, Chrysler's DeSoto, Hudson, and Kaiser-Frazer's Frazer model were the competitors in the upper-middle segment. Finally, Chrysler, Packard, Lincoln, and Cadillac were the competitors in the upper segment.[38]

The assumption here is that consumers probably considered the models in the price segments specified above as their market options, although the potential for overlap existed, especially between adjacent segments. Studebaker drew buyers from both the lower and lower-middle segments. The Kaiser, Hudson, and DeSoto models were priced between the upper ranges of the lower-middle segment and the lower ranges of the upper-middle segment. The Frazer model was priced in the upper ranges of the upper-middle segment. It was within the price and taste reaches of those buying the cheaper makes of the upper segment, especially those attracted to the lower-priced Chrysler and Packard models. All of these models were purposely placed in the price range of adjacent market segments to draw buyers from both without spurring price competition.

Tables 6.2 and 6.3 report market-share behavior in the lower and lower-middle segments. Sales here made up between 73 and 75 percent of the industry's total. The absolute values of the divisions' market-share gains or losses from the previous year are reported in parenthesis below the annual market-share figures in each of the tables. I consider a percentage share change of two percent or more to be significant. By analyzing annual percentage changes in divisions' segment shares, I can pinpoint which divisions gained shares at whose expense. The data evinces relative market stability.

The average market-share change experienced by the divisions selling in the lower segment from 1946 to 1952 was 1.55 percent. While eleven of the thirty-two annual cells show that divisions gained or lost two percent or more in market share from the preceding year, most of these changes can be explained in reference to extraneous factors, such as sales losses because of national strikes. Chevrolet's 4.5 percent gain came the year after the 1946 GM strike, an event which depressed GM sales significantly. The 1947 gain represents less of a market invasion than simply Chevrolet keeping its plants running steadily throughout the year. This readjustment also explains the Ford and Plymouth 1947 losses. Plymouth's big loss in 1950 reflects the influence of the national Chrysler strike, as do the gains which Ford and Chevrolet made that year. The 1951 market shifts were imposed on the industry by the government.

Table 6.2
Division-Level Performance in the Lower Segment

	Market-Share Percentages					
Year	Plymouth	Ford	Chevrolet	Studebaker	Henry J	Crosley
1946	22.8	35.2	35.5	6.2	—	0.3
1947	19.5 (-3.3)*	33.2 (-2.0)	40.0 (+4.5)	6.4 (+0.2)	—	1.0 (+0.7)
1948	20.3 (+0.8)	28.4 (-4.8)	41.4 (+1.4)	8.4 (+2.0)	—	1.5 (+0.5)
1949	20.5 (+0.2)	31.3 (+2.9)	40.0 (-1.4)	7.7 (-0.7)	—	0.4 (-1.0)
1950	16.0 (-4.5)	34.1 (+2.8)	41.5 (+1.5)	7.8 (+0.1)	0.4 (+0.4)	0.3 (-0.2)
1951	19.8 (+3.8)	31.5 (-2.6)	39.0 (-2.5)	7.5 (-0.3)	1.9 (+1.5)	0.1 (-0.2)
1952	19.6 (-0.2)	33.2 (+1.7)	38.6 (-0.4)	7.1 (-0.5)	1.4 (-0.1)	—**
1947-1952 Totals	+0.1	0.0	-1.4	+0.7	+1.4	-1.0

*Absolute values of market-share changes from the previous year are in parentheses. Market-share changes greater than 2 percent are underlined.

**Crosley went out of business in 1951. No sales were reported for 1952.

Source: Automotive Industries, various years.

The story in the lower-middle segment is much the same. The average market-share change experienced by the divisions in the segment was 2.68 percent, a percentage considerably higher than that experienced in the lower segment. Eleven of the twenty-eight annual cells in table 6.3 show that divisions gained or lost two percent or more market share, but most of these changes can again be accounted for by extraneous factors not related to market invasion policies. Both the Dodge loss and the Mercury gain in 1950 reflect the influence of the national Chrysler strike. Dodge's 6.9 percent gain in 1951 reflects gains made up from the strike loss during the previous year and the federal governments' Korean War readjustments.

Table 6.3
Division-Level Performance in the Lower-Middle Segment

			Market-Share Percentages		
Year	Dodge	Mercury	Pontiac	Kaiser	Nash
1946	34.0	15.4	28.4	0.9	21.4
1947	30.6 (-3.4)*	16.2 (+0.8)	30.1 (+1.7)	8.1 (+7.2)	15.0 (-6.4)
1948	27.0 (-3.6)	17.3 (+1.1)	28.9 (-1.2)	13.7 (+5.6)	13.1 (-1.9)
1949	28.1 (+1.1)	19.2 (+1.9)	32.9 (+4.0)	6.0 (-7.7)	13.9 (+0.8)
1950	22.7 (-5.4)	24.1 (+4.9)	33.4 (+0.5)	6.5 (+0.5)	13.3 (-0.6)
1951	29.6 (+6.9)	23.1 (-1.0)	33.5 (+0.1)	—**	13.9 (+0.6)
1952	29.3 (-0.3)	22.1 (-1.0)	31.7 (-1.8)	—	16.9 (+3.0)
1947–1952 Totals	-1.3	+5.9	+1.6	-8.1	+1.9

*Absolute values of market-share changes from the previous year are in parentheses. Market-share changes greater than 2 percent are underlined.

**Information not available.

Source: Automotive Industries, various years.

I interpret the evidence presented in tables 6.2 and 6.3 as suggesting that the GM divisions were following Sloanist market prescriptions. The GM divisions gained 2 percent share or more only once, and then only with the apparent aim of making up the market share lost to the 113-day 1946 strike. Pontiac's behavior is most interesting. Pontiac did not regain this lost share until 1949, when it picked up 4 percent. Pontiac management may have waited for the segment to stabilize to regain its lost market. Kaiser-Frazer introduced its Kaiser model in 1946, and gained an 8.2 percent share in 1947. The Kaiser model's gain came mostly at the expense of Nash sales. Had Pontiac made up its losses in 1947, it would have likely hurt its competition badly.

The overall segment share changes from 1947-1952 in the lower and lower-middle segments evince considerable stability. Even with a new entrant into the lower segment, and an exit from the lower-middle segment, the market segment share held by Plymouth, Ford, and Studebaker changed less than one percent. That held by Chevrolet, Henry J, Crosley, Dodge, Pontiac, and Nash changed less than two percent. Ford's Mercury Division was the only division to gain substantially in these markets during the period.

Market Instability in the Upper-Middle and Upper Segments

The divisional behavior in the upper-middle and upper segments is presented in tables 6.4 and 6.5. Sales here made up between 25 and 27 percent of the industry's total. These data indicate instability. In the upper-middle segment (table 6.4), the average market-share change experienced by the divisions was 2.6 percent. Divisions' absolute market shares changed by two percent or more in sixteen of the thirty annual cells. Unlike in the lower-middle segment, this instability cannot be explained away as the outcomes of extraneous forces. Again the entry of a new model—Frazer—had a disruptive effect on the balance of competitive forces. In 1947, Frazer gained 7.6 percent, while Hudson lost that much. When both Buick and Olds lost in 1948, Hudson regained 3.1 percent. Both Frazer and Hudson lost significantly in 1949, when Buick gained about five percent and Olds gained about four percent. In 1950, both GM divisions gained again, while Hudson suffered the most.

In this segment the GM divisions were marching to the beat of the same drummer, but this drummer wasn't pounding out the civil rhythm of the Sloanist regulatory ideology. Together, Oldsmobile and Buick gained 4.3 percent segment share from 1947-1952 and their gains came at the expense of the weaker independents. Both Frazer and Hudson, who concentrated sales in this segment, lost 2.6 percent respectively. This represented about 20 percent of sales for Hudson, and 32 percent for Frazer.

In the upper segment (table 6.5), the average market-share change experienced by the divisions was 3.1 percent. Divisions' absolute market share changed by two percent or

Table 6.4
Division-Level Performance in the Upper-Middle Segment

		Market-Share Percentage			
Year	DeSoto	Buick	Olds	Frazer	Hudson
1946	15.6	36.3	26.7	0.5	20.8
1947	11.5	38.8	28.4	8.1	13.2
	(-4.1)*	(+2.5)	(+1.7)	(+7.6)	(-7.6)
1948	12.3	36.5	26.2	8.7	16.3
	(+0.8)	(-2.3)	(-2.2)	(+0.6)	(+3.1)
1949	11.5	41.4	30.0	1.8	15.3
	(-0.8)	(+4.9)	(+3.8)	(-6.9)	(-1.0)
1950	9.8	45.8	31.9	1.0	11.5
	(-1.7)	(+4.4)	(+1.9)	(-0.8)	(-3.8)
1951	12.1	42.3	29.5	5.6	10.4
	(+2.3)	(-3.5)	(-2.4)	(+4.6)	(-1.1)
1952	12.4	42.0	29.5	5.5	10.6
	(+0.3)	(-0.3)	(0.0)	(-0.1)	(+0.2)
1947–1952 Totals	+0.9	+3.2	+1.1	-2.6	-2.6

*Absolute values of market-share changes from the previous year are in parentheses. Market-share changes greater than 2 percent are underlined.

Source: Automotive Industries, various years.

more in fourteen of the twenty-four annual cells. From 1947 to 1952, Cadillac gained more than 5 percent, while Chrysler lost as much. Again, we see the GM division increasing its share at the expense of its competition.

Wildcats, Shop-Floor Authority, and the Market

Table 6.6 presents the conjunctural associations between the variables of interest. It groups the divisions vertically into two market categories—those selling in the Sloanist-regulated segments, and those selling in the unstable segments. Those selling in unstable segments are grouped into three subcategories: those invading the markets of their competitors;

Table 6.5
Division-Level Performances in the Upper Segment

	Market-Share Percentages			
Year	Chrysler	Lincoln	Cadillac	Packard
1946	48.0	7.9	17.3	26.7
1947	42.8	11.0	24.4	21.8
	(-5.2)*	(+3.1)	(+7.1)	(-4.9)
1948	38.3	11.9	21.6	28.3
	(-4.5)	(+0.9)	(-2.8)	(+6.5)
1949	37.6	10.9	23.3	28.2
	(-0.7)	(-1.0)	(+1.7)	(-0.1)
1950	42.0	9.5	28.2	20.3
	(+4.4)	(-1.4)	(+4.9)	(-7.9)
1951	44.0	7.6	28.6	19.7
	(+2.0)	(-1.9)	(+0.4)	(-0.6)
1952	38.2	9.8	29.6	22.4
	(-5.8)	(+2.2)	(+1.0)	(+2.7)
1947–1952 Totals	-4.6	-1.2	+5.2	+0.6

*Absolute values of market-share changes from the previous year are in parentheses. Market-share changes greater than 2 percent are underlined.

Source: Automotive Industries, various years.

those holding stable shares there; and those losing market share to the invaders. Table 6.6 also groups automotive divisions horizontally as to whether they legitimated quota-based authority systems. In addition, the table reports the number of divisional wildcats occurring during the period that were not heat strikes.

The Findings

The evidence supports the existence of the conjunctural associations specified in chapter 5. Let's begin with the relatively stable segments. We can interpret the evidence as suggesting that the quota-based system enabled the divisions experiencing Sloanist regulation to operate their production systems without frequent work stoppages and labor unrest. The four divisions legitimating such a system experienced only six-

Table 6.6
Market Environments, Shop-Floor Authority, and Wildcat Frequencies, 1946–1952

Division's Position in Market Segment	Managerial Orientation to Quota-Based Authority			
	Accepting	Wildcat Strikes*	Antagonist	Wildcat Strikes*
1. Producers in Sloanist-Regulated Segments	Chevrolet	1	Ford	20
	Pontiac	1	Dodge	20
	Studebaker	5	Plymouth/Briggs	27
	GM/Fisher	5	Lincoln/Mercury	14
	Nash	4	——	
Totals		16		81
2. Producers in Unregulated Segments				
Market Invaders	Cadillac	0	——	
	Buick	0	——	
Stable Shares	Oldsmobile	0	DeSoto	10
	Packard	5	Briggs-Packard	8
Share Losers	Hudson	22	Chrysler	14
	Kaiser-Frazer	11	——	
Totals		38		32

*Heat strikes are excluded.

Source: Reports from the *Wall Street Journal* and *New York Times*.

teen total wildcats, while the four that refused to do so experienced eighty-one. These findings suggest tentatively that Sloanist regulation is functionally compatible with the legitimation of quota-based authority. Later, I present evidence suggesting that all adopted quota-based shop-floor policies as their position in Sloanist-regulated segments stabilized.

The wildcat activity occurring in the divisions selling in unstable markets is interesting. The number of wildcats occurring in the plants that refused to legitimate quota-based authority were quite similar—in the double digits, regardless of market conditions experienced. The number of wildcats occurring in divisions beginning the period with quota-based systems, but experiencing severe unstable market conditions, were similar to those that refused to legitimate quota-based systems. This suggests that serious market-share instability is functionally incompatible with the reproduction of quota-based shop-floor authority.

That the market share invaders, who legitimated quota-based authority, did not experience significant wildcat activity might appear to contradict the theory. The GM invaders did not experience serious wildcats. However, I argue that the time frame examined is too narrow to provide the reaction time required to affect these divisions' shop-floor relations. What is of critical theoretical significance in the case of market-share invaders is their shop-floor responses to the actions of the competitors whose markets they invade. If, in response to such invasions, these competitors revolutionize their productive forces in order to cut prices, they force the invaders to follow suit. Only then do we expect to see shop-floor ramifications. We do not begin to see this chain reaction until the middle and late 1950s.

The Hudson shop-floor response to the GM invasion is critical, for it adumbrated what was to come industrywide as the market foundation supporting quota-based authority collapsed in the middle 1950s. Faced with severe market losses, Hudson's management assaulted the types of shop-floor activities and relationships which it had encouraged and accepted in the past. It assaulted production standards on critical operations, especially in its trim and body-building departments. In doing so, it also met fierce resistance from a labor force that had grown accustomed to stable production standards—a labor force that perceived these assaults as violations of the norm and reacted to them with moral outrage. Shop-floor disputes over production standards were waged for years in the late 1940s and early 1950s, and a series of daily wildcats and lockouts dragged on in the trim department for more than thirty days in 1951. I will discuss these episodes in detail in the next chapter, along with similar episodes occurring at DeSoto, Dodge Main, Plymouth Body, and Studebaker in response to the breakdown of the sellers' market.

Definitional Foundations of Workers' Revolts at Chrysler and Ford

My conceptualization runs into difficulty in explaining militant worker behavior in the divisions with managements that were antagonistic to quota-based authority—particularly Chrysler and Ford. I argued that Chrysler's and Ford's managements never fully legitimated the quota-based system during the late 1940s. How, then, did workers learn to define managerial assaults on their production standards and working conditions as being unjust and illegitimate? What were the definitional foundations of their shop-floor revolts?

My discussion of the Chrysler authority system carried a response to this critical question. At Chrysler, workers came to accept a quota-based definition of a fair day's work as legitimate in their informal negotiations over production standards with shop foremen. In order to get production in a chaotic organizational structure, I argued that these foremen legitimated the quota-based definition of a fair day's work. Jefferys' history of labor relations at Dodge Main provides support for this interpretation.[39] It is reasonable to generalize to all Chrysler division plants, because the labor-relations structure affecting relationships was the same in those plants. Chrysler workers then drew from their experiences in informal dealings with foremen who accepted the legitimacy of "running-for-time" shop practices in defining assaults upon their production standards as illegitimate and unjust. I contend that this definition, legitimated in informal shop practice, was the trigger precipitating the wildcat action taken by Chrysler workers.

The situation at Ford is more difficult to assess because there is less evidence with which to construct a plausible explanation. Where did the notion of earned time—an idea so alien to the definition of the situation legitimated in the early Ford drive system—take root? I argue that it began to emerge on the shop floor as Ford's centralized management structure under Harry Bennett's reign began to lose its production competence in the 1940s. The Ford managerial structure was always a centralized, authoritarian structure. Few intermediary levels of management existed off the shop floor, and those in control ruled by arbitrary will. During the latter years of World War II, Harry Bennett and Henry Ford II waged a severe power struggle for corporate control. This power struggle diverted the attention and resources of the managerial organization from its everyday business functions. Whatever production competence Ford management had in the past was lost during the Bennett regime, which was as likely to use terrorism as anything else to assert and maintain control. After the young Henry II won his battle with Bennett, the Ford organization was in a state of severe disarray. It further underwent a trying transition period when Ford's new management team instituted the Sloanist organizational controls.[40] I argue that the Bennett-Ford control struggle, coupled with the organizational transition following it, left a power vacuum on the Ford shop floors much like–or perhaps even more expansive–than the ones that developed at Chrysler and Briggs.

As it attempted to gear up for the postwar boom in 1946, Ford's corporate management did not have a strong grip on the shop floor. Yet, even during the most chaotic years of the reorganization, Ford workers managed to get the product out. They met specialized production needs during World War II; they produced 399,000 cars in 1946, and 668,000 in 1947. What won their commitment to producing at these levels? What was the nature of the authority inspiring this immediate commitment?

It seems quite reasonable to argue that, in the wake of the power vacuum, Ford's foremen made the same informal deals with their workers that Chrysler's foremen had made. Such deals ceded to workers earned time in exchange for consistent, stable production outcomes. From the point of view of those in charge of meeting production schedules in a chaotic, undependable structure, this option would likely appear as the best of the available alternatives. Of course, legitimating "running-for-time" pursuits through such dealing would also establish the definitional foundation for interpreting subsequent managerial assaults on earned time as illegitimate violations of time-honored, traditionally legitimated norms. The feeling of outrage generated in this definitional frame—coupled with memories of worker resistance in the past, when cost-plus contracts during the war gave management less incentive to fight for tighter rates—was sufficient to spur militant action. While corporate-level management never accepted nor legitimated this definition, I argue that Ford shop-floor management was inclined to do so,[41] and that Ford workers drew upon these experiences to define assaults on their production standards as illegitimate. This was, most likely, the trigger precipitating their wildcat activity as well.

Stabilization in the Later Years of the Period

The data seem to suggest that something other than a mere taste for authoritarianism and labor strife was driving the behavior of those managements refusing to legitimate quota-based authority in the 1946–1952 period. The divisions embracing the drive system were often those experiencing the most market instability. They appear to have been assaulting their production standards and shop-floor relationships in direct reaction to this instability. With the waning of market instability—which, I argue, would have resulted if Sloanism had become institutionalized in all segments—these firms might have eventually embraced the quota-based systems that were profitable for those companies which were securely established in stable segments.

There is evidence suggesting that those initially antagonistic to quota-based authority in the 1940s were closer to embracing it by the early 1950s. The annual number of wildcats occurring in the industry declined significantly after the 1951 mark of thirty-one. There were only twelve wildcats in 1952, thirteen in 1953, and seven in 1954. Chrysler and Briggs experienced fifteen major wildcats in 1952–1954, compared to 104 in 1946 to 1951. While I argue that the market structure which regulated industry competition began to change significantly in 1953, and that this shift changed managements' shop-floor orientations thereafter, I believe that the wildcat declines from 1952–1954 might have resulted from a greater acceptance of quota-based authority.

Where's the evidence for this? Two sources of evidence exist for Ford. Robert Asher reports that Ford's Industrial Relations management encouraged their plant managers to set and maintain the constant production rates called for in the 1949 strike agreement in the early 1950s.[42] Managers were to honor the time-studied production rates stipulated and balance their lines so as not to exceed them. They were also to provide their unions with accurate information on rates. This orientation toward production rates was similar to that purportedly practiced by GM's management in this period.

I have found other archival evidence from Ford, such as their wildcat decline from 1952–1954 which appears to correlate with a shift in Ford's grievance-handling policy. In late 1950, Ford took action to decentralize its labor-relations system, granting its foremen more authority in resolving grievances.[43] This policy gave that level of management closest to workers' daily activities and concerns a greater role in settling disputed production standards. I have postulated that this level of management would be more sympathetic to workers' "running-for-time" cultures than levels farther removed from the shop floor—such as engineers from the Ford Automation Department and Ford's corporate labor relations staff. When Ford's shop management was given greater authority in settling labor disputes, wildcats declined. I contend that, with the decentralization of Ford's labor-relations structure, a system more in line with GM's was beginning to take root on the Ford shop floor.

The outcome of the late 1952 labor dispute at Dearborn Stamping supports this contention. This labor dispute revolved around union charges that management was retiming jobs arbitrarily. UAW Local 600 representatives demanded that management stop all time studies of jobs not affected by technological change. Archie Acciacca, the union president at Dearborn Stamping at the time, claims in *Ford Facts* that management agreed to honor this demand, even though it was not codified in the collective bargaining agreement. He claims that Dearborn management also agreed to consider fatigue and personal time in setting new rates—which they were contractually required to do—as well as a proposal to discipline working foremen attempting to speed up production.[44] I have found no evidence suggesting that Dearborn management reneged on this agreement.

To underscore the significance of this position, we simply need to review management's position at Ford in the 1949 production standard strikes. Before the 1949 strikes, Ford's management would accept only "a clear danger to the health and safety of its operators" as a brake on its prerogative to establish production rates. In 1952, Dearborn management in the Stamping Division tacitly accepted as binding the existing rates on production operations until it changed the technology structuring them. This policy was honored at Studebaker and also in GM plants, even though it was not then codified in contract language at GM. I contend that the newly decentralized Ford labor-relations structure which granted shop foremen and superintendents the right to set disputed rates, encouraged the tacit acceptance of this principle.

I have not found strong evidence suggesting a similar policy shift at Chrysler. However, the protected market situation which the Chrysler divisions experienced during the Korean War may have diverted its corporate managements' concerns away from the shop floor, allowing the informal shop-management/union-steward bargaining system to reign. Chrysler did not mount a full-scale assault on its production standards until the mid-1950s. After this assault, Chrysler's new management refused to allow its foremen to settle production rate disputes. Prior to this, they had routinely bypassed formal labor-relations channels and set production standards in dispute.[45]

The Market/Shop-Floor Linkage

For our concerns, the most significant industrial behavior reported in table 6.6 is that of the stable producers in Sloanist-regulated market segments who legitimated quota-based authority. These firms operated quite successfully during 1946–1952, with the behavior of the smaller independents being especially illuminating. Until 1952, Studebaker and Nash did not suffer unduly in a market segment in which they competed with the Big Three divisions. Studebaker actually increased its share during the period. Nash's share held fairly constant after the 1947 readjustments.

By the criteria with which Sloanists define their success—that is, rate or return criteria—Studebaker's and Nash's successes exceeded those of Ford, Chrysler, and Packard. Table 6.7 reports the annual rate of return on net worth earned by the auto firms. For 1947–1952, GM's annual rate of return averaged 30.0 percent. Nash's averaged 21.6 percent, and Studebaker's averaged 21.5 percent. This compares to the 20.9 percent earned by Chrysler, the 13.2 percent earned by Ford, the 12.4 percent earned by Hudson, and the 10.1 percent earned by Packard. While Nash's and Studebaker's rates of return dropped considerably below GM's during the Korean War, these rates were still higher than Ford's. During the war, both firms had engaged in a high percentage of government work which typically provided protected but lower margins. While they were earning handsome profit rates, these firms were also keeping pace proportionately with the Big Three's investments in plant and equipment as well.[46]

Studebaker and Nash also played leadership roles in the industry during this period. Studebaker marketed the first all-new postwar model in 1946, while Nash pioneered unibody construction, a method of body building that would eventually spread to the Big Three in the late 1950s and early 1960s.

Thus, I argue that, for a short time, quota-based authority was a viable alternative to the despotic drive system. Firms as diverse in other respects as GM, Nash, and Studebaker all profited with quota-based authority systems. These systems enabled their managements to co-opt workers' experiential knowledge and skill in the pursuit of orderly, efficient production. And the GM variant of quota-based authority also demonstrated that it was not necessarily a fetter to productivity increases so long as these increases followed procedural patterns which workers had come to define as legitimate.

However, in order for quota-based authority to become hegemonic, it seems that the expansionary designs of firms in a given market segment must be held in check. It appears that quota-based authority can meet the demands of rapid expansion only when there is room in the industry's market segments for all firms to expand in step with one another. When a firm begins to lose market share to a competitor—especially an aggressor—it tends to react to the invasion with shop-floor assaults. This type of instability seems to threaten the authority system's viability, driving managements to assault production standards and to breach traditionally legitimated role expectations. As we shall see, this, in turn, provokes solidary workers with notions of legitimate shop-floor expectations weaned in the quota-based authority systems to initiate rebellions.

The Specter of an Interventionist State

Finally, we examine the political, economic, and corporate foundations of the initial hegemonic order. Specifically, we ask why GM played the role of the Sloanist hegemon and acted in ways that preserved, for the most part, the balance of competitive forces in the dominant market segments. Considering GM's market position at the end of the war, this question is important. Had GM made the massive invest-

Table 6.7
Firms' Net Profit after Taxes, Divided by Net Worth, 1946–1952

Year	GM	Ford	Chrysler	Nash	Hudson	Studebaker	Packard	Kaiser	Total for Auto Manufacturers	Manufacturing Corporations
1946	6.1	-1.1	5.3	5.2	5.8	2.3	8.2	-56.1	3.3	10.3
1947	48.3	8.3	20.7	28.0	12.6	19.0	6.5	32.6	16.2	13.4
1948	24.5	11.5	23.2	25.8	23.0	30.1	21.6	15.7	21.0	13.4
1949	31.4	18.0	28.1	26.6	15.6	32.3	11.0	-84.8	25.8	9.8
1950	35.0	22.5	24.9	25.2	16.7	22.5	6.9	- 5.9	27.5	13.4
1951	20.0	10.1	13.8	13.5	-1.6	12.1	7.3	-12.0	15.2	10.2
1952	20.5	8.8	14.4	10.2	10.9	12.7	7.2	- 8.6	15.6	8.0
1947–1952 Average	30.0	13.2	20.9	21.6	12.9	21.5	10.1	-10.5	20.2	11.4

Source: Automotive Industries, various years.

ments in plant and equipment in the late 1940s that it was to make in the middle and late 1950s, it could have expanded in all segments with reasonably high return rates well within the 15 to 20 percent range long accepted as the GM target. To explain why it did not, we must examine the political stage and the manner in which GM and the Democratic Administration danced upon it.

State Prescription for the Strong; State Beneficence for the Weak

As discussed in chapter 1, the industrial policy of the Roosevelt administration shifted after the 1936 election. As the NRA promoted a collusive relationship between the state and industry, the Second New Deal dusted off the nation's antitrust laws and used them as weapons prohibiting firms from taking destructive courses of business action. The Roosevelt administration appeared to be especially concerned with preventing greater monopoly concentration in key industries, using its antitrust laws against dominant, expansionist firms who were driving their competitors out of the market. The administration's punitive actions against such firms served as deterrents to the expansionary designs of the like-minded. GM was hit with just such a suit in 1937, and, while its consequences were slight, Cray reports that it had a considerable effect on GM.[47] In response, GM began to restrict its market share.

At the end of World War II, the course of development taken by the key U.S. industries was not preordained, and the relationship between the state and the leading firms was not well-defined. In the immediate postwar years, the Truman administration sent signals to business suggesting that its stance would not change. The Truman administration held to Roosevelt's commitment to industrial pluralism and aggressive antitrust action. In 1946, it filed antitrust suits against ALCOA and American Tobacco, charging each firm with unfairly monopolizing their industries. These actions defined the political terrain upon which GM was to act.

Of course, GM took a 113-day UAW strike in 1946, and it didn't crank up its production system until May of that year. If GM had not taken the long strike in this potentially hostile political environment, its wisest political decision might well have been simply to let its productive forces lie fallow until the competition had begun to reestablish themselves in the market. In 1949—a year in which GM gained 2 percent in market share—the Justice Department filed an antitrust suit against it, charging that the DuPont investments in GM during the 1910s and 1920s violated the Clayton Act. Following the popular literature, I argue, that this potentially hostile political environment was decisive during the early postwar period in steering GM toward more civic market policies in the lower and lower-middle segments.

However, not all auto firms experienced this hostility. The state, for example, played an important role in launching Kaiser-Frazer's entry into the industry. Kaiser-Frazer entered the market a weakling. In August 1945, Kaiser-Frazer's total investment came to about $5 million. This compares to GM's working capital of $600 million and Chrysler's $150 million. Its plant—the old Graham-Page factory—was an outdated facility and too small for volume production. In 1946, the government's Reconstruction Finance Corporation sold the Willow Run Bomber plant that Ford had managed during the war to Kaiser-Frazer. This plant was newer and larger, and Kaiser-Frazer got a good price! They sold their old Graham-Page facilities back to RFC for the price which they had paid for Willow Run.[48] This state beneficence was a godsend to a struggling company during its first critical year of operation.

The state's effect on the balance of forces in the industry was greatest during the Korean War. The federal government established the National Production Authority to regulate war production. The NPA also effectively controlled domestic production schedules of auto firms by allocating their steel supplies. Firms were not allowed to produce beyond the market-share quotas set by the NPA's steel allocations. These allocations were based on production rates of 1947 to 1949. This hurt Ford because the figures did not account for the effects of expansionary programs that the company had instituted in 1949 and 1950. Meanwhile Chrysler regained what market share it had lost through the NPA's beneficence.

Studebaker and Packard also benefitted considerably from federal policy during the latter years of the period. Both were large defense contractors. In 1953, 42 percent of Packard's and 36 percent of Studebaker's sales went to government contracts.[49] These firms had vested interests in the type of interventionist/militarist polices to which the Truman administration turned.

State intervention threatened to extend much further than control over production schedules during the Korean War. In December 1950, Truman's Office of Price Stabilization placed the industry under another price freeze. Nevins and Hill report that profit controls were also in the air.[50] All of this understandably alarmed the dominant auto firm managements, who resented state infringement on their autonomy.

From hindsight, of course, the significance of the regulatory constraints imposed upon the industry during the Korean War appear to be slight. They proved to be temporary impediments to free enterprise in support of a relatively short war. However, from the point of view of the dominant firms, these types of controls did not bode well for the future of free enterprise, given the Truman administration's shift to a more militarist/interventionist foreign policy. Such controls, while restricting managerial prerogatives and autonomy, might have been used to create more permanent space in the market within which the weaker independents could survive and prosper—a condition that an unregulated market could not guarantee. At least, this is what the NPA actually accomplished during 1951–1952.

The dominant firms—especially Ford—vehemently opposed this form of statist regulation. Calling upon the time-honored American political traditions of free enterprise, laissez faire, and self-help, they mobilized public support against profit-control proposals. Congress passed the Capehart amendment to the Defense Production Act of 1951 which explicitly forbade all forms of profit control.[51] With the election of a probusiness Republican administration in 1952, the heyday of this type of industrial regulation had passed.

Fault Lines

I stated in chapter 1 that, by 1946, all of the surviving auto firms were ready to embrace Sloanist business strategies. I've also presented evidence in this chapter suggesting that, from 1946 to 1952, these firms behaved, for the most part, in accordance with Sloanist precepts in the lower and lower-middle market segments which constitute 73–75 percent of the total market. Yet, the foundations of Sloanist regulation were still rather weak.

First, the power structures of the dominant firms were, over the long haul, incompatible with Sloanist regulation. That is to say, the management groups in control of these firms were more likely to define corporate success in terms of market-share gain and industry-level dominance than by Sloanist criteria. Surprisingly, these firms were Ford and GM.

Of course, Henry Ford II recruited Ernest Breech and several officials from GM after World War II to restructure his company's managerial organization along GM's lines. However, this, in itself, did not signal a clear and lasting commitment to Sloanist courses of action. Early on in the Ford-Breech relationship, it became clear that Breech's job was to prepare the young Henry as the heir to his grandfather's autocratic throne. Henry II asserted dominance over a company whose assets remained family controlled and—true to its founder's wishes—never became beholden to Wall Street's interests. It doesn't appear that earning high rates of return on investments was as important to Ford's management as it was to others. Ford's rates, during the period, were much lower. Its dividends were about one half those paid by GM and Chrysler. Because of Ford's financial structure, the corporate interests and commitments that would tend to lead toward safe, predictable courses of market action were never strong. This freed Ford's management to deviate from Sloanist precepts at opportune times.

Of all the auto firms, Ford's commitment to increasing market share appeared to be the strongest. Ford's pronounced goal was to target the lower and lower-middle segments and attain market-share parity with Chevrolet. Then, it planned to challenge GM's hegemony over the more lucrative, higher priced segments.[52] When the federal government lifted its production controls in February 1953, Henry Ford II found nothing holding him back. He would act upon his dream of challenging GM for industry dominance.

The power of GM's operations management was also stronger in the early postwar years than it had ever been. As discussed in chapter 1, Sloan centralized GM's managerial structure during the 1930s, and he allowed operations management much more leverage in responding to Depression conditions than they had experienced previously. In 1946, on the eve of Sloan's retirement, C. E. Wilson pushed for a proposal that would, in essence, strip the chairman of GM's powerful finance committee of an executive function. Wilson's proposal would place the finance chairman under the authority of the C.E.O. and would replace the position of president. Donaldson Brown, GM's finance chairman, opposed this move, seeing it as a threat to finance's position in the corporate power structure. The alternative proposal was to have Brown succeed Sloan as GM's board chairman, a position from which Brown could preserve the balance of forces between GM's operations management in Detroit and the finance management in New York. Wilson's proposal carried the day. Sloan retained his position as Chairman of the Board, and he allowed Wilson a free hand in managing the firm.[53] Not favoring this arrangement, Brown resigned. This reorganization again strengthened GM's operations managements' power. Wilson surrounded himself in the general office with successful like-minded division managers.

While GM's management would always have to concern themselves with rate-of-return criteria, it was in such a strong position in the late 1940s that it could both expand and conform to such criteria. The major brakes on expansionary designs in the 1946–1952 period were political ones. With Eisenhower's victory in 1952, and with C. E. Wilson and two other GM officials taking positions in Eisenhower's cabinet, these political brakes were lifted.

While I argue that the fickle Sloanist commitments of the industry's dominant firms were the leading factors in the breakdown of the initial hegemonic order in the mid-1950s, the early regulatory system suffered from other defects as well. A major prop was the great sellers' market of the early postwar years. For most of this period, this market would absorb what firms produced. Because of government price regulation in 1946 combined with the threat of further regulation when those controls were lifted later in the year, prices were kept below market clearing levels. Patterns of price-and-style leadership did not emerge to regulate the market, for they were unnecessary.[54] The auto firms' levels of commitment to price maintenance strategies were also untested. What would happen when the sellers market collapsed?

Thus, the foundations upon which the industry experienced stability in the 1946–1952 period were weak. This regulatory system operated only in the lower and lower-middle segments, and it was propped up even here by the specter of an interventionist state and an exceptional sellers' market.

Yet, I have argued that the orderly expansion that occurred enabled key firms to institute a type of shop-floor authority compatible with "running-for-time" cultures and the quota-based definition of a fair day's work that legitimated them. Those firms instituting such systems performed quite well in the stable segments.

The Anomalies

The ideal types developed in chapter 5 proved useful in interpreting historical developments taking place in the early postwar period. Workers and managers in those firms and divisions which embraced quota-based authority, and operated in stable and unstable market segments, behaved in the predicted manner. The Ford and Chrysler cases, however, are difficult to reconcile in terms of the theoretical model. They stand as anomalies to it.

Ford operated in a relatively stable market segment. Yet, workers in the Ford plants initiated numerous wildcat strikes from 1946 through 1951. With considerable pressure from the corporate level, Ford's managers appear to have embraced the drive system. However, this is understandable in the terms which the model specifies. The organizational chaos Ford experienced throughout the 1940s, coupled with a management change at the onset of the period, left it unprepared to enter the new postwar market arena. Ford management did not have sufficient control over its operations to compete in the Sloanist-regulated environment. The new Ford management had to establish its authority and control over the labor process before it had the luxury of stabilizing relations. Had it not done so, its ability to prosper would have been in serious doubt, even in the relatively benign years of the sellers' market.

What is most significant to the model is the adjustments that Ford's management made after it asserted initial control over operations. The evidence suggests that Ford moved in the expected direction after its Automation Department improved key operations, after its supervisory ranks stabilized following the 1947 foreman's strike, and after it adjusted to the arbitrators' ruling in the 1949 strikes which set production-standard procedures at River Rouge and the Lincoln plant. Ford appears to have moved toward the GM position with regard to production-standard practices by the early 1950s. When it did so, the number of wildcat strikes experienced in its plants declined significantly.

The Chrysler case, however, can not be so easily reconciled to the model. Chrysler experienced serious and numerous wildcat strikes during the period. Yet, in many ways, it experienced conditions similar to the independents. Chrysler's profit margins were high during the period, and it placed many of its makes in the more stable segments of the market. Chrysler's industrial relations should have been more stable than Ford's, because Ford faced massive reorganization and earned lower profit margins, or Hudson's, because Hudson was forced to compete in an unstable segment experiencing new entries and expansion by two GM divisions.

All we can say is that, even with a market foundation supportive of stable industrial relations, Chrysler's chaotic management structure was quite slow to take advantage of the opportunities open to it. This points to the limitations of the theoretical model used here, and to a host of variables likely to trigger wildcat activity that were not incorporated in the model—such as corporate-level ideologies hostile to unionization and collective bargaining, interunion rivalries, personality factors, and so forth.

Importantly, however, Chrysler's labor relations stabilized in the early post-Korean War years, along with those of the Sloanist-run firms. Evidence suggests that its managements, like Ford's, began to accept quota-based authority as legitimate.

In summary, expectations weaned on experience in quota-based authority systems had developed in all of the industry's plants by the early 1950s. At different rates and in different degrees, managements had grown to accept quota-based authority as legitimate, and they won real benefits from doing so. A standardized production quota—rather than management's arbitrary command—became the legitimate expectation regarding a fair day's work. Once management accepted this definition, workers in operator-paced jobs could "run for time" and gain some control over their production experiences. This set expectations regarding rightful managerial behavior. These expectations were also in place to guide workers' collective action when the return to competitive market conditions forced management to revert to the drive system of years past.

CHAPTER 7

Bursting Two Seams in the Early Hegemonic Order: Market Breakdown and Shop-Floor Response, 1953–1958

Eisenhower won the 1952 election by promising to usher in a new era of industrial self-regulation. His administration frowned upon the types of production and price controls that were currently practiced, and the types of profit controls that were advocated during the Korean War. The Eisenhower administration denounced prescriptive and statist forms of business regulation as socialistic and as fetters to business initiative and productivity. The Eisenhower administration also criticized the Justice Department's aggressive use of the Clayton Act, defining big business' interests as consistent with national interests.

Eisenhower's election victory confirmed auto managements' belief that public opinion would eventually swing to its favor once again—and it apparently had. When the federal government lifted its production controls in March 1953, the industry was left to itself. As the early postwar sellers market quickly evaporated, auto firms had to manage the readjustment to normal market conditions on their own. For the first time since World War II, auto managements ran their affairs unhindered by government prescription or its threat. As a consequence, the props supporting Sloanist regulation in major market segments collapsed. As we shall see, the industry succumbed quickly to the driving forces of capitalist dynamics with predictable results—overproduction, glutted markets, company failures, massive unemployment, and profit-rate declines.

The first section of this chapter documents the breakdown of Sloanist regulation in the market arena and discusses company's market responses to the increased competition and their failures.

The second section of this chapter examines both managements' and workers' shop-floor reactions to the breakdown of the early hegemonic order. It shows that, as market conditions became increasingly unstable, firms abandoned their commitments to honoring shop-floor expectations legitimated in the quota-based authority systems. Managements assaulted established production standards with vigor and attempted to coerce workers' acceptance of an authority system legitimating its prerogatives to establish and change production standards at will. These assaults were most fierce in the plants hardest hit by the intensifying market competition—Hudson, DeSoto, Plymouth Body, Dodge Main, and Studebaker. However, the evidence suggests that such assaults had spread industrywide by the end of the period.

This chapter's final section examines in detail solidary workers' responses to these shop-floor assaults. These were the workers whose conceptions of legitimate shop-floor expectations were forged in the quota-based authority systems of the early postwar years. These were the workers with structurally generated capacities for initiating militant collective action against such assaults. The section first presents critical cases of plant-level struggles over production standards. Then it presents more aggregated evidence of worker responses, focusing especially on industrywide protests during the 1955 and 1958 national contract negotiations.

The evidence presented in this chapter will suggest that, by the late 1950s, the industry had steered itself onto a destructive course. Firm-level reactions to the unregulated market undercut the industry's capacities for controlling the disruptive effects of competition. In response, managements were disrupting established shop-floor expectations and relationships and the conflicts resulting from these disruptions were delegitimating the postwar authority structures established in the industry.

Market Breakdown, 1953–1958

Auto firms reacted aggressively to the political signals sent by the Eisenhower administration. Ford continued its challenge to GM's dominance and planned to expand its share of the middle priced segments.[1] Ford's expansionary designs promised to destabilize the hegemonic order.

In response to the new political climate and to Ford's aggressiveness, GM abandoned its commitment to Sloanist-market precepts. Like Ford, GM committed its resources to increasing sales and market penetration at the expense of its weaker competitors. GM's rate of investment in plant and equipment during the period matched Ford's. GM invested heavily in new plant and equipment, increasing its plant capacity to 74 percent above its 1946 level. GM was determined to check Ford's expansionary designs and to teach the new Ford management a lesson in the dynamics of market power.

A new GM administration initiated these market policies. In 1953, the GM board elected Harlow Curtice, an expansion-minded salesman, as president and C.E.O. Curtice's appointment represented another victory for operations management over finance. Curtice centralized his control over GM's general office and rendered ineffective finance management's customary brake on division management's expansionary designs.[2]

The GM and Ford expansionist signals in the early 1950s did not bode well for the market positions of Chrysler and the independents. Those firms began to prepare themselves for the inevitable consequences. Chrysler introduced its first completely new postwar Plymouth and Dodge models in 1953, and its new Chrysler and DeSoto models in 1954. Chrysler's styling on these models bucked the industry trend toward bigger and more ostentatious cars. The sales slogan for the new models was "smaller on the outside, bigger on the inside." These cars were much shorter than the GM and Ford competitors, but were taller, allowing people to sit in them with their hats on.[3]

Lacking the resources to defend their markets successfully against direct assaults from the Big Three firms, the independents' survival was threatened by the GM-Ford competition for market dominance. In the 1946-1952 period, as we have seen, the independents' models were priced between major segments. These models, while relatively lighter, less powerful, and more expensive, competed successfully by offering buyers options that were unavailable on models sold in the established segments.

Unfortunately, the auto market was squeezed during the mid-1950s precisely where the independent makes were located. Plymouth, Chevrolet, and Ford all increased production and sales of their larger and more luxurious models, extending their market penetration into the middle-price range of the market. The independent makes could not compete head-on with the Big Three makes. The independents did not enjoy similar economies of scale, nor did they have the facilities to meet changes in demand, especially for the larger V8 engines.

Yet, the independents did take measures to strengthen their positions. They brought out compact models, testing the market for small, lower priced cars. They also merged. Nash and Hudson combined to form the American Motors Corporation. Studebaker and Packard combined to form Studebaker-Packard. Thus, it appears that the independents were moving toward GM's full-line marketing strategy, selling different models in different market segments.[4]

In sum, Ford and GM began to pursue expansionary policies that were out-of-step with those prescribed by the Sloanist marketing strategy. They refused to respect the existing balance of competitive forces established in the market segments, and they attempted to increase their market share. They moved increasingly to the middle-priced segments with larger and more expensive cars. Chrysler appeared to counter these moves with styling innovations, while the independents merged to increase economies of scale, market coverage, and visibility. They also tested the market for small, lower priced cars. How did these firm-level policies weather the increasing competition?

Table 7.1 reports the industry's firm-level market performances. Several developments are worth noting. First, we see that unit sales increased by 39 percent in 1953 over their 1952 levels. Sales then decreased slightly in 1954, and increased again in 1955 by 30 percent. In 1956, 1957, and 1958, the industry skidded into recession.

Columns for manufacturers in table 7.1 show the firm-level consequences of this instability on the balance of com-

Table 7.1
Firm-Level Market-Share Data, 1953–1958

Year	Total Units*	% of Change in Unit Sales	GM	Ford	Chrysler	Independents
			Market-Share Percentages			
1952	4,087	—	42.5	23.2	21.7	12.6
1953	5,666	+39	45.7 (+3.2)**	25.5 (+2.3)	20.6 (-1.1)	8.5 (-4.1)
1954	5,489	- 3	51.1 (+5.4)	31.1 (+5.6)	13.0 (-7.6)	4.8 (-3.7)
1955	7,112	+30	51.2 (+0.1)	27.8 (-3.3)	17.0 (+4.0)	4.0 (-0.8)
1956	5,853	-18	51.7 (+0.5)	28.9 (+1.1)	15.8 (-1.2)	3.6 (-0.4)
1957	5,771	- 1	46.5 (-5.2)	31.5 (+2.6)	19.0 (+3.2)	3.0 (-0.6)
1958	4,269	-26	50.5 (+4.0)	28.8 (-2.7)	15.2 (-3.8)	5.5 (+2.5)
(1952–1958) Totals	—	—	+8.0	+5.6	-6.5	-7.1

*In thousands.

**Absolute values of market-share changes from the previous year are in parentheses. Market-share changes greater than 2 percent are underlined.

Source: Automotive Industries, various years.

Table 7.2
Divisional Performances in the Lower Segment, 1953–1958

			Market-Share Percentages			
Year	Chevrolet	Ford	Plymouth	Studebaker	HenryJ	Rambler
1952	38.6	33.2	19.6	7.1	1.4	—
1953	41.5	34.5	18.6	5.0	0.4	—
	(+2.9)*	(+1.3)	(-1.0)	(-2.1)	(-1.0)	
1954	43.0	42.5	11.6	2.9	—**	—
	(+1.5)	(+8.0)	(-7.0)	(-2.1)	(-0.4)	
1955	41.5	39.8	16.4	2.4	—	—
	(-1.5)	(-2.7)	(+4.8)	(-0.5)		
1956	43.8	38.5	13.5	2.1	—	2.0
	(+2.3)	(-1.3)	(-2.9)	(-0.3)		(+2.0)
1957	40.4	39.4	16.1	1.7	—	2.5
	(-3.4)	(+0.9)	(+2.6)	(-0.4)		(+0.5)
1958	42.7	35.6	13.5	1.7	—	6.5
	(+2.3)	(-3.8)	(-2.6)	(0.0)		(+4.0)
1952–1958 Totals	+4.1	+2.4	-6.1	-5.4	-1.4	+6.5

*Absolute values of market-share changes from the previous year are in parentheses. Market-share changes greater than 2 percent are underlined.

**Production of Henry J model was halted in 1953.

Source: Automotive Industries, various years.

Table 7.3
Divisional Performances in the Lower-Middle Segment, 1953–1958

		Market-Share Percentages			
Year	Pontiac	Mercury	Dodge	Nash	Edsel
1952	31.7	22.1	29.3	16.9	—
1953	35.1 (+3.4)*	26.2 (+4.1)	26.3 (-3.0)	12.5 (-4.4)	—
1954	41.4 (+6.3)	31.2 (+5.0)	17.9 (-8.4)	9.6 (-2.9)	—
1955	41.4 (0.0)	29.1 (-2.1)	22.2 (+4.3)	7.3 (-2.3)	—
1956	40.8 (-0.6)	31.2 (+2.1)	25.1 (+2.9)	2.9 (-4.4)	—
1957	36.6 (-4.2)	29.8 (-1.4)	29.5 (+4.4)	—** (-1.8)	3.1 (+3.1)
1958	42.5 (+5.9)	25.2 (-4.6)	25.1 (-4.4)	— (-1.1)	7.1 (+4.0)
1952–1958 Totals	+10.8	+3.1	-4.2	-16.9	+7.1

*Absolute values of market-share changes from the previous year are in parentheses. Market-share changes greater than 2 percent are underlined.

**Production for model was halted in 1956.

Source: Automotive Industries, various years.

Table 7.4
Divisional Performances in the Upper-Middle Segment, 1953–1958

			Market-Share Percentages		
Year	Buick	Olds	DeSoto	Hudson	Kaiser-Frazer
1952	42.0	29.5	12.4	10.6	5.5
1953	46.7	31.4	12.6	6.9	2.3
	(+4.7)*	(+1.9)	(+0.2)	(-3.7)	(-3.2)
1954	49.3	39.1	7.4	3.4	0.9
	(+2.6)	(+7.7)	(-5.2)	(-3.5)	(-1.4)
1955	49.5	39.6	7.9	2.9	0.1
	(+0.2)	(+0.5)	(+0.5)	(-0.5)	(-0.8)
1956	49.0	40.6	9.3	1.1	—**
	(-0.5)	(+1.0)	(+1.4)	(-1.8)	(-0.1)
1957	45.1	42.5	11.9	0.5	—
	(-3.9)	(+1.9)	(+2.6)	(-0.6)	
1958	42.8	49.5	7.8	—	—
	(-2.3)	(+7.0)	(-4.1)	(-0.5)	
1952–1958 Totals	+0.8	+3.2	+20.0	-10.6	-5.5

*Absolute values of market-share changes from the previous year are in parentheses. Market-share changes greater than 2 percent are underlined.

**Production for model halted.

Source: Automotive Industries, various years.

Table 7.5
Divisional Performances in the Upper Segment, 1953–1958

	Market-Share Percentages				
Year	Cadillac	Lincoln	Chrysler	Imperial	Packard
1952	29.6	9.8	38.2	—	22.4
1953	27.2 (+1.0)	10.8 (-2.4)*	42.4 (+4.2)	—	19.6 (-2.8)
1954	38.5 (+11.3)	12.6 (+1.8)	35.5 (-6.9)	—	13.4 (-6.2)
1955	36.6 (-1.9)	9.1 (-3.3)	40.6 (+5.1)	—	13.5 (+0.1)
1956	41.2 (+4.6)	13.7 (+4.6)	33.1 (-7.5)	3.2 (+3.2)	8.8 (-4.7)
1957	43.7 (+2.5)	11.5 (-2.2)	32.9 (-0.2)	10.2 (+7.0)	1.6 (-7.2)
1958	55.1 (+11.4)	11.9 (0.4)	26.3 (-6.6)	6.7 (-3.5)	— (-1.6)
1952–1958 Totals	+25.5	+2.3	-11.9	+6.7	-22.4

*Absolute values of market-share changes from the previous year are in parentheses. Market-share changes greater than 2 percent are underlined.

Source: Automotive Industries, various years.

petitive forces in the industry. The message is clear. Overall, GM gained 8 percent market share by the end of the period.[5] Ford gained 5.6 percent. We might interpret this as a standoff, although GM did beat back Ford's assault as well as establish its position as the industry's styling and pricing leader. In making these gains, however, GM lost a critical antitrust case in the Supreme Court, placing itself thereafter under increasing Justice Department scrutiny. We examine the consequences of this in more detail in the next chapter. The independents were the big losers. All of their established models were driven out of the market.[6] Chrysler was a big loser as well.

As tables 7.2–7.5 show, the market performances of the divisions competing in the four segments followed the firm-level trends.

All segments experienced considerable instability. The absolute values of the divisions' annual market-share gains and losses exceeded 2 percent frequently. The averages of these changes show this instability. The average change for the divisions selling in the lower segment was 2.3 percent during 1953–1958, compared to 1.6 percent in 1947–1952. This average was 3.5 percent for those selling in the lower-middle segment during 1953–1958, compared to 2.7 percent in 1947–1952. It was 2.3 percent in the upper-middle segment during 1953–1958, compared to 2.6 percent in 1947–1952. It was 4.2 percent in the upper segment during 1953–1958, compared to 3.1 percent in 1947–1952. Thus, the market segments became highly unstable during 1953–1958. The numbers illustrating this actually underestimate the extent to which the market destabilized, as much of the flux in 1947–1952 was because of effects of outside forces, rather than divisions invading one another's established markets.

Table 7.6 reports firms' annual rates of return on net worth after taxes during the period. Table 7.6 allows us to gauge the effect of market instability on firms' financial performances. We see that, while expanding from 1953–1955, both GM and Ford were earning rates of return roughly comparable with those that they earned during 1946–1952, while the rates of Chrysler and the independent firms dropped below their 1946–1952 marks. During the recession years of 1956–1958, the rates of return of all firms declined, reflecting the effects of increased competition.

Table 7.6
Profits After Taxes, Divided by Net Worth, 1953–1958

Year	GM	Ford	Chrysler	AMC	Studebaker-Packard	Industry-wide
1953	20.1	11.5	13.1	—	—	15.3
1954	24.1	14.3	3.2	-6.8	-17.7	16.9
1955	28.0	22.8	15.3	-4.8	-25.0	23.9
1956	18.5	11.7	3.1	-15.9	-662.	13.2
1957	17.2	12.8	16.4	-10.6	-249.	15.3
1958	12.6	5.0	-4.9	19.0	-22.2	8.9
1953-1958 Average	20.1	13.0	7.7	-3.8	-196.	15.6

Source: White 1971.

Thus, the GM and Ford divisions increased their market shares at the expense of Chrysler and the independents, but they may have paid for this in terms of decreasing profit margins in the late 1950s. The strategies employed by the weaker firms to buffer their market positions against GM and Ford's expansions failed. Chrysler's new models failed to sell in 1953 and 1954. The independent mergers did not help sales in the segments where they had established positions.

Managements' Market Definition of a Fair Day's Work

As a response to the increasing competition, auto firms embraced shop-floor policies aimed at decreasing production costs and increasing labor productivity. The direction the industry took after 1958 is, in large measure, a response to the failures of these policies to bring about the desired results. Not only did these policies produce fierce shop-floor militancy from the solidary workers whose conceptions of legitimacy were forged in the quota-based authority systems, but they also produced a considerable amount of technical inefficiency and chaos. Here, we examine the content of these policies and rank-and-file workers' reactions to them.

The shop-floor responses of Chrysler and Studebaker-Packard managements were strikingly similar. Each placed the fate of their production operations in the hands of outside engineers without direct experience in the production operations which they were charged with redesigning. Packard management took control over Studebaker-Packard in 1955, using Packard engineers to study, evaluate, and redesign operations in the old Studebaker South Bend complex. Chrysler's new management hired an outside engineering firm to study operations in 1954 and 1955. Chrysler also employed engineers who formerly worked in GM's and Ford's work redesign programs to revamp its aged production processes.[7]

In revising operations and production standards, these engineers adopted the drive system's managerial prerogative. Their goal was to reach parity with the standards which GM and Ford employed, defining the production standards of the most efficient firms as reasonable and just.[8] They rationalized rate increases with the exchange-value-equivalency demand.[9]

At Chrysler, formal contract provisions—provisions granting management the prerogative to set rates as it saw fit—legitimated management's assault on production standards.[10] At Studebaker-Packard, management won similar contract provisions on 12 January 1956, after it opened its books and pleaded to the UAW International for relief.[11]

These new managements' interpretations of a fair day's work was expressed succinctly by Frank W. Misch, a Chrysler financial vice president.

> We have developed new work standards. These standards are comparable to those on the same jobs at Ford and General Motors, and they are fair in themselves. Meeting these new work standards means only that each of us will do on his job as much work as the employee doing the same job at Ford and General Motors. It takes that much effort to give us the job security and progress we are all shooting for.[12]

The new managements were contemptuous of their firm's workers, the "running-for-time" cultures they honored, and the shop managements legitimating them. They refused to see the rationality embedded in established methods of operations. They blamed workers' slovenly work habits and managements' accommodative policies toward them for their firms' plights. The new managements refused to be bound by past agreements legitimating earned time and they defined nonproductive labor time as illegitimate. In an effort to delegitimate "running-for-time" cultures, the new management teams excluded shop-level managements from participation in redesigning labor processes, in setting production standards, and in negotiating production standard grievances.[13] In general, these managements mounted heated assaults on all standards in virtually all of their departments and operations. To gauge the extent of these assaults, we must examine them on a plant-by-plant basis.

At Plymouth Body, the 1954 changeover from Briggs to Chrysler management marked the onset of the shop-floor assault. Anticipating what was to come, the president of UAW Local 212 sent letters to all shop committeemen advising them to save recorded evidence of minutes, agreements, and Briggs policy statements for use in negotiations with Chrysler. By October 1954, the number of grievances had tripled, and the formal procedures for resolving them ground to a standstill. Chrysler management refused to negotiate.[14] A UAW Local 212 official, interpreting the new Chrysler policy, states in *Voice of Local 212*

> Workers will do exactly what supervision says regardless of past policies, or any previous agreement, or even the bargaining procedure, and firings or lesser penalties will be given for "insubordination."[15]

The assault was widespread. It affected the Mack Avenue trim department, the Eight Mile and Outer Drive stamping plants, as well as the maintenance departments servicing the complex.[16] By September 1956, Chrysler began reevaluating every job in the complex. UAW Local 212 officials claimed that management was sending teams of supervisors into GM and Ford plants to study their methods and standards for implementation at Plymouth Body.[17] The speedup affected all workers in the complex, regardless of plant or occupation.

The story was much the same at Dodge Main. The speedup actually began there as early as 1951 in the trim department, and particularly on operations off the main line. Management retimed jobs on key operations and threatened operators refusing to meet them with stiff disciplinary sanctions. Dodge management fired both the trim department committeeman and the chair of the plant committee. In March 1952, it fired two trimmers and disciplined twenty-two others over a rate dispute.

Management's position in the dispute was expressed clearly in a letter sent to UAW Local 3's Recording Secretary on 4 April 1952. The Dodge Works manager claimed that management had instituted technological changes modernizing the trim department after the war, but that output had not increased accordingly. Now, Chrysler insisted on a fair day's work, regardless of the consequences.[18]

The speedup spread throughout Dodge Main in the latter 1950s. By 1958, Chrysler management had sped up almost every operation, reneging on the informal agreements that were made in the past between line foremen and shop stewards. In the stamping-press room, management assaulted the customary fifty-minute on/ten-minute off schedule.[19] Management increased production standards in the body-in-white department by 32 percent, in trim by 30 percent, in final assembly by 20 percent, and in motor assembly by 43 percent.[20] The speedup spread to nonproduction jobs as well. By 1958, the number of janitors per department at Dodge Main had been cut in half, and the difficulty of the work performed by inspectors increased phenomenally due to a marked decrease in quality production. Of the 1950s speedup, a headlight installer stated that "I've had 27 years working in this plant, and I've never seen workers driven this hard."[21]

The story was much the same at Studebaker. Management at South-Bend abandoned the old piece-rate system that had governed shop-floor practices for decades. In 1955, it increased production standards across the boards by 25 percent, reduced wages, and replaced piece-rate incentives with tighter supervision and discipline.[22]

Thus, from the point of view of the new managements taking over the firms hardest hit by market competition, workers were duty-bound to produce at levels comparable to the industry's most efficient plants. This conception detached management's expectation of workers' work-role performances from existing practice. Past practice and customs—as well as the rationality embodied in them—were not taken into account in their definition of a fair day's work. From their point of view, to limit expectations to these past practices would run their firms out of business—an outcome that was not in the best interests of anyone employed.

Workers' Responses

As in the 1930s, auto workers responded to the corporate-wide speedups of the 1950s with shop-floor militancy. This militancy was in many ways as fierce and as significant to the development of the industrial structures regulating subsequent shop-floor practices as any that preceded it.

Yet, such militancy was different in two fundamental respects than that which occurred in the 1930s. First, this militancy was not nurtured in the larger political economic environment. Second, it was spurred on by a quota-based conception of fair shop-floor practices spawned in the "running-for-time" cultures that managements legitimated in the 1940s and early 1950s. To illustrate these differences, we compare the 1950s shop-floor revolts with those of the 1930s, emphasizing their relationships to their respective external environments.

The 1930s militancy was spawned to a considerable extent in the political-economic environment. Section 7 of the NLRA in 1933 and the Wagner Act in 1935 were interpreted by labor as legitimating strikes as viable means of resolving grievances. Public opinion in general, while never fully supportive of militant labor action, had at least shifted away from big business. Business' corporatist hegemony had been broken following the stock market crash of 1929. Until 1938, there were no labor contracts signed in auto industry with curbs on striking.

UAW organizers mobilized this sentiment in support of pivotal strikes—such as those waged at GM Flint, at Chrysler, and, later, at Ford. Most importantly, the UAW International encouraged and supported the militant local initiatives of rank-and-file workers, providing them with leadership, resources, and direction. All of this encouraged workers to act in unprecedented ways with a boldness and a determination that broke managements' grip on the shop floor.

The situation was quite different in the 1950s. Where the political-economic environment of the 1930s nurtured shop-floor militancy, that of the 1950s was openly hostile to it. Public opinion, the state, and the UAW International supported managements' efforts to increase productivity in its most vulnerable plants. All were antagonistic to the militant strikers, defining their protest action as detrimental to the interests of the majority employed. The Eisenhower election marked a dramatic shift in public opinion toward the large corporations' position, a shift that had begun with the passing of Taft-Hartley. Aggravated auto workers could not turn to the public or the state for support in their struggles.

The UAW International was especially hostile to militant shop-floor demands from workers in the firms hardest hit by the intensifying competition. The International accepted managements' utilitarian rationalization for their speedups. In its view, working with tighter production standards in line with the most efficient producers in the industry was preferable to no jobs at all. The International was also sympathetic to the plight of the smaller firms squeezed by the GM-Ford expansionist policies, taking a hard line against unauthorized strike activity and placing the most militant of its locals under administratorships. The UAW International was reluctant to authorize the strike requests it received from its locals in the disadvantaged firms, although it began doing so in the late 1950s in response to intense pressure. Thus, the auto workers most affected by the 1950s speedups could not turn to the UAW International for support in their struggles. As will be shown, they were forced to fight the International as well as management in pursuing militant courses of action.

But fight they did. Even in such an environment, auto workers confronted management with shop-floor protests, waging some of the most intense and persistent plant-level struggles in the industry's history. What enabled them to do so, I contend, was their experiences in both the solidarity-generating labor processes defined in chapter 3, and the quota-based authority systems under which managements legitimated the notion of earned time as the right of those workers competent to earn it.

The first of these enabling conditions—experiences in solidarity-generating labor processes—gave workers the organizational capacities necessary for initiating collective courses of action independently of management and the UAW International. The production workers primarily responsible for initiating the militant shop-floor activity in both the 1930s and the 1950s hailed from these types of processes. Their collective experiences were perhaps a necessary condition enabling them to act collectively through noninstitutionalized means.

What differentiates the 1950s militancy from that of the 1930s was the definitional foundations precipitating the protest action. While managements during the 1930s breached their implicit promise to provide for workers' financial security in the leading firms, the ideological foundation for militant courses of action was not anchored securely in workers' everyday shop-floor experiences. Workers' experiences prior to the Great Depression were in managerially dominated drive systems—that is, systems that did not offer workers much space on the job for carving out independent collective identities.

In the absence of such an experientially rooted ideological foundation, the material and moral support which workers received from powerful actors in the external political environment was probably necessary for precipitating militancy. After all, it was only after the passage of Section 7a of the NIRA that local revolts began to occur with frequency, and only after the passage of the Wagner Act and the formation of the UAW that auto workers became emboldened enough to mount serious threats against firm-level managements. Prior to this legislation, auto workers, for the most part, acquiesced to rather severe speedups during 1929–1932. It was only after contract ratification, and after workers' experiences in mounting recognition strikes, that workers began to pursue courses of militant action on the shop floor independent of the UAW's leadership and direction. While these independent actions caused many headaches for both auto firms and the UAW, their occurrence took a rather undisciplined form.

By the 1950s, auto workers in solidarity-generating labor processes had had some experiences with quota-based authority systems. These systems accepted, and, therefore legitimated, earned time as workers' rights. They allowed workers to pursue work ends on the shop floor outside of managements' sphere of domination and interest. They defined a fair day's work as a given production output, leaving room for workers to carve out a free space for themselves on the job, channeling their collective activities toward this pursuit. Long tenure in such systems reinforced workers' belief in the rightness of such pursuits. It provided them with an ideological foundation for defining managements' shop floor assaults as illegitimate, for critiquing these assaults as counterproductive, and for redressing the sanctity of the shop-floor traditions violated. Next, we examine both the ideology legitimating noninstitutionalized militancy and workers' initial responses to these managerial assaults.

The Ideological Foundation

The terms *guess-o-matics* and *pencil-pushing fiends* express the ideological foundation of workers' shop-floor protests during the 1950s. *Guess-o-matics* is a term which Arthur Hughes, a UAW-Chrysler official, used to label Chrysler management's approach to work redesign and production standard revision. *Pencil-pushing fiends* is a term used by Walter Rosser, an official from UAW-Ford Local 600, to ridicule the industrial engineers responsible for automating the Rouge's frame plant. Of course, both terms are pejorative.

In auto workers' definitional frame, guess-o-matics is a pseudoscience of production without a rational basis. For guess-o-matics is detached from actual production experiences and the knowledge emanating from them. Driven by guess-o-matics, managements redesign production processes and establish production standards in ignorance of what it actually takes to produce value on the shop floor. Guess-o-maticians take for granted the translation of designs derived from the realm of pure theory into actual shop practice. They refuse to acknowledge the different situational contingencies affecting production outcomes and the problematic nature inherent in transforming raw materials into saleable commodities.

From the point of view of the workers experiencing quota-based authority systems, the "running-for-time" shop cultures legitimated in these systems, and the efficient, orderly production outcomes they produced day in and day out, the new management teams were nothing more than guess-o-maticians. They were demanding production standards comparable to those set on GM and Ford operations, basing their demands on studies of data found in their competitors' books. Yet, these managements appeared totally ignorant of how the faster rates were actually accomplished in the more efficient plants. These "pencil-pushing fiends" were ignorant of the real differences in plant layouts, numbers of changeovers, production flows, and the like that made comparable operations in, say, a GM and a Studebaker plant unacceptable.[23]

This charge of noncomparability was rooted in more than simply workers' rationalizations of the looser production rates. As Moritz and Seaman point out,[24] both GM and Ford used more dedicated or captive component assembly lines than did Chrysler and the smaller producers. The formers' lines were set up to manufacture or assemble production runs of single parts, while the smaller firms often produced multiple parts per line. This not only caused production losses due to changeovers, but it made it more difficult for workers to attain maximum production rates as well.

The arbitrary, irrational feature of Chrysler's demands was illustrated vividly to workers at Dodge Main in 1958. According to a press release from the UAW-Chrysler Department, management kept demanding increased production on a job that did not even exist in the plant. The company's production engineers, while apparently copying GM's records, had set rates on a nonexisting job.[25] This incident demonstrated clearly, to workers and union officials, that Chrysler management's newly revamped standards were not grounded in production knowledge. Those responsible did not know what was actually going on on the shop floor which they were trying to command. They were guess-o-maticians, nothing more. From the workers' point of view, their demands were unfair and illegitimate. Workers were justified in rebelling against them regardless of who supported them outside the shop. They reacted accordingly.

The First "Armies of Redressers"

Auto workers' protests were initially localized affairs, beginning in the plants hardest hit by market dynamics—namely, Hudson and DeSoto. Initial struggles were waged autonomously in heated opposition to both managements' and the UAW-International's call for restraint. Later, protests appear to have spread, becoming corporate and even industrywide.

Workers actually waged serious local rebellions against managements' assaults on their production practices and standards before the 1953–1958 periodization. These rebellions began in the late 1940s in the divisions competing in the unstable upper-middle market segment.

The Hudson labor strife began in the trim department in the late 1940s, and those conflicts appear to have revolved around the legitimacy of "running-for-time" practices. In 1948, for example, operators in the seat-building and sewing-and-pasting departments wildcatted over disciplinary action which management took against workers leaving their jobs during working hours, a common practice when earned time is accepted.

In 1949, trim operators took protest action against management once again. This time they waged a slowdown, and their actions won sympathetic support from maintenance crews who shut down the plant in March, and from truckers who shut down eight thousand workers.[26] This dispute culminated in a request for official authorization on 3 August. The UAW International denied the request, however, after receiving correspondence from management claiming that local UAW officials were encouraging illegal wildcats. Management also claimed that the local was demanding that its officers be permitted to dole out work assignments in the plant.[27]

Entering the Korean War years, Hudson management clamped down hard on its militant local in an attempt to establish the labor discipline and production standards which it felt it needed to compete with GM. Market conditions favored management's hand. Reduced sales, coupled with a market protected by government quota allocations of steel, gave management considerable leverage. It could take strikes without losing ground to its competition. Striking workers, however, were not protected. They paid for their militancy with lost wages and jobs.

Nonetheless, the Hudson workers responded with fierce resistance. This resistance was greatest in the trim department, where management eliminated ninty-four workers on eleven operations and increased production standards. Workers responded with wildcats, slowdowns, and blatant refusals to meet the new standards. As a result, auto bodies moved down the conveyor unfinished. In June 1951, management began shutting down the plant in response to the slowdown, and sending workers home for refusing to meet the new standards. However, the trim workers held fast to their position, refusing to honor the new rates, even in the face of lost wages. For thirty-four consecutive days management shut down the plant. In 1951, *Business Week* described this labor skirmish as the first serious test of union resolve to fight for production standards established in the early postwar sellers' market.[28]

The Memorandum on Production Standards resolving the dispute was rather ambiguous. It contained contractual language supporting elements of both the quota-based and managerial-prerogative definition of a fair day's work. The Memorandum stated that

> It is recognized as fundamental to good management-labor relations that the working conditions of employees should be disturbed as little as possible and that employees should be notified in advance of changes affecting them together with the reason for change. It is likewise fundamental that it is management's right to establish the time standards. It is likewise management's function to plan for efficient operations and to improve capacities by better methods and to make technological improvements.[29]

The memorandum's first sentence binds management, in principle, to undisturbed working conditions. Such a commitment would support the type of routinization compatible with "running-for-time" practices. The second and third sentences reaffirm management's prerogative to set production standards as it sees fit, and to adjust them when changing methods or technology. While these provisions probably gave management more leverage over production standards than it had previously, the authority system it legitimated was still quite far from the drive system defined in chapter 5.

How did this agreement actually work itself out on the shop floor? Paragraph 9 of the 1951 agreement set formal procedures for establishing production standards. At the start of a new model run, the Hudson Time Study department set estimated standards on all jobs. It was given the right to revise these standards on the basis of time-study conclusions. These standards would become finalized and locked in after six months. Management could change them later only when it changed methods or technologies. Disputed standards were to be resolved through joint union-management time studies. On a three-year model run, this agreement locked in the quota-based system for thirty months, leaving the six-month period at the beginning of the model run as the period for rate struggles and inevitable conflict.[30]

While management won ratification of this agreement at the union hall, it quickly ran into opposition on the shop floor. The shop-steward body apparently refused to cede to management its right to set production standards on operations. On 11 June 1952, Hudson's labor relations manager sent a letter to the local UAW president, claiming that stewards were obstructing time-study operations.[31] On 27 January 1953, Hudson management telegraphed Walter Reuther, pleading with him to halt a wildcat led by the shop stewards over the time-study dispute.[32] The Hudson rank-and-file wildcatted again on 23 July, and again on 15 October, in protest of disciplinary sanctions against their stewards.

Labor relations at Hudson were, thus, stalemated with neither management nor workers buckling to the demands of the other over the content of a fair day's work or the procedures for determining it. Management fought hard to establish the type of production standards it defined as vital to its survival. Workers fought back tenaciously in defense of standards which they had come to accept as right and just. This stalemate ended only with the closing of the Hudson plant shortly after the Nash-Hudson merger.

The labor strife at Chrysler DeSoto parallels that occurring at Hudson. The DeSoto division was affected by the GM Buick and Olds expansions in the early postwar period. Like Hudson, the DeSoto management responded by revamping production methods and tightening standards in line with its more efficient competitors. These changes were accompanied by Chrysler's expansion of its Warren Avenue plant. DeSoto transferred its welding, trim, and paint departments to the new plant, which also housed the latest body-building technology.[33] With the protection provided by state-regulated steel allocations during the Korean War, management was ready to play its hand.

The rank-and-file of UAW Local 227 responded militantly to the new production standards at the Warren plant. DeSoto trimmers were the first to wildcat over production standards, shutting down both the DeSoto and the Chrysler Kercheval and Jefferson Avenue plants.[34] A series of wildcats occurred in June 1951. Eighteen arc welders walked on the 6 June to back up their demands for two more workers on the job. Twenty-six metal finishers on the coupe body line refused to work on 13 June, apparently in protest of management's disciplinary actions against earlier wildcatters. Thirty-nine arc welders walked again on 22 June. These strikes shut down both the DeSoto Warren and Wyoming plants.[35] The labor conflict continued into July. Management shut down the plant on 10 July in response to an alleged slowdown by the body builders.[36] The rank and file walked on 20 July in protest of disciplinary actions doled out to thirty-two body builders for leaving the plant six minutes before quitting time.[37]

DeSoto management was forced to call on the UAW International for assistance. On 24 July, the International took over the administration of the local, cracking down on its militant rank and file and their stewards, denying them the privileges spelled out in their union constitution. While DeSoto survived into the 1960s, the fate of the Warren plant workers mirrored that of the Hudson workers. Chrysler shut down body-building operations there in late 1958, transferring them to the Kercheval and Jefferson plants and to various stamping plants.[38]

Workers at Chrysler's Dodge Main and Plymouth Body reacted to managements' assaults with a tenacity rivaling the earlier militants at Hudson and DeSoto. Trim workers at Dodge Main wildcatted for five days in July 1954, protesting the new production rates set on trim subassemblies. This strike shut down 80 percent of the units operating at Dodge Main, and won sympathy-support from the Chrysler truckers.[39]

In mid-March 1956, fourteen trimmers wildcatted, refusing to work in protest of the suspension of five workers for "failure to make any effort to meet fair work standards." Twelve hundred trim department workers walked out in January 1957 to protest the suspension of two employees for failing to meet standards.[40] On 28 February, the metal polishers walked out, protesting new work standards which removed two relief workers from the group. Chrysler management and the UAW-Chrysler Department attempted to cool down the conflict with a negotiated Memorandum of Understanding spelling out production standards procedures.[41]

The speedup at Dodge Main intensified during the 1958 recession.[42] Chrysler stockpiled a tremendous inventory prior to the slump, and used it against its rank and file. Determined to break the back of its militant trim department, Dodge management sent workers home early every day from 27 January until 2 March for failing to make production standards. Dodge Main workers averaged only eleven to twenty hours of work per week during the two months of conflict, and they were ineligible for unemployment, supplemental employment, or welfare. Yet, the trimmers refused to buckle under.[43]

The dispute was resolved on 4 March with an agreement requiring management to lay off those not needed to meet the reduced production schedules and to run a forty-hour weekly production schedule for those remaining. Management also agreed to time-study disputed production rates.[44]

Chrysler had a sixty-eight-day inventory when it began to negotiate for a new UAW contract on 1 May 1958 and refused any concessions. The UAW International allowed its contracts with the Big Three to expire in June, waiting for market improvements before entering into serious negotiations. Not legally bound by contract restrictions during this period, Chrysler took ruthless action against the Dodge Main union stewards.[45] Wildcats and labor disputes reached crisis proportions throughout the summer.

The situation was much the same at Plymouth Body. In May 1955, the trimmers wildcatted, protesting the firing of twelve operators for failing to make standards. Four of the fifteen affected were fired initially. Then, fourteen hundred trim department workers struck, shutting down ten thousand jobs in the complex. Management responded by reinstating the twelve who were fired.[46] In June 1955, sixty metal finishers walked out, protesting changes introduced after the trimmers' wildcat.[47]

The labor strife continued into 1956. In February, 1,030 workers wildcatted over the discharge of a committeeman accused of using abusive language.[48] In June, trim workers shut down the plant for six days over a speedup and disciplinary action against the steward leading it. This strike shut down sixteen thousand.[49]

Labor tension did not ease in 1957, as Chrysler began to outsource work done at Plymouth Body, and as workers' responses became more organized. Workers wildcatted for three consecutive days in May, shutting down 50,500. This wildcat was waged by both skilled and unskilled workers, and involved the tool-and-die craft workers at Vernor South, stamping-press workers at the Outer Drive plant, and truck drivers in the transportation unit. On 8 May, UAW Local 212 took a strike vote that was approved by a 96.5 percent of the membership.[50]

To end the 1957 strife, Chrysler agreed to honor existing production standards for the duration of the model run, unless it changed tools, methods, or procedures. It reduced fourteen firings to disciplinary layoffs, withdrew eighty-one disciplinary reports, and set up machinery for handling group grievances involving more than one plant management. A factor in Chrysler's concessions was its decision to phase out body-building operations at Plymouth Body.[51]

However, the Chrysler agreement did not tame the labor strife. On 2 February 1958, four hundred trimmers refused to work in protest of new production standards, charging that management changed the standards without increasing manpower or introducing new technology.[52] In mid-February, the company began sending home the trim workers early for allegedly instigating a slowdown. This shut down 9,700 workers in the Plymouth complex.[53]

Chrysler hit UAW Local 212 hardest of all its locals during the summer of 1958, when they worked without contract protection. Management refused to recognize the local's chief steward. It created new districts, reduced the ratio of stewards to workers, and restricted time allowances for investigating grievances.[54] Workers reacted immediately. One hundred walked in the trim department in early June after their steward was dismissed.[55] In late June, the trimmers wildcatted for three consecutive days after management gave workers a three-day suspension for poor work. Two of the disciplined shoved their supervisor, and management retaliated by firing them. After the trimmers returned, they resorted to sabotage, ruining more than sixty bodies in a two-week period.[56] In late July, workers wildcatted again.[57] After two full months of intense conflict, the UAW filed suit against Chrysler.[58]

Tragically, the Dodge Main and Plymouth Body militants suffered fates similar to those at Hudson and DeSoto. Plymouth body-building operations were cancelled in late 1958. Component trim and welding operations were outsourced. Operations performed on the moving line were transferred to Plymouth Final Assembly, and technological developments there—which we will examine in chapter 9—structurally atomized them. Similarly, the Dodge Main complex was decentralized in 1959, and the main building became a double-line, final-assembly operation. As at Plymouth, component trim and body-assembly operations were outsourced, and new technologies atomized those remaining there.

Finally, Studebaker workers responded to management assaults with parallel intensity. They responded to the shift to day-rate incentives with a two-day wildcat in mid-January 1955.[59] They won a memorandum clarifying procedures for establishing production standards. The memorandum granted stewards the right to observe management's time studies and to receive information obtained from them. Yet, it denied them their customary right to challenge or question the time-study conclusions until after the standard was put into effect.[60]

However, the procedural clarifications specified in the February memorandum did little to ease the tension at Studebaker. In early July, UAW Local 5 sent a letter to its regional director charging that the company was refusing to provide the union with time-study information used to reestablish production standards. The local took a strike vote on 12 July. Two days later, before official authorization from the UAW International, fifty-five men walked off the line, protesting new bumping procedures that violated time-honored seniority rights. UAW Local 5 supported the strike and stayed out for more than two weeks. To get workers back on the job, management agreed to grant the fifty-five strike leaders their seniority rights. However, management refused to cede concessions regarding production standards, and they communicated to reporters that it wanted much faster rates on the 1956 model changeover.[61]

When the Studebaker collective bargaining agreement expired in September 1955, UAW Local 5 struck for thirty-six days over production standards. This was the first official strike since Studebaker's wagon-making days. The strike ended only when the UAW International ordered workers back amidst chants and boos from strikers.[62]

The collective bargaining contract that was forced upon the rank and file granted management key concessions. It contained the first Studebaker management-prerogative clause, reduced relief time from forty-three to twenty-four minutes per shift, and cut the ratio of stewards to employees from 1:50 to 1:75. Management also won a transfer clause which restricted plant-wide seniority.[63] However, management's contractual victory in the fall of 1955 was not easy to transfer into shop-floor gains, and workers continued to resist production standard assaults throughout the 1950s.

Thus, while the new Studebaker management instituted day-rates, and demanded increased production from its workers, it never fully succeeded in establishing the type of drive system for which it hoped. Workers resisted the speedup until Studebaker management decided to withdraw completely from the U.S. auto market in the early 1960s.

The Theoretical Significance

The local rebellions at Hudson, DeSoto, Dodge Main, Plymouth Body, and Studebaker share a number of characteristics. First, the occupational groups leading them hailed from the solidarity-generating labor processes identified in chapter 3—the trimmers at Hudson, Dodge Main, and Plymouth Body, the body builders at DeSoto, Hudson, and Plymouth Body, and the paint sprayers working the forty-minute-on/twenty-minute-off schedule at Studebaker. While managements' speedups affected virtually all production workers in these plants, it was usually body-department workers who led the protest action.

Second, these workers worked in authority systems in which managements had legitimated a quota-based definition of a fair day's work prior to the speedups. They were accustomed to earning time on the job, and perceived earned time as an accepted part of their work routines, day in and day out. This pursuit motivated their efforts on the shop floor. The combination of these two factors gave these workers capacities and incentives for mounting non-institutionalized collective protests against managements' assaults on their production standards without support from external authority.

Third, each of these rebellions displayed a nonrational character which is difficult to comprehend when using instrumental or utilitarian cost-benefit criteria. These rebellions occurred during sales slumps when managements could afford to take production losses, or when managements were outsourcing work to other plants. The strategic implication of this inopportune timing did not seem to affect these workers' actions, however. They struck in direct response to the speedups, regardless of the odds against them. They refused to buckle to market pressure, even with tremendous personal sacrifice. I think it best, therefore, to interpret these rebellions as motivated by workers' reactions to perceived norm violations. Workers were acting to redress serious wrongs, regardless of the types of outcomes they could calculate to produce in advance of their actions.

Fourth, neither of the conflicting parties in these plant-level disputes realized their objectives. In each plant, management failed to successfully impose the drive authority system on the shop floor, and management failed to force its solidary workers to honor its managerial prerogative to adjust production standards at will to market pressures. In each case, workers fought management to a bitter stalemate. These prolonged labor conflicts came to an end only when managements shut down the affected plants or departments. Neither party budged from its position. However, neither party prevailed in the struggle.

Finally, the type of production processes spawning these rebellions did not survive into the 1960s. A characteristic differentiating the old-timer trimmers and body builders in the historic Hudson, DeSoto, Dodge Main, Plymouth Body, and Studebaker plants from the type of occupational groups replacing them was the skill content involved in their work. Each of the militant wildcatting groups were semiskilled production workers, controlling their operations with experienced hands.

Management deskilled many aspects of these operations in the new or remodeled plants of the late 1950s and early 1960s. Automated technologies (which we examine in chapter 9) were either replacing operators' control of the actual welding or fabric-forming processes, or were atomizing the group work typically conducted in stationary fixtures. As the militants in the old plants were waging their battles with managements over production standards, auto firms were rapidly investing in plants and technologies designed to make their skills and job control obsolete.

The significance of these rebellions lies then, not in their immediate effects, but in their consequences for the industry and the subsequent developments they helped set in motion. First, these workers' rebellions prevented firms and divisions—such as Hudson, DeSoto, Studebaker and Packard—from making the types of labor process changes which they defined as critical to their survival in the increasingly competitive market. The failures of these firms and divisions to survive affected the type of market structure that was to consequently emerge. Second, these workers' rebellions influenced workers in the newer body-parts plants who were to replace them. These workers, while nonskilled, followed the early protesters with rebellions of their own.

The New "Armies of Redressers"

The types of struggles waged in the older Chrysler and independent plants spread throughout the industry in the late 1950s. These later struggles were to affect substantially the development of the shop-floor authority systems governing production activities in the 1960s and early 1970s. These struggles not only threatened managements' abilities to impose their designs on the shop floor, but they began to threaten the UAW International's authority as well.

Table 7.7 shows the number of aggregated annual wildcat and authorized strikes reported in *Wall Street Journal* and *New York Times* during 1946-1958. Three findings are noteworthy.

First, the numbers of wildcats occurring in both the 1946-1952 and 1953-1958 periods were similar. The average number of wildcats occurring annually during the 1946-1952 period was thirty-three, while the average for the latter period was thirty-one. The average number of local-issue strikes, or authorized strike votes, doubled in the latter period, from six to twelve. Second, the sequencing of wildcat occurrences changed considerably in the latter period. With the institution of longer term agreements, wildcat activity tended to peak during contract years. Finally, the frequency of wildcat activity increased substantially in the latter period after the declines in 1952-1954.

While illustrative, the wildcat data reported mask the significance of strike changes in the later 1950s. The wildcats waged in the latter period tended to be more intense and to center on production standard issues affecting production costs, sales prices, and profits.

The number of multiple-day wildcats reported in *Wall Street Journal* and *New York Times* for the two periods (1946–1952; 1953–1958) suggest an increase in intensity. Thirty-eight percent of the reported wildcats in the latter period lasted two or more days, while only 21 percent in the earlier period did so. Sixteen percent in the latter period lasted more than five days, while only eight percent in the earlier period did so. Seven percent in the latter period lasted more than eight days, compared to only three percent in the former period.

Finally, information concerning the issues provoking wildcats in the two periods provides additional support for the argument that the intensity of militant activity increased in the latter period. First, wildcats over either production standard or contract-related issues made up 44 percent of the total wildcats waged during 1953–1958. They made up only 26 percent of the total waged during the earlier period. This suggests that, in the latter period, issues concerning produc-

Table 7.7
Strike Activity in the Automobile Industry, 1946–1958

1946 to 1952			*1953 to 1958*		
Year	Wildcat	Authorized	Year	Wildcat	Authorized
1946	25	10	1953	14	6
1947	39	5	1954	7	3
1948	31	9	1955	60	15
1949	57	5	1956	14	9
1950	34	5	1957	12	16
1951	31	4	1958	80	23
1952	12	5			
Total	229	43	Total	187	72

Sources: Wall Street Journal and *New York Times*, various years.

tion outcomes and the methods to regulate them were more likely to spur militant worker activity than during the former period. This is not surprising, considering the types of workplace changes which managements were instituting during the period.

Second, strikes over status issues provoked 15 percent of the wildcats waged during the latter period, with only 7 percent of those waged in the earlier period. This reflects the awakening of craft-worker militancy in the latter period, as craft workers' wages began to slip in comparison to comparable trades represented by AFL unions, and to the production workers working alongside them.

Thus, the evidence suggests that shop-floor militancy intensified throughout the auto industry during the 1953-1958 period. The number of wildcat strikes increased significantly from their low levels in the early 1950s. These wildcats were more intense, and were waged over issues much more likely to have consequences for firms' labor costs and profit margins. These shifts were especially dramatic at GM, and less dramatic but significant at Studebaker-Packard and Budd. These firms experienced relatively low levels of wildcat activity in the 1946–1952 period and had taken steps toward legitimating quota-based shop-floor authority systems. While the numbers of wildcats occurring at Ford and Chrysler during the latter period paralleled those occurring there in the earlier period, they increased considerably after 1954 and in direct response to fierce market competition.

While we have no evidence to suggest that GM and Ford managements initiated corporatewide assaults upon production standards comparable in scope to those initiated by Chrysler and Studebaker-Packard managements, archival evidence does suggest that the GM and Ford managements responded to the intensifying competition of the late 1950s with their own brand of speedup. Elmer Yenney, a local UAW official from the Janesville, Wisconsin, Chevrolet assembly plant, claims, for example, that his local began having production standard conflicts in the spring of 1953. Yet Yenney suggests that GM management was selective in speeding up operations in his plant.[64]

Where the new managements at Chrysler and Studebaker brutally and openly assaulted production standards with corporatewide campaigns, GM managements may have tightened standards in more strategically calculated ways—snipping away at loose rates discretely to avoid direct plant-wide or firm-wide confrontations. This may explain why the GM workers tended to wait until contract periods to mount their protests. The corporate-wide character of the contract protests, however, does suggest that this cold, calculated snipping was something more than a local, isolated problem. Production standard relief was frequently a key issue in GM plants' local contract negotiations.

Ford managements' assaults on production standards during the 1953–1958 period also appear to have been more strategic than that of either Chrysler or Studebaker managements. Ford workers appear to have had most trouble with speedups in older assembly plants—such as the Missouri and New Jersey plants—in the newly automated parts plants with established locals—such as the militant UAW Local 723 at Monroe, Michigan—or during major model changeovers.

The wildcat strike waves occurring during the 1955 and 1958 contract negotiations caused considerable alarm for both the UAW International and auto managements. Both the GM and Ford workers took direct protest action against their working conditions during these years. They demonstrated a willingness to act independently of the UAW International and initiated coordinated work stoppages both before and after national contract settlements.

While media coverage of these strike waves tended to focus on national negotiations rather than local initiatives, I have collected information on all plant-level work stoppages reported during these negotiation periods. Several important characteristics of these strikes are worth noting.

First, many of the wildcats were waged by skilled craft workers, particularly the tool-and-die workers throughout the industry. The wages of the UAW skilled-trade groups compared to those represented by the AFL craft unions fell considerably in the postwar period, and skilled-trades workers pushed hard for relief during the 1950s contract negotiations.

However, skilled trades groups were not the exclusive instigators of the protest activity during these negotiations, and skilled trades issues were not the only ones that the rank and file attempted to resolve through direct action—not by any means. Contractual relief from speedups was also a major issue here. As we have seen, production standard disputes sparked numerous conflicts in the older Chrysler plants during contract negotiations, particularly in the trim and body building departments. Production standard disputes were also major factors sparking wildcats at several of the newer or newly renovated stamping plants in the industry, such as the stamping plants at Ford Monroe in Michigan, at GM West Mifflin in Pennsylvania, and at Chrysler Nine-Mile Detroit and Twinsburg, Ohio.

A second characteristic of these rebellions concerns the occupational status of the production workers initiating them. Workers in stamping and body-parts plants tended to initiate more of these work stoppages than did workers in final assembly. Based on available information reported in the *New York Times* and *Wall Street Journal*, we find that forty-five occurred in stamping, body-parts, and body-assembly plants; while twenty occurred in final-assembly plants. The final-assembly plants in which wildcats occurred tended to be the older plants—such as the Ford St. Louis and Chicago plants, or the GM St. Louis, Kansas City, and Tarrytown, New York, plants. These older plants were more likely to house solidary generating, body-building operations than were the newer plants using more modern automated production technologies. This evidence could suggest that workers in solidarity-generating labor processes were initiating the wildcats waged by production workers. This is consistent with the theoretical predictions developed in chapter 3 and justifies our focus upon the fates of these groups.

A third characteristic worth noting here is that these plant-level wildcats often occurred in conjuncture with other plant-level wildcats. Seven wildcats, for example, occurred in Ford plants on 6 June 1955, one day before Ford and the UAW International reached agreement on a new contract.[65] Fifteen two-day wildcats occurred in GM plants on 9 June 1955. Ten more occurred on 13 June 1955.[66] On 1 July 1958, a wave of sabotage also occurred in GM stamping, hardware, and body-assembly plants. Twenty-four car bodies were damaged at the Flint Fisher Body #2 plant; 106 were damaged at GM's Euclid, Ohio, hardware and trim plant, 9 were damaged at GM's Baltimore plant, and 73 were damaged at GM Kansas City.[67]

The timing of these protest actions itself suggests some sort of strategic coordination and communication between the local militants initiating the protests. What agency was responsible for this coordination? This is an important question, for the auto firms often blamed the UAW International for sponsoring such actions. Yet, Solidarity House responded to these accusations both with denials and with orders to the wildcatting locals to return to work.

Some of the most spectacular local strike waves occurred after the International had reached an agreement on the national contract with the affected firm. Workers then struck for relief on issues neglected in the contract—typically, production standards. Stanley Weir claims that these rebellions were initiated at the local level and were coordinated by the rank-and-file delegates serving on the General Council during the negotiations.[68] The concerted character of many of these local strikes made them dangerous—not only to managements, but to the UAW International. They threatened the union's legitimacy.

To what extent did these coordinated actions represent a united front made up of both skilled and production workers? This is an important question that is difficult to answer. In most cases, I suspect that these wildcats were led by one group or the other, because the issues tending to spark the protests of the two groups—such as wages and status privileges for the skilled; production-standard relief for production workers—were occupationally specific. These issues were not likely to unite the sentiments and resolve of the other group. The exception to this were the cases in which locals were responding to management actions, such as outsourcing, which affected all workers. In this instance, we find both skilled and production workers locking arms against management.

Summary

The conjuncture associated with an increase in militant activity crystallized in the late 1950s. This conjuncture included: (1) increasingly competitive and unstable market conditions triggered by the breakdown of firm-level commitments to Sloanist-marketing strategies; (2) the institution of centralized managerial structures granting corporate-level managements, far removed from the shop floor, authority in determining shop practices and standards; and (3) open managerial assaults on existing shop practices and production standards legitimated through the managerial-prerogative definition of a fair day's work. In turn, this conjuncture triggered (4) prolonged rebellions by the solidary workers whose work expectations were forged in quota-based authority systems in the early postwar period.

This conjuncture occurred in the Hudson, Studebaker, DeSoto, Dodge Main, and Plymouth Body plants. It produced some of the most intense, prolonged shop-floor conflicts in the industry's history. These rebellions began to spread throughout the industry by the late 1950s as competition intensified.

The fact that these rebellions were being waged—not only in the older body-building plants, but in the newer stamping plants employing automated equipment as well—assured managements and the UAW of a stormy future if they failed to take action addressing the demands of those leading them. However, their abilities to do so were limited by unbridled market forces.

CHAPTER 8

Repairing the Seams of the Hegemonic Order: State-Inspired, Sloanist-Regulated Market Relations, 1959–1973

The industry did not hold to the destructive course it blazed during 1953-1958. By 1960, auto firms had, once again, committed themselves to Sloanist market strategies. These commitments led to an avoidance of destructive market-share competition, and the market environment that was created enabled firms to respond to the 1950s crises in innovative ways. In this chapter, firm-level marketing strategies at the company level and their structuring effects are examined.

Corporate-Level Marketing Shifts

Ford's shift to Sloanist marketing strategies is quite understandable. With all of its effort, Ford could not make ground on GM's market dominance during the 1950s. Ford's attempt to penetrate the middle-priced market failed, its profit margins declined, and its expansionist policies proved to be quite costly. By 1960, Henry Ford II had soured on his fantasy of regaining industry dominance. Ford's marketing policies from 1960-1973 reflected this. For the most part, these policy shifts were market driven.

Summarizing Ford's 1960s marketing policy, Schnapp states

> Ford's approach here was to chip away at GM's market dominance rather than competing with it head on. To do this, Ford subsegmented the auto market to exploit niches not being filled by GM, and created a product mix rich in specialty products (with potentially greater profit margins) at the high end of its product line.[1]

Ford backed away from head-on competition with GM and became the industry's product innovator, pursuing untapped markets with new product concepts. Ford was the first to introduce the subcompact car, the Falcon; the "sports car for the masses," the Mustang; the luxury sports car, the Mercury Cougar; and the luxury compacts, the Ford Granada and Mercury Monarch. Ford also continually upgraded its new models in order to broaden their appeal. These strategies promised higher rates of return than did expansionist strategies.[2]

In contrast, GM's Sloanist marketing shifts were not, for the most part, market driven. After all, GM asserted unquestioned dominance in the industry. GM also needed considerable sales volume in order to employ the fixed capital it invested in plant and machinery during the 1950s expansion. Following Fligstein's general argument,[3] I argue that GM's marketing changes were political responses to antitrust threats. After the Supreme Court forced DuPont's divestiture of GM stock in 1957, GM's political fate was uncertain. In 1958 a New York grand jury demanded a sweeping investigation of GM for antitrust violations.[4] In 1961, the Justice Department began studying the possibility of breaking the Chevrolet Division away from GM and established a special unit to oversee GM cases.[5] These aggressive investigations continued throughout the period.

This threat created a peculiar business environment for the industry's hegemon. Successful market penetration could potentially threaten GM's future. As Robert Sheehan, a noted industry journalist, states

> Admiration of those awesome figures is accompanied by recurrent rumblings in Washington and elsewhere that General Motors is "too big." The Justice Department, for one, keeps a team of eight antitrust attorneys busy pondering and probing GM. . . . The atmosphere becomes tense whenever GM's penetration of the domestic market exceeds the 50 percent mark.[6]

The rational response to this antitrust predicament was simply to embrace Sloanist marketing and investment strategies, restrict market-share penetration, target those segments that promised the most investment return, and leave substantial market space for competitors. For the most part, these were the strategies that GM adopted. After 1963, GM kept its market-share penetration below 50 percent, and refrained from entering new markets until they proved large enough to support multiple suppliers. GM concentrated its sales in the segments promising higher profit margins.

By 1958, Chrysler's future was uncertain. Chrysler's 1950s marketing strategies failed. Chrysler failed both to exploit untapped market niches with innovative styling in the early 1950s and to follow its competitors' styling trends in the late 1950s. As a result, Chrysler began the 1960s with severe financial, labor, and engineering problems.

As grave as these were, Chrysler survived. I attribute Chrysler's survival to the Sloanist strategies adopted by its competitors. These strategies created survival spaces in the lower-margin segments for Chrysler to service. In order to survive and prosper modestly, Chrysler moved to these spaces, resigning itself to the lower-priced, lower-margin segments—segments which were relatively safe from competition from the more efficient GM and Ford organizations.[7] Unable to pick and choose markets, Chrysler took whatever returns it could earn on whatever was leftover.

The dynamic compact segment was the major market untouched by Sloanist regulation. No one could claim leadership or dominance here. This segment was very unstable, and this affected the fate of the surviving independents. For a short time in the late 1950s, the AMC Rambler was this segment's sole domestic occupant. AMC bucked the industry trend toward bigger and more expensive models with its Rambler, withdrawing altogether from the segments experiencing severe competition and instability. AMC reaped the lucrative rewards accruing to this position, reversing its early 1950s business decline in stunning fashion.[8]

Some have argued that the invasion of AMC's market niche by the Big Three producers during the 1960s was politically motivated. George Romney, AMC's president, testified before the Kefauver Senate subcommittee investigating the industry's pricing practices in 1958. Against the advice of industry leaders, Romney claimed that the industry practiced monopolistic pricing and boldly advocated antitrust action that would break up GM. Industry leaders responded to Romney's testimony with outrage and, as a consequence, Romney reportedly lost favor in Detroit's business circles.[9]

After that incident, both GM and Ford invaded the compact field and continued to expand their penetration there. GM, for example, followed its 1960 Chevrolet Corvair into this segment in 1961 with compact Pontiac, Oldsmobile, and Buick models and, in 1962, with an upgraded Chevrolet model, the Chevy II.

This invasion adversely affected the fates of the remaining independent firms. The first casualty was Studebaker. After abandoning its full-line strategy in 1959—and earning modest success with its compact Lark—Studebaker's fortune declined. Studebaker's auto division operated at a loss every year after 1959, and the company halted domestic operations in late 1963.

AMC responded to the market invasion with multiple product-line strategies. While it still concentrated models in the lower reaches of the established segments, AMC began upgrading its products and introducing bigger and more expensive models. This strategy was designed to protect AMC from head-on competition with GM and Ford in the compact market. Rather than take this risk, AMC chose to pursue the Chrysler strategy, repositioning its product lines in safer segments.

Thus, for various reasons, each of the surviving producers turned to Sloanist marketing strategies during the 1960s. GM reasserted itself as the industry's hegemon and committed itself, for the most part, to Sloanist market-sharing strategies. GM's competitors respected its hold on the more lucrative markets, targeting for themselves those segments that GM had neglected.

GM's commitment to such policies, more than anything else, was a strategic response to the threat of antitrust action, while GM's competitors' commitments to these policies were more market driven. These policy shifts promised to ease the tension and crises which the industry experienced during the late 1950s by bridling the competitive dynamics that produced them. How successful were these strategies in doing so? We address this question with a review of market data.

Market Data, 1959–1973

A review of market-share data at firm and division levels allows us to gauge the extent to which market behavior during 1959-1973 conformed to expectations. The data show relative stability at the firm level. At the division level, however, the data show instability in approximately one-third of the market. This instability has important implications for a hegemony theory linking the stabilization of shop-floor relations to the stabilization of market dynamics.

Market Stabilization at the Firm Level

Table 8.1 reports firm-level market data from 1959-1973. Three findings are worth noting. First, the market was relatively stable throughout the period. Second, market invaders during the period were not the domestic firms, but foreign importers. The only domestic to gain over the period spanning 1960 to 1973 was GM, and it gained less than one percent of the market. Third, GM gradually increased its market share from 1960 to 1963 to the 50-percent mark. Thereafter, its share decreased to the middle-40-percent range.

The average of the absolute values of annual market-share changes experienced by firms also express the level of market stability achieved. This average is 1.2 percent for the period. By contrast, the average for 1953-1958 was 2.9 percent and 2.0 percent for 1947-1952. Thus, the auto market stabilized considerably during 1959-1973. Firms' market shares were more stable during this period than in any preceding it.

Stability and Instability at the Division Level

Did the stability experienced at the corporate level translate into uniformly stable market segments? Before we address this, the categorization scheme used in previous chapters must be adjusted for two reasons. First, as discussed previously, the divisions which concentrated sales in the lower and upper market segments placed their product lines in the middle-priced segments in the late 1950s, thus blurring traditional pricing classifications. I adjust for this during the 1959-1973 period. Second, all divisions—except Cadillac, Lin-

Table 8.1
Firm-Level Market-Share Data, 1959–1973

		Market-Share Percentages					
Year	Total Units*	GM	Ford	Chrysler	AMC	Studebaker	Imports
1959	6,041	42.1	28.1	11.4	6.0	2.2	10.2
1960	6,577	43.6	26.6	14.0	6.4	1.6	7.6
	(+8.9)	(+1.5)	(-1.5)	(+2.6)**	(+0.4)	(-0.6)	(-2.6)
1961	5,855	46.5	28.5	10.8	6.4	1.2	6.5
	(-11.)	(+2.9)	(+2.1)	(-3.2)	(0.0)	(-0.4)	(-1.1)
1962	6,938	51.9	26.3	9.6	6.1	1.1	4.9
	(+18.5)	(+5.4)	(-2.2)	(-1.2)	(-0.3)	(-0.1)	(-1.6)
1963	7,558	51.0	24.9	12.4	5.7	0.9	5.1
	(+8.5)	(-0.9)	(-1.4)	(+2.8)	(-0.4)	(-0.2)	(+0.2)
1964	8,065	49.1	26.0	13.8	4.7	0.3***	6.0
	(+6.7)	(-1.9)	(+1.1)	(+1.4)	(-1.0)	(-0.6)	(+0.9)
1965	9,313	50.1	25.5	14.7	3.5	—	6.1
	(+15.5)	(+1.0)	(-0.5)	(-1.2)	(-1.2)		(+0.1)
1966	9,009	48.1	26.1	15.4	3.0	—	7.3
	(-3.3)	(-2.0)	(+0.6)	(+0.7)	(-0.5)		(+1.2)
1967	8,362	49.5	22.2	16.1	2.8	—	9.3
	(-7.2)	(+1.4)	(-3.9)	(+0.7)	(-0.2)		(+2.0)

Year	Total Units	GM	Ford	Chrysler	AMC	Studebaker	Imports
		Market-Share Percentages					
1968	9,404 (+12.5)	46.7 (-2.8)	23.7 (+1.5)	16.3 (+0.2)	2.8 (0.0)	—	10.5 (+1.2)
1969	9,447 (+0.5)	46.8 (+0.1)	24.3 (+0.6)	15.1 (-1.2)	2.5 (-0.3)	—	11.2 (+0.7)
1970	8,388 (-11.2)	39.7 (-7.1)	26.4 (+2.1)	16.1 (+1.0)	3.0 (+0.5)	—	14.7 (+3.5)
1971	10,024 (+19.5)	44.2 (+5.4)	24.2 (-2.8)	14.0 (+1.0)	2.9 (+0.5)	—	14.8 (+0.1)
1972	10,487 (+4.6)	44.2 (-0.9)	24.3 (+0.7)	14.0 (0.0)	2.9 (+0.4)	—	14.6 (-0.2)
1973	11,343 (+8.2)	44.5 (+0.3)	23.5 (-0.8)	13.3 (-0.7)	3.5 (+0.6)	—	15.2 (+0.6)
1960–1973 Total Market-Share Changes		+0.9	-3.1	-0.7	-2.9	-1.6	+7.6

*In thousands. Annual percentage changes in parentheses.

**Absolute values of market-share changes from the previous year are in parentheses. Market-share changes greater than 2 percent are underlined.

***Studebaker ceased domestic operations in 1963.

Source: Schnapp, *Corporate Strategies of the Automobile Manufacturers*, vol. 3.

coln, and Chrysler—marketed models in the new compact segment. As divisions eventually upgraded their initial models, this segment itself was differentiated into at least four distinct segments during the period.

By 1960, three distinct full-sized segments were established—the upper segment, in which cars sold for more than $4,400 in 1960; the middle segment, with cars selling from $2,501 to $4,000; and the lower segment, with cars selling from $2,000 to $2,500. Cadillac, Lincoln, and Chrysler sold models in the upper segment. Pontiac, Oldsmobile, Buick, Mercury, Chrysler, and Dodge sold models in the middle segment. Chevrolet, Ford, and Plymouth sold full-sized models in the lower segment. While overlap existed between the lower and middle segments, it makes sense to use these distinctions because industry analysts and the auto firms themselves used them.

The compact segment emerged as a viable market in the late 1950s, and most of the Big Three divisions plus AMC marketed models in that category after 1961. The only exceptions were Cadillac, Lincoln, and Chrysler. Fortunately, *Ward's Automotive Yearbook* reports separate annual sales figures for these compact models. This enables us to examine their performances independently of other models marketed by their respective divisions.

The compact segment actually became the spawning ground for the development of new segments. The compact segment spawned the popular intermediate-sized models in the middle 1960s, as Mercury and Dodge in 1964, and then Pontiac, Olds, and Buick in 1965, stretched and upgraded existing compact models to differentiate them from the established ones. This segment also spawned the subcompacts in the early 1970s.

Perhaps the most important segment to emerge from the compact segment was the popular-priced sports/specialty segment. Ford's Mustang and Dodge's Barracuda pioneered this segment's development in 1964. These models were followed by Chevrolet's Camaro and Dodge's Charger in 1966, Pontiac's Firebird and AMC's Javelin in 1967, and Chevrolet's Monte Carlo, Olds' Toronado, and Dodge's Challenger in 1969. This segment encouraged the development of a higher-priced sports/specialty segment in the late 1960s when Cadillac, Mercury, and Lincoln introduced models to compete with the established Ford Thunderbird and Buick Riviera.

Table 8.2 summarizes division-level market performances. Column 2 reports averages of the absolute values of annual market-share changes experienced by the divisions in each distinct segment during the period. Market segments are listed in rank order by these averages, beginning with the segments with the lowest averages or those most stable.

Table 8.2 shows that only about 47 percent of the auto sales during the period were transacted in relatively stable market segments. The intermediate, the middle-priced full-sized, the early compact (1959–1963), and the high-priced full-sized segments were all relatively stable. The averages of the annual market-share percentage changes experienced by divisions here ranged from 1.3 percent to 2.3 percent.

We can trace the lineage of two of these stable segments—the middle-priced full-sized and the high-priced full-sized segments—to prior periods. When we compare averages of the annual market share percentage in the middle-priced segments across periods, we see that the latter period was more stable than the prior ones. The 2.0 percent average for the middle segment during the latter period is lower than the 3.5 percent and the 2.3 percent averages for the lower-middle and the upper-middle segments during 1953–1958 (not in table 8.2). It is lower than the 2.7 percent and the 2.6 percent averages for these respective segments during 1947–1952. Similarly, the 2.3 percent average for the high-priced segment during the latter period is much lower than the 4.2 percent average for the segment during 1953–1958 and the 3.1 percent average during 1947–1952. Thus, the upper-full-size and the middle-full-size segments did experience stabilization. Commitments to Sloanist-marketing strategies appear to have been effective in taming fierce market-share competition.

In contrast, the lower-priced full-sized, the later compact (1964–1973), the popular sports, the high-priced sports, and the subcompact segments all experienced instability. The average of the annual market-share percentage changes experienced by the divisions competing in these segments range from 3.3 percent to 4.0 percent.

We can trace the lineage of only one of these segments to prior periods—the lower-priced full-sized segment. The 3.3 percent average of the annual market-share percentage

Table 8.2
Summary of Aggregate Market-Segment Behavior, 1959–1973

Market Segment	Annual Average of Market-Share Changes by Percentages*	Total Units Sold Per Period**	Percentages of Total Units Sold Per Period	Annual Unit Range**
Relatively Stable Market Segments				
Intermediate 1961–1973***	1.3	21,149	18.0	1,729–2,257
Middle-priced/ Full-Sized	2.0	21,600	18.4	1,026–1,757
Early Compact 1959–1963	2.1	9,282	7.9	643–2,360
High-Priced/ Full-Sized	2.3	3,473	3.0	138–281
Relatively Unstable Market Segments				
Lower-Priced/ Full-Sized	3.3	36,186	30.8	1,822–3,150
Later Compact 1964–1973	3.4	14,107	12.0	558–2,360
Popular Sports 1964–1973	4.0	6,593	5.6	600–861
High-Priced Sports	4.0	2,380	2.0	138–281
Subcompacts 1970–1973	—	2,801	2.4	139–1,066

*The annual average of market-share changes by percentages is the sum of the absolute sales of each division's market share in the period of observation subtracted from the division's market share in the previous year, divided by the number of division/year changes in the segment for the period covered.

**In thousands.elcome datacomp

***Statistics for each segment cover the full period spanning 1959 to 1973, unless a more restrictive periodization is noted.

Source: Ward's Automotive Yearbook, various years.

changes in this segment during the latter period is higher than the 2.3 percent and the 1.6 percent averages for the lower segments during 1953–1958 and 1946–1952, respectively. This suggests that stabilization did not occur, that market-share fluctuations increased. Was this fluctuation because of intense market-share competition? I argue momentarily that it was not.

The division-level market data reported in table 8.3 and 8.4 gives us keener insight into the segment patterns emerging during the period. These tables report the segment-level net gains and losses for the divisions in percentages of market share from 1959 to 1973. For discussion, we partition the segments into two groups: full-sized segments, and those developing from the compact segment.

In reviewing the division-level performances in the lower-, middle-, and upper-full-sized segments, two points are noteworthy. First, the instability reported for the lower segment in table 8.2 and 8.3 is misleading. For one thing, this segment lost considerable volume over the period—from a bit less than 3.2 million units to 1.8 million units (not reported in the table). Firms were abandoning this segment in search of higher profit margins.

Market-share fluctuation in the lower-priced, full-sized segment reflects this abandonment and regrouping. As a case in point, Ford split its model lines in 1961 with the introduction of its Fairlane, its pioneer model in the intermediate market. The strategic decision to pull out of this segment accounts for Ford's 6.6 percent segment-share loss. Chrysler, moreover, attempted to retreat completely from this segment in 1962 and 1963 by shortening the wheelbase of its lower-full-sized Plymouth models in line with the Fairlane. It reentered the lower-full-sized segment in 1964, as others began crowding the intermediate segment and began to cut into its market share there. In addition to Chrysler's reentry, AMC enlarged the wheelbase of its Ambassador in 1967 to that of other lower-full-sized models, largely as a defensive response to the invasion of the Big Three firms into the smaller-sized segments.

In this light, I reclassify the lower-full-sized segment as Sloanist regulated. Increasingly, this segment represented a market that the major producers were loath to serve, preferring instead to sell in the higher margin segments. Chevro-

Table 8.3
Summary of Division-Level Market-Share Data for the Full-Sized Divisions, 1959–1973

	Percentage of Share in 1959	Percentage of Share in 1973	Net Percentage Gain or Loss for Models	Net Percentage Gain or Loss for Firms
Lower-Priced Segment				
Chevrolet	43.2	47.0	+3.8	
Ford	44.6	38.0	-6.6	
Plymouth	12.1	11.6	-0.5	
Ambassador	—	3.3	+3.3	
Middle-Priced Segment				
GMC Models				
Pontiac	26.8	21.6	-5.2	
Oldsmobile	25.2	23.7	-1.5	
Buick	17.2	25.6	+8.4	(GM +1.7)
Ford Models				
Mercury	11.1	10.2	-0.9	
Edsel	2.9	—	-2.9	(Ford -3.6)
Chrysler Models				
Chrysler	4.5	11.2	+6.7	
Dodge	9.4	7.8	-1.6	
DeSoto	2.9	—	-2.9	(Chrysler +2.2)
Upper-Priced Segment				
GM				
Cadillac	73.8	78.7	+4.9	
Ford				
Lincoln	15.9	17.0	+1.1	
Chrysler				
Imperial	10.4	4.3	-6.1	

Source: Ward's Automotive Yearbook, various years.

let's hold on the lower-full-sized market segment—with its superior and more efficient production system—blocked the least efficient producers from considerably expanding their share of this segment.

The second point of interest is that much of the market shifts in the middle-full-sized segment in table 8.3 can be explained by Edsel's and DeSoto's withdrawal and by interdivisional shifts among the GM divisions. The net market share gained by the GM divisions over the fifteen-year period was only 1.7 percent. Ford lost 3.6 percent, largely due to its catastrophic experience with the Edsel, while Chrysler gained 2.2 percent. Thus, both unit volume and interfirm market-share behavior were quite stable here. These findings are consistent with those reported in table 8.2. They strengthen our interpretation of this segment as a stable, Sloanist-regulated one.

The market-share shifts among the GM divisions in the middle-full-sized segment are interesting. I cannot definitively ascertain whether this shifting was the result of strategic calculations by GM's general office staff, or the result of genuine interdivisional rivalry. Given that GM's general office embarked upon a corporate policy centralizing decision-making authority and placing GM's production schedules under tight general office control, the latter interpretation seems suspect.

At any rate, the rationale behind GM's decision to allow this shifting is clear in light of its political situation and its renewed commitment to Sloanism. The profit margins on the more expensive Buick models were higher than those which GM earned on comparable Pontiac and Oldsmobile models. Because GM was forced by political pressure to limit its overall market-share expansion, the growth of Buick sales at the expense of Oldsmobile and Pontiac sales promised higher rates of return without disrupting GM's competitors' market shares.

GM's 4.9 percent market-share gain in the expanding upper-full-sized segment in table 8.3 can also be explained in light of its renewed commitment to Sloanism. Profit margins were higher for Cadillac than on any other GM line. Because this segment made up only approximately 3 percent of the total market, GM could expand in this area without much political risk.

In sum, the data suggest that the full-sized market segments—in which slightly less than 52 percent of total unit sales were transacted—stabilized considerably during the period. The fierce competition for market share that disrupted both interfirm and shop-floor relations in 1953–1958 had abated. I suggest that this outcome was the result of company-level commitments to Sloanism.

In general, the data reported in table 8.4 suggest that the newer, smaller-sized segments were more unstable. These segments have a common lineage. They all developed from the low-priced-compact segment. We review the data for each segment in turn.

The strongest firms were quite reluctant to service the low-priced-compact segment after World War II—as seen in table 8.4—for fear that sales would not return desired profit rates. Both GM and Ford entered this segment briefly to attract buyers with low-priced models. Then they upgraded their entry models with more luxurious styling, trim, and larger size. This pattern is reflected in annual unit sales (not reported in table). In 1959, 643,000 units were sold in this segment. In 1961, sales jumped to more than two million. However, with the introduction of the Big Three intermediates in 1965, unit sales dropped to less than one million. Only 558,000 units were sold in this category in 1967. Afterwards sales began to climb. After 1970, more than one million units were sold each year.

While this segment was more unstable than the full-sized segments already reviewed, much of the fluctuation can again be explained by market-share shifts among the models of a given firm. For example, much of the 21.8 percent share lost by Chevrolet's Corvair was picked up by Chevrolet's Chevy II/Nova, Pontiac's Ventura, Oldsmobile's Omega, and Buick's Apollo. Examining firms' performances in this segment from 1965 to 1973, we see that GM and AMC both lost shares, while Ford and Chrysler gained.

However, this pattern should not suggest that Chrysler beat GM out of the segment. GM simply did not desire to service this low-margin market. It left the segment as the "mop-up" market for its weaker competitors. Indeed, in 1973, Chrysler's percentage share in this area was more than three times its total percentage market share. AMC's was 2.4 times its total, Ford's was about 98 percent, and GM's was about 60 percent.

This pattern is reversed in the intermediate segment. From 1964–1973, GM and AMC gained 4.5 percent and 2.3 percent, respectively. Ford's share did not change. Chrysler lost seven percent. When we combine these findings with

Table 8.4
Summary of Division-Level Market-Share Data for the Compact Divisions, 1959–1973

	Percentage of Share in 1961	Percentage of Share in 1963	Net Percentage of Gain or Loss for Models	Net Percentage of Gain or Loss for Firms
*Early Compact, 1961-1963**				
GMC Models				
Chevrolet Corvair	15.3	10.4	-4.9	
Chevrolet II	1.7	13.3	+11.6	
Pontiac Tempest	5.3	5.9	+0.6	
Oldsmobile F85	3.4	4.8	+1.4	
Buick Special	4.4	6.1	+1.7	(GM +10.4)
Ford Models				
Ford Falcon	23.5	13.8	-9.5	
Mercury Comet	9.0	6.0	-3.0	(Ford -12.5)
Chrysler Models				
Plymouth Valiant	5.9	7.5	+1.6	
Dodge Dart	7.2	4.7	-2.5	(Chrysler -0.9)
Independant Models				
AMC Rambler	17.9	18.1	+0.2	(AMC +0.2)
Studebaker	3.5	2.8	-0.7	(Studebaker -0.7)

	Percentage of Share in 1965	Percentage of Share in 1973	Net Percentage of Gain or Loss for Models	Net Percentage of Gain or Loss for Firms
Later Compact, 1965-1973				
GMC Models				
Chevrolet Corvair	21.8	—	-21.8	
Chevrolet II and Nova	14.7	21.0	+6.3	
Pontiac Ventura	—	4.6	+4.6	
Oldsmobile Omega	—	3.1	+3.1	
Buick Apollo	—	2.2	+2.2	(GM -5.6)
Ford Models				
Ford Falcon	21.0	1.2	-19.8	
Ford Maverick	—	16.9	+16.9	
Mercury Comet	—	4.8	+4.8	(Ford +1.9)
Chrysler Models				
Plymouth Valiant	13.5	20.4	+6.9	
Dodge Dart	19.2	17.6	-1.6	(Chrysler +5.3)
AMC Models				
AMC Rambler	9.7	8.4	-1.3	(AMC -1.3)

Table 8.4 (continued)

	Percentage of Share in 1964	Percentage of Share in 1973	Net Percentage of Gain or Loss for Models	Net Percentage of Gain or Loss for Firms
Intermediate Segment, 1964–1973				
GMC Models				
Chevrolet Chevelle	18.2	16.4	-1.8	
Pontiac	13.9	12.4	-1.5	
Oldsmobile	10.0	16.2	+6.6	
Buick	10.5	11.7	+1.2	(GM +4.5)
Ford Models				
Ford	14.6	19.6	+5.0	
Mercury	10.8	5.8	-5.0	(Ford 0.0)
Chrysler Models				
Plymouth	19.6	8.0	-11.6	
Dodge	2.5	7.1	+4.6	(Chrysler -7.0)
AMC Models				
Ambassador	—	—	—	
Rebel	—	2.3	+2.3	(AMC +2.3)

	Percentage of Share in 1969	Percentage of Share in 1973	Net Percentage of Gain or Loss for Models	Net Percentage of Gain or Loss for Firms
Popular-Priced Sports/Specialty Segment, 1969–1973				
GMC Models				
Chevrolet Camaro	21.6	12.3	-9.3	
Chevrolet Monte Carlo	2.8	34.5	+31.7	
Pontiac Firebird	7.5	5.9	-1.8	
Pontiac Grand Prix	11.6	17.1	+5.5	
Oldsmobile Toronado	3.4	5.4	+1.9	(GM +28.2)
Ford Models				
Ford Mustang	32.8	16.8	-16.0	(Ford -16.0)
Chrysler Models				
Plymouth Barracuda	4.0	2.1	-1.9	
Dodge Charger	9.0	—	-9.0	
Dodge Challenger	2.4	2.8	-0.4	(Chrysler -11.3)
AMC Models				
Javelin	4.3	3.1	-1.2	
AMX	0.8	—	-0.8	(AMC -2.0)

Table 8.4 (continued)

	Percentage of Share in 1967	Percentage of Share in 1973	Net Percentage of Gain or Loss for Models	Net Percentage of Gain or Loss for Firms
High-Priced Sports/Specialty Segment, 1967–1973				
GMC Models				
Cadillac El Dorado	8.3	17.8	+9.5	
Buick Riviera	17.8	10.0	-7.8	(GM +1.7)
Ford Models				
Ford T Bird	24.1	28.1	+4.0	
Mercury Cougar	49.8	20.6	-29.2	
Lincoln Mark III–IV	—	23.5	+23.5	(Ford -1.7)

	Percentage of Share in 1970	Percentage of Share in 1973	Net Percentage of Gain or Loss for Models
Domestic Subcompact Segment, 1970–1973			
Chevrolet Vega	16.6	42.4	+25.8
Ford Pinto	54.7	45.1	-9.6
AMC Gremlin	28.8	12.5	-16.3

*The restrictive periodizations mark the year in which the segment became established, and the year, if prior to 1973, the segment collapsed or was recognized as new segments.

Source: Ward's Automotive Yearbook, various years.

those reported in table 8.2, we see a relatively stable segment within which GM was gradually increasing its domination at Chrysler's expense. Comparing the GM divisions, we see the same pattern observed in the middle-priced/full-sized segments. Chevelle and Pontiac, the lower-margin GM divisions, lost share. Oldsmobile and Buick, the higher-margin divisions, gained.

The most truly competitive segment was the newly emerging, popular-priced sports/specialty segment. Ford's Mustang dominated the segment's early development, but, by 1969, all divisions—except Cadillac, Chrysler, and Lincoln—marketed models in this segment. From 1969 to 1973, GM gained 28.2 percent market share. Ford lost 16 percent,

Chrysler lost 11.3 percent, and AMC lost two percent. By 1973, GM had 75 percent of this market. Of course, this was a higher-margin segment.

Surprisingly, this pattern did not hold in the upscale version of the sports/specialty market. While the GM and Ford divisions' share here fluctuated considerably in this market, most shifting took place among the parent firm's divisions rather than among firms. From 1967 to 1973, GM gained only 1.7 percent. Buick's Riviera, however, lost 7.8 percent, all of which was picked up by Cadillac's El Dorado. Ford's Mercury Cougar lost 29.2 percent, but this was picked up by Lincoln-Mercury's Mark III and Mark IV and Ford's Thunderbird. Thus, GM and Ford were practicing classic Sloanism, upgrading buyers within the segment to higher-margin models.

Summary of the Market-Share Review

Thus, two distinctive market environments developed during the period. One was regulated by company-level commitments to Sloanist marketing strategies. These strategies enabled firms to avoid head-on competition for market share, and provided relatively stable environments within which to transact business. This environment supported approximately 70 percent of the industry's domestic business, and included the three full-sized and the newly emerging intermediate segment. This environment was considerably more stable than was the turbulent 1953–1958 market. Other market environments were relatively unstable, and included the low-priced compact, both sports/specialty segments, and the subcompact segments. Divisions entered, withdrew, and then reentered these segments, often redefining them with new product concepts. In violation of Sloanist prescriptions, these divisions, at times, attempted to increase their market-share penetration at the expense of competitors. These conditions affected approximately 30 percent of the industry's transactions during the period.

The Centralization of Managerial Authority

New organizational structures and operations policies accompanied the marketing shifts in the 1960s, and these structural developments affected shop-floor relations. GM, Ford, and Chrysler centralized their decision-making structures, and stripped operations managements of their authority to plan marketing strategies and set production schedules.

GM's managerial structure began to develop along these lines in 1958, the year in which Frederic Donner, a finance manager, was appointed to the positions of both GM's chairman and C. E.O. According to DeLorean and others, Donner stripped the GM presidency of much of its power, and concentrated decision-making authority in the positions which he occupied.[10] The power shift from operations management to finance came to its zenith in 1971, when the GM board appointed finance managers as both chairman/CEO and president.[11]

According to DeLorean,[12] Donner publicly blamed Curtice's policies for leading GM down a path to ruin in the 1950s, crediting his own policies for restoring order and profitability to the company. While DeLorean questions the accuracy and motive of Donner's claims, Curtice's expansionary policies played a major role in triggering the Justice Department's antitrust investigations. The fear of antitrust action may well have motivated GM's board to elect executives who were willing and capable of keeping the expansionary designs of division-level managements tightly bridled. This is what GM's corporate finance-oriented management did from 1959 to 1973, and the Justice Department did not break up the GM divisions.

During the 1960s and early 1970s, corporate-level policy groups increased their control over operations.[13] The most famous of these was the General Motors Assembly Division which in the late 1960s and early 1970s took over management of most GM body-assembly and final-assembly plants, stripping the divisions of control over production scheduling.

DeLorean describes the effect of this policy on his operations as Chevrolet's general manager. DeLorean claims that GM's general office typically gave his assembly plant managers their production schedules only a week in advance. This created "panicville," as managers rushed orders for parts and supplies. DeLorean critiqued this policy as inefficient and costly.[14]

DeLorean's criticism, however, may well have missed the

significance of such a policy in a hostile political environment. I argue that this type of tight production control was necessary in order for GM's general office to restrict its market share to politically safe levels. With such a policy, the general office could synchronize both its divisions' production schedules to one another and to that of its competitors over short periods of time. The general office could manipulate its schedules so as not to exceed the Justice Department's market-share flashpoints. It could increase production on the more profitable product lines, while decreasing production on the lower-margin lines. This tight control enabled GM to maintain a politically safe market share, while maximizing its rate of return. The market data suggests that this is precisely what GM was doing during this period.

After 1960, Ford's divisions also were stripped of their independence, as Henry Ford II centralized control. All of Ford's North American production facilities were consolidated under a "centralized, functional organization."[15] Such an organization enabled Ford to put brakes on his division managers' expansionary policies—those very policies that pitted Ford in head-on competition with GM in the 1950s.

Chrysler also centralized decision-making authority in its general office which was dominated by managers with finance backgrounds.[16] Chrysler's automotive divisions were stripped of their autonomy. Under Townsend, the general office staff made all of Chrysler's significant engineering, investment, and production scheduling decisions. Chrysler's divisions were transformed into sales organizations.[17]

Finally, the increasing centralization of corporate decision-making authority was accompanied by a shift in the financial structures of the auto firms. In 1960, GM, Ford, Chrysler, and AMC each relied upon internally generated funds to finance their expansions. By the mid-1960s, Ford, Chrysler, and AMC were forced to abandon this policy. They borrowed money from the capital markets and increased their debt-to-equity ratios.[18]

The situation at GM was different, but not by much. GM managed to keep its debt-to-equity ratio quite low throughout the period. GM management protected its internal policies from outside domination. However, DuPont's divestiture had an impact upon GM's financial structure, because it diffused the automaker's stock ownership. DeLorean claims that, after the DuPont divestiture, much of GM's corporate stock was controlled by large financial institutions which owned 1 to 2 percent. While institutional investors did not take an active role in GM management, DeLorean claims that their short-term orientation affected company policy.[19] These institutional financiers were instrumental in electing finance managers to positions of power in GM's general office—managers with orientations compatible with their interests.

Thus, it seems reasonable to assert that the centralization of decision-making authority in the hands of finance management reflected the increasing influence of Wall Street financiers. These managements favored high investment returns and avoided expansionist policies that might have lowered margins and invited price competition. Their policies and structures actualized these investors' short-term interests.

Summary

Thus, the industry's firms reembraced Sloanism and turned away from the destructive market courses which they blazed during the 1950s. Commitments to such strategies at company levels led to the reemergence of Sloanist regulation, and provided necessary space for the surviving firms to prosper in a period of relatively stable growth.

However, we must temper this image of effective market rationalization. Sloanist strategies themselves led to the development of new market segments that proved to be unstable and at times highly competitive. These new segments represented about 30 percent of the industry's business, as well as the growth segments of the market.

What were the consequences of these market and corporate-level developments for noninstitutionalized, shop-floor militancy and the development of workplace authority structures? This is the critical question.

I begin by stating simply that the type of two-faced market environment emerging during the period belies a simple response. In chapter 5, I predicted that Sloanist regulation might spur the emergence and legitimation of quota-based authority. Yet, the significant unstable component of the market environment during the 1959–1973 period would likely block such a development, as would the centralization of decision-making authority in the hands of managements far removed from the points of production.

Furthermore, the partial reemergence of Sloanist regulation did not lead to increasingly inflated prices. GM, the industry price-setter, kept new-car price increases below those of the consumer price index throughout the period. GM did this in spite of wage, raw material, liability, and recall costs that rose well above the consumer price index levels.[20] The antagonistic political environment within which GM operated during the period undoubtedly affected its pricing policies. GM tried hard to maintain its reputation as a civic-minded industry leader.

GM's pricing policy had the effect of squeezing the profit margins of its competitors somewhat. These competitors accepted GM's pricing structures as guidelines for setting their own prices. They had little choice. If they raised their prices considerably higher than those set by GM, they would not have been able to sell their products. This squeeze is reflected in the rate of return data reported in table 8.5.

Thus, market and organizational forces were exerting contradictory pressures on the shop floor during the 1959–1973 period. While experiencing real pressures to increase productivity and control costs, managements were not driven to the brink of catastrophe by competitive market forces, as many had been during the late 1950s. I argue that this more benign environment provided auto managements with leverage to experiment, innovate, and even err in responding to solidary workers' militant reactions which allowed them to stumble eventually onto a course of resolution that sufficed.

Implications for the Hegemony Model

The conjuncture theorized to produce a decline in noninstitutionalized shop-floor militancy in chapter 5 consisted of three components: Sloanist-regulated market segments; managerial structures that grant shop management the authority to set and change production standards; and the legitimation of quota-based authority systems on the shop floor. These components did not come together in the

Table 8.5
Return on Equity Expressed as a Percent, 1959–1973

Year	GM	Ford	Chrysler	AMC
1959	16.2	17.3	(0.8)	31.6
1960	16.5	14.8	4.6	21.6
1961	14.8	13.1	1.6	10.4
1962	21.9	14.1	8.5	13.7
1963	22.4	13.1	17.6	13.8
1964	22.8	12.6	19.0	9.4
1965	25.8	15.6	14.7	1.9
1966	20.6	13.0	11.1	4.9
1967	17.6	0.2	10.0	(42.4)
1968	17.8	12.7	13.8	6.2
1969	16.7	10.5	4.1	2.4
1970	6.2	9.4	(0.3)	27.6
1971	17.9	11.8	3.7	4.8
1972	18.5	14.6	8.8	12.4
1973	19.1	14.2	9.4	25.0

Source: Schnapp, Corporate Strategies of the Automobile Manufacturers, vol. 3.37.

post-1958 period. While the chapter suggests evidence of partial Sloanist-regulation of major market segments, this did not trigger the other developments linked to declines in noninstitutionalized militancy. Authority over labor-process outcomes was not passed down to the shop-floor level. Rather, authority became increasingly centralized in the hands of corporate-level management. The more benign market environment did not ease pressures at the company level to increase productivity, either. Profit margins declined somewhat in the later years of the period.

The failure of the hegemonic conjuncture to materialize fully during the period points to the importance of nonmarket influences left unaccounted for in the model developed in chapter 5. The most important of these appear to be those emanating from the political arena—specifically, the influence of aggressive antitrust enforcement by the federal government. For example, the specter of antitrust action forced GM to back away from the more expansionary policies it pursued in the market during the 1950s.

The effects of the antitrust threat were much more complex than anticipated in the model, and were instrumental in shaping GM and its competitors' managerial structures and labor policies in unanticipated ways. Political motivations played a key role in GM's decision to strip its divisions of key decision-making prerogatives and to plan production schedules from its general office. The complex structure resulting from this centralization made the Justice Department's prospect of breaking a major division away from GM infeasible.[21]

Moreover, the Justice Department's intensive surveillance over GM's activities played a key role in its decision to use restraint in setting prices for the industry. This restraint led,in the latter years of the period, to reduced profit margins for the industry's firms, and to renewed drives to tighten production standards and productivity levels. Political pressures were key factors in driving management away from the quota-based authority systems linked theoretically in the model to Sloanist market regulation. They appear to have blocked managements from embracing them.

It is best to view these contradictory pressures as emanating from the American political culture. This culture has long lauded free enterprise, and has shunned corporatist- and state-regulatory solutions to the contradictions generated by capitalism. Yet, when these markets were most free in industries such as automotive—and when the firms competing within them pursued their self-interests without the threat of state interference, the natural results were greater industry concentration and the specter of complete monopoly control, as the self-interested actions of the most efficient producers drove out the least efficient. These outcomes were not politically acceptable, either.

The developments discussed in this chapter were the compromised solution to these contradictory tendencies. The industry avoided the types of head-on competition that may have led to price wars and single-firm dominance. Although in position to become the dominant firm, GM realized that it could not continue along its expansionary path. Yet, the logical alternative—market sharing with oligopolistically regulated pricing and profits—was also unacceptable. Because of this, GM was forced to act in ways that held the line on price increases, even when this lowered profit margins in the industry and forced its firms toward a more driving productivity-oriented labor policy that had, in the past, provoked militancy.

CHAPTER 9

Repairing the Seams of the Hegemonic Order: Labor Process Dualism, 1959–1973

The complex market and organizational structures described in chapter 8 were incapable of laying a stable foundation for the industry-wide institutionalization of quota-based authority systems. While Sloanist regulation, to some extent, buffered the effects of intense competition on the operation of the auto firms, real pressures to increase productivity continued into the post-1958 period.

How, then, did the auto managements tame the noninstitutionalized militancy that threatened their authority during the 1950s? The argument developed on this point is that managements eventually separated the operator-based labor processes that generated team solidarity from those that tended to atomize workers. They then responded to each type of worker in different—but strategically rational—ways. Managements allowed production standards in the solidary plants to routinize—in effect, honoring a quota-based definition of a fair day's work. Managements refused, however, to respect this definition in the final assembly plants, and they continued to drive for increased productivity. This, I argue, was the development that reduced the incidence of wildcat activity within the industry. It was not well-planned. Management stumbled upon it after experimenting with other programs that had failed.

The Technological Solution

Of course, the optimal solution—from managements' point of view—was deskilling and atomizing solidary work groups. This would have muted their capacities for shop-floor militancy and allowed for the institutionalization of a drive-authority system which whould grant managements the uncontested right to set and change production standards at will. Indeed, managements experimented with this program in the late 1950s and early 1960s when they decentralized multioperational plant complexes and established separate single-component parts plants in suburban and rural locations throughout Michigan, Indiana, Illinois, and Ohio. However, this simple solution proved to be much more problematic than expected. The automation experiments, for the most part, failed to produce intended results.

My analysis of the auto industry's experiences with automated technologies will challenge the deskilling perspective developed most forcefully by Braverman.[1] This perspective posits a linear trajectory for industrial development, assuming that competitive dynamics inevitably propel capitalist managements to increase their control over the pacing and direction of their employees' work processes. The labor processes found in auto manufacturing are often depicted as embodying the essence of such a developmental trajectory.[2]

There is good reason for this. Many of the technological developments pioneered in the industry were designed specifically to simplify and limit the number of tasks performed by workers in their daily routines, to reduce the scope of workers' discretionary input in critical production processes, and to replace skilled workers with less-skilled ones. Machine-paced final-assembly lines, specialized machine tools used extensively since the 1910s, and automatic transfer lines employed since the late 1940s and early 1950s were all designed and used as deskilling devices.[3] Many of the developments introduced in body production during the 1950s were inspired by the promise of a production process in which every function was totally controlled by management.

The problem with the deskilling thesis does not lie in its claim that technologies are developed with an aim toward stripping workers of control over their work tasks or blunting their resistance capacities. Indeed, as Noble's analysis suggests,[4] machine-tool vendors are often quite explicit about this in their advertisements and sales pitches to potential buyers. The problem lies in the deskilling thesis' over-estimation of two critical management capacities.

The first is managements' capacity to impose its will upon its external environments. Deskilling theorists often neglect critical environmental constraints—such as a product market unresponsive to mass-produced goods[5]—that limit management from effectively instituting deskilling programs. If such constraints are real, we should not ignore them. Instead, we should specify both their content and how they affect shop-floor relations.[6] This, however, is seldom done.

The other is industrial engineers' capacity to design and implement effectively automated technologies. Deskilling theorists often neglect industrial engineers' dependence on the intervention of workers' experientially grounded knowledge and skill in implementing new technology in the workplace. A growing body of literature questions industrial engineers' capacity to develop effective production systems from a reified symbolic medium divorced from everyday, practical production experience.[7] If this is problematic, we must follow Noble in documenting the effects of this technical incapacity on shop-floor practices and relationships and examine how these failures are dealt with over time.[8] We must address the consequences of this technical incompetence for power relations in the shop.

I contend that an approach that both questions managements' capacities to actualize their market and shop-floor designs, and closely documents both the intended and unintended consequences of managerial actions, will enhance our general understanding of labor process development.[9] I take such an approach in examining the outcomes of technologies introduced in automotive body-building operations.

My thesis is that managements' successes in implementing deskilling and atomizing technologies on those production processes which spawned capacities for noninstitutionalized shop-floor militancy were limited at best. The most ambitious of these attempts proved to be ineffective in producing desirable market outcomes and in quelling workers' propensities to wildcat. These failures forced managements, for the most part, to accept and legitimate quota-based authority systems on key body-building operations.

By the late 1940s, industrial engineers had developed and implemented automated technologies on machining operations. Automatic machines took loading, activating, and unloading operations out of human hands. Limit switches with electronic sensors performed these functions on the various machines employed on the lines. Operators merely watched and monitored the automated tools that performed the operations they used to do manually. This transfer-line technology promised to displace workers, as well as increase machining precision and productivity. By taking loading and activating processes out of workers' hands, it also promised to mute worker capacities to pace operations.

Ford pioneered the use of this automatic transfer line in the machining of engine and transmission components. By the early 1950s, Ford successfully installed it at the new Cleveland and revamped Dearborn Engine plants.[10] The technology quickly spread throughout the industry.

However, the industry's success with this particular technology was somewhat mixed. Evidence revealed during a Society of Automotive Engineers panel discussion suggests that the new machines were "not doing the jobs expected of them" and were not living up to their vendor's billing.[11] The reliability of the technology's electronic sensors was suspect and, while the technology did decrease direct labor costs, it also considerably increased indirect costs.

In-line transfer technology's major limitation was inflexibility. The transfer devices were highly specialized machines, designed for use in loading and unloading a given part. They would not accommodate even the most simple design change. Such changes required management to replace every automatic machine tool on the line. While this was generally true of specialized machine tools, the additional costs of the electronically activated equipment prohibited frequent changes. This was not overly problematic with regard to machine processes performed in the manufacture of engine blocks and parts, because engines typically had a planned product life of ten years.[12] However, this shortcoming would eventually limit its use on other operations.[13]

Ignoring such limitations, managements increased in-line technology's use in the 1950s. It held the promise of automating stamping and welding processes, as well as traditional machining operations. This was looked upon as the solution to management's labor problems with the occupational groups employed there.

Stamping Press Automation

The first target was stamping. As with machining operations on engine manufacture, the stamping technology used prior to in-line automation had already taken the shaping and forming of metal out of the press operators' hands. These shapes were built by skilled tool and die workers into the dies used in the stamping press prior to operation. The pre-formed dies mechanically pressed their shape onto the sheet metal piece when activated by the push of a button. A nonskilled operator simply placed the piece into the die at the base of the press, activated the press mechanically, watched the matching die at the top of the press stamp its imprint onto the piece, then unloaded the finished piece from the press.

In-line transfer technology was designed to displace this type of unskilled labor, and, in the 1940s and early 1950s, managements began to install it on stamping presses. This threatened to wrest control over pacing from workers' hands, and thereby wipe out workers' "running-for-time" shop cultures.

However, the threat never fully materialized. Only the automatic unloading devices remained on the stamping presses in the 1960s. Rather than stamp out "running-for-time" shop cultures, I argue that they enhanced workers' capacities for attaining the goals valued in them. Next, we examine the industry's experience with both loading and unloading technologies.

The auto industry experimented with automatic loading and activating devices in stamping soon after they were installed in the engine and transmission plants. Ford installed these devices in the early 1950s in its new Monroe, Michigan, and Buffalo stamping plants. At Monroe, iron hands were attached to both ends of many of the stamping presses in use, loading and unloading parts automatically. Joseph Geshelin, a noted industry journalist, describes this technology system as accomplishing "automatic control of work movements on the line."[14]

This technology spread during the late 1950s. Ford installed it at its new Cleveland and renovated Chicago Heights stamping plants.[15] Chrysler installed it at its new Twinsburg, Ohio, plant,[16] and GM installed it at its Flint and Pontiac Fisher Body plants.[17]

Perhaps the most ambitious experiments occurred in the frame plants. Prior to automation, underbody frames were first shaped in large stamping presses, and then welded together by teams in stationary welding bucks. Frame plants developed reputations for being hotbeds of labor militancy. The Ford River Rouge Frame plant is the most striking example.

Working conditions in this plant were reputed to be among the poorest of the plants at the Rouge, and most of the production workers in the plant were African-American. Smoke and heat were constant problems, as was fatigue caused by heavy lifting. The Ford Frame plant developed a host of pejorative nicknames, such as "Hell's little acre," "plantation north," "Henry's slave palace," and "the hellhole of the Rouge."[18] The absenteeism rate was often the highest of all Rouge plants,[19] and the frame plant rank and file elected some of the most militant of UAW Local 600's unit leaders.

In-line transfer technology promised to wipe out the source of frame workers' militancy, for it promised to deskill and atomize frame operations. Automatic welding-press lines promised to take the welding torch out of buck welders' hands. Limit switches and automated loading devices also promised to wrest control over the pacing of the stamping operations from workers. Together, these developments promised to link frame manufacture and assembly operations into a centralized production unit which would be activated, paced, and monitored by electronic sensors. Such systems were put into effect in the 1950s at both Ford's Dearborn Frame and A. O. Smith's Granite City, Illinois, plants.[20]

Gartman cites the industry's experimentation with these technologies to support his general thesis that labor processes in auto manufacturing developed along a deskilling trajectory that increased managements' domination and control, and turned workers' everyday worklives into "auto slavery."[21] Of course, it is difficult to argue that such devices were not, at least, intended for such purposes.

The problem with Gartman's thesis is that his detailed historical account ends at 1950 and, thus, assumes that trends then in evidence would continue into the future. Gartman's analysis also assumes that automation engineers had the production competence to make the new complex systems work effectively. It also assumes that the market would be receptive to the products produced by them.

Such assumptions are wrong in the case of automation used in stamping and frame production as automated technologies proved unreliable. They were ineffective in wrenching control over pacing from workers as well as in muting their resistance. Further, the auto market became increasingly unreceptive to the standardized products demanded by the automated equipment.

The industry's experience in fully automating frame-building operations is the most striking case of the technical and labor problems associated with in-line transfer. The automated line installed at A. O. Smith lasted only three months. The outcomes were: (1) operating losses of $5 to $10 million; (2) serious labor trouble, culminating in slowdowns and a sit-down strike; and (3) a decline in frame orders from Chevrolet. To keep the lines running, management doubled its workforce and turned to manual assembly to meet production schedules.[22]

Ford installed a similar system at Dearborn, and local union officials reported that, in line with the demands of the new equipment, management reorganized every job in the plant in September 1956.[23] The results were immediate. Bill Collett, president of UAW Local 600's transportation unit, reported that, in September 1956, the plant was producing 90 percent scrap and that 50 percent of all frames were rejected by final assembly.[24] By mid-October, the new system had caused total pandemonium, putting the entire Ford production system behind schedule. Plant management was forced to add 1,200 additional workers to the unit in order to make the system operate. The Frame Plant editor noted that "congestion abounds as hundreds of men had to be utilized in the place of faulty automation." He ended his column on a cautious note, however, stating

> When I recall that, a few months ago, the company's shop pencil boys were around bragging about these completely

> new set-ups for the 1957 model chuckling to themselves about the hundreds of workers to be displaced—the first thought is to laugh and say that, for once, the dilemma of the automatic factory has backfired. But from past experience, I know that these job-killing artists will eventually learn to function with this Frankenstein they created and get it to live up to most of its potential, if not all of it.[25]

Did the frame engineers get the bugs out of their "Frankenstein"? This is difficult to ascertain with any certainty. Yet, some union reports suggests that they did not. At Dearborn, for example, problems continued into the late 1950s and 1960s. In September 1957, Carl Stellato, UAW Local 600's president, was called in to negotiate serious frame-plant grievances. The union won an agreement with the company to lock the line speeds and to keep the key in the plant manager's office. At this time, the traditional stationary welding bucks were still being used.[26] In June 1960, the frame plant took a strike vote over production standards issues and won a resolution adding 25 percent more welders on the lines in critical departments.[27]

Perhaps the most telling pronouncement on the viability of automated frame technology comes from a more contemporary example. Management installed an automated frame-welding line in the 1980s in the stamping plant where I interviewed informants. Of the plant's experience with this operation, a union official stated

> They have a line now that is supposed to run with nine people. . . . They can't get it going. They're running it with twenty-nine people. They don't know how to run the line.

Local union leaders linked management's failure to manage the automated line with the financial difficulties this particular plant experienced.

Managements experienced similar problems with the loading devices and the limit switches activating operations on stamping lines. The Fisher Body stamping plant at Pontiac, for example, ran into serious problems with its transfer shuttles when, in 1959, it began changing the designs on component parts more frequently. The plant experienced serious production delays and increased maintenance costs.

The automatic transfer lines proved to be highly sensitive to even the smallest changes in design. The automatic controls also proved to be unreliable in activating the presses. In response, management ripped out its automatic transfer devices and reverted to manual loading. This cut their production costs on hood operations by 25 percent.[28]

The effectiveness of the new technology as a tool for restricting operator control and muting militancy also proved to be quite limited. The most striking failure to pacify a militant labor force was Ford's experience at its Monroe, Michigan, plant. Its UAW Local 723 quickly gained a reputation for being one of the most militant in the Ford-UAW system. Its workers revolted constantly against management's attempt to increase production standards, waging slowdowns and wildcats throughout the 1950s.

A key factor in limiting the use of in-line transfer technology in stamping and welding-press operations was a shift in marketing strategies during the late 1950s. Firms resorted to more frequent styling changes in response to the increasingly competitive market environment. The proliferation of body styles led to shorter production runs and more frequent retooling and changeovers.[29]

These marketing strategies rendered in-line transfer automation ineffective because changes on these lines required new fixtures and automated loading equipment on every press. Costs on the automated lines proved to be much higher than on manual ones. As a result, stamping and welding-press operators continued to pace most of these lines in the industry into at least the mid-1970s.[30] The exceptions were stamping operations that produced parts with multiple-year runs.

These marketing strategies transformed production in the typical stamping plant into "a batch-type operation—a job shop on a large scale."[31] They demanded that skilled workers change stamping dies in the presses over short-term intervals. The major technological innovation developed in stamping plants after the mid-1950s was a tool designed to facilitate these frequent changeovers—the rolling bolster press. This technology allowed craft workers to slide stamping dies into and out of the press quickly and easily. While facilitating swift changeovers, it also assured operator control over pacing.

Rolling bolster presses quickly spread throughout the industry. They were used at GM's Grand Rapids, Michigan, and Hamilton and Cleveland, Ohio plants in the 1960s.[32] Ford installed them at Walton Hills, Ohio; Chicago Heights, Illinois; Dearborn and Woodhaven, Michigan.[33] Chrysler used them at its Nine-Mile, Detroit, and Twinsburg, Ohio, plants.[34]

Thus, both market forces and technical limitations checked managements' attempt to break workers' control over stamping and welding-press lines. Workers on these lines maintained collective control over loading and activating functions. Such control preserved their structural capacities for initiating outlawed collective action on the shop floor, as well as their interest in "earning time" on the job. Managements' reliance on formally trained production engineers for an automated solution to their labor problems failed, forcing them to turn elsewhere for relief.

Not all automated stamping and welding-process technologies suffered the fate of the in-line loading and activating devices. Sahlins "iron hand" was a successful case of semiautomation. This tool was developed to extract stampings from dies automatically, lifting parts out of presses after they are stamped. It rotates from the back of the press, first lifting the part then swinging it out onto a moving conveyor which transports it to the next press. Limit switches, tripped by the presses as they complete their cycle, automatically swing iron hands into motion.

One factor in this tool's success is simply that the unloading process does not require the type of precision placement that is required in the loading process. However, another critical factor was workers' responses to this technology. I have not found evidence suggesting that this tool's introduction and dissemination triggered any wildcat activity. We should also note that this tool displaced the conveyor-belt attendants that once pulled finished parts out of the presses and placed them on the conveyors, causing a substantial decrease in hourly worker employment. Finally, we should note that the iron hands were used by managements to increase productivity.[35]

Why was this tool successful, then, when others failed? The key to explaining this lies in understanding how iron hands affected workers operating in "running-for-time" shop cultures. While iron hands are labor-displacing, they do not really deskill or atomize because they do not remove pacing from the remaining workers' collective control. In controlling the loading of parts and the activation of the stamping cycles, operators still control how fast lines move with iron hands. The incentive of earned time is as collectively real for the workers after the installation of iron hands as it was before.

In truth, iron hands held the potential to enhance operators' capacities to earn time on the job—the valued goal in "running-for-time" cultures—by removing a major obstacle which had prevented its attainment in the past. This obstacle was fatigue which limited operators' capacities for attaining consistent production rates. A seasoned press operator whom I interviewed expressed this. He stated

> At the end of the day, he's done more than seventeen tons of lifting. . . . In the beginning it was tremendous. I've seen so many people go down in here. We've had tremendous turnover. . . . I've seen a lot of people just throw down their gloves and walk out. They just couldn't take it. The mental was there for a lot of them to do the work, but the physical just wasn't there. It was physically impossible for a lot of them to keep up with the line. When I first came in here they'd say: Stick it out. You'll get used to it. It wasn't true. I never got used to it.

The fatigue factor, then, functioned as a threat to the viability of "running for time." It created conflicts of interest between fatigued workers desiring to slowdown production and those desiring to run fast and earn time. This tension was expressed in another interview I conducted with a seasoned press operator. She stated

> One work rule that divided workers was the rule that allowed workers to finish early if they exceeded their rate. This caused a lot of people to work fast and dangerously so they could go upstairs and take it easy. The rub came if there was someone on the line who could not keep up. If such a person kept everyone else later, they resented that person and would try to get him or her kicked off the line.

Iron hands displaced the people on the back of the presses placing metal stampings on conveyors, but they proved to be more reliable than manual operators. Unlike humans, they didn't get tired, fall behind, and force the faster operators to hold up on their account. Instead, they kept up automatically with whatever speed the press operators in front of them chose to run. In essence, they could "run for time" consistently and enhance the remaining operators' capacities to achieve a valued goal—earned time—in ways in which few human beings could. I argue that, for this reason, they were accepted on the line, and appropriated by workers into their "running-for-time" shop cultures.

Technological Developments in Body Building

The typical early postwar body-building operation was a far less likely candidate for complete automation than was stamping. Body builders not only controlled the loading and activating processes for which they were responsible, but they also guided their welding torches with semiskilled hands. Although by the 1940s some welding operations were performed on moving assembly lines, body builders typically worked in teams in stationary fixtures or body-building bucks. Welding was a semiskilled operation in this period, and, before the automatic transfer technology could be employed, management had to first replace hand welding with machine welding.

Industrial engineers were successful at displacing welders' semiskilled hands with automatic welding subassemblies. Separate welding machines were tooled to perform specific welding functions. On these machines, stationary fixtures held the pieces of the subassembly precisely into place, while the welding-press operator loaded the machine and pushed a button to activate the process automatically. Management grouped these machines in lines, and transported subassemblies from machine to machine along conveyors. These lines looked and functioned much like the typical stamping lines.

In essence, welding-press operators became stamping-press operators. While this development considerably reduced the skill content of the operation, it did not strip operators of their abilities to pace the process. The same dynamics linking operators on the stamping-press lines to a community of fate—and the same dynamics giving rise to the development of "running-for-time" shop cultures on those lines—affected workers in welding operations. While the transfer of the welding torch to machines made this process technically susceptible to in-line transfer automation, the same market and technical dynamics which rendered that technique ineffective on stamping lines also rendered it ineffective on the welding line.

So, we can say that while this development deskilled body builders, it did not take pacing completely out of their control, nor did it atomize work groups. As did the workers on the stamping line, machine welders retained their structural capacities for initiating collective protest action against unpopular managerial policies. As in stamping, the industrial engineers who automated welding-press lines failed to provide an acceptable deskilling response to managements' labor problems.

In many cases, such as in body framing, management could not transfer the welding torch to the machine. Working in groups in massive stationary bucks, body framers had established and reinforced their reputations for militancy throughout the 1930s, 1940s, and 1950s. Managements' technological response to this group's militancy was both ingenious and effective. It became known as the "gate-line" system.

The gate-line system sets the framing buck in motion on the moving conveyor. It holds all of the subassemblies of the complete body in gate fixtures, swinging them into their preset place as the welder welds them together. Here, body builders are no longer required to work together in the buck. They do not coordinate their actions with one another as they load the fixture, weld the body together, and then unload the body from the fixture. As in other final-assembly jobs, body-frame welders work alone on the task, walking along the moving conveyor as they work.[36]

There is some confusion over the origins of this technology. Analysts typically cite Ford Dallas as its first successful employer in 1953.[37] Yet it appears that GM used a similar setup as early as 1947 to assemble Chevrolet bodies at Flint Fisher Body,[38] and as early as 1948 to assemble Futurama bodies at Lansing.[39] GM's early use of such moving-line systems may explain why it experienced much fewer body-builder wildcats.

Once this system was installed at Ford Dallas assembly, however, it quickly disseminated throughout the industry. Ford installed it in both its new and renovated final-assembly plants during the 1950s. Experiencing frequent body-builder wildcats in the past, Chrysler's management embraced the system wholeheartedly. In 1956, L. L. Colbert, Chrysler's president, met with Walter Reuther and UAW-Chrysler department officials to discuss its installation in Chrysler body-building divisions.[40] In late 1959, Chrysler installed it at Dodge Main, Plymouth Final Assembly, and Chrysler Final Assembly.[41]

In sum, the gate-line system should not be thought of as a deskilling device, for it left the welding torch in welders' hands, and it required the same types of welds as performed in the old system. Although not a deskilling tool, this technology did atomize task-oriented work groups. In the new system, body welders no longer worked together in a common space, coordinating their moment-by-moment activities. Instead, the gate-line system individuated workers' on-the-job experiences and struggles which had been shared collectively under the old system. In doing so, the new system muted body builders' capacities for initiating outlawed work stoppages.

With the dissemination of this system throughout the industry, body-building welders initiated patterns of protest activity similar to those working on the final-assembly line. Rather than challenge management's authority directly on the shop floor, gate-line welders appear to have channeled their grievances through the formal bureaucratic procedures. I suggest that this was a factor in the marked decline of wildcat activity in final-assembly plants after 1958.

Trim Shop Reorganization

Trim operations have always posed problems for industrial engineers hell-bent on deskilling or atomizing them. The nature of trim operations did not lend themselves readily to either deskilling or atomization. As a trim foreman stated in an interview with Leonard Sayles

> With steel, it either fits or it doesn't, but cloth is another matter. It takes a good man to know just how much it should stretch and how much it shouldn't, and to fit it into

> place with the right amount of tension. There is no tool that can do that. . . . only the experienced hand of a good trimmer. That's why you can never make an unskilled job out of trimming.[42]

For the most part, the foreman's prediction has been correct. Trim operations were resistant to the type of automation introduced in machining, and, to a more limited extent, in stamping and body welding. While staple guns replaced trimmers' magnetic hammers and tacks in the 1940s, they could not replace their experienced hands in stretching and placing the cloth along the metal or pasteboard. The reliance of this process on experientially acquired feel and knowledge left trimmers in control.

Because panels were typically too large to be handled individually, and because progressive subassembly operations in trim left operators in control over pacing, management could not readily break up the task-coordinated work groups formed on these lines. Both of these limitations led management to seek organizational, rather than technological, solutions to trim-worker militancy.

What made the trim workers' control over their work processes so troublesome to management in the 1940s and 1950s was its effects upon other workers. First, work practices of seasoned trimmers—practices such as finishing an eight-hour production quota in six hours on subassembly operations, pursuing down-time activities, or doubling up in a thirty-minute-on, thirty-minute-off schedule—could give the impression that trimmers did not work hard and were not required to do so. This was the impression of the UAW International representative whom Sayles interviewed.

> Many of them don't do anything approximating a day's work. It is embarrassing for us sometimes to try to negotiate a new rate for them when they are only working half as hard as the men in the body shop.[43]

Such practices undoubtedly affected other workers' motivations and expectations, making management reluctant to assault their standards.[44] Trimmers' willingness to shut down operations to protect customary production standards encouraged other workers to take similar actions. As shown in chapter 7, trimmer wildcats often sparked waves of wildcat shutdowns in body plants. Trim militancy—and trimmers' success in imposing their will upon managements—was often infectious.

In response, management transferred the building of trim component panels, seat cushions, and garnish moldings from the body and final-assembly plants to centralized trim component plants. The former operations were those involving handwork, operator pacing, and collective effort coordination. This uncoupled the effects of the solidarity-generating operations from the other increasingly atomized body and final-assembly operations.

Prefabricated trim components built in the trim supplier plants were shipped to final assembly. Workers in what remained of the trim departments there installed them in car bodies. They simply screwed or fastened these component panels onto bodies moving down the machine-paced line, much like other final assemblers there.[45]

The most brutal form of uncoupling was the outsourcing of trim work to suppliers, a strategy which left trimmers out of work. This was Chrysler's direct response to militant cushion builders in the Plymouth Body and Dodge Main plants.[46] However, much of the trim work went to other trim plants within the Chrysler system.

One deskilling technology was developed in the early 1950s which molded seat cushions and trim panels together, thereby eliminating sewing and hand fastening. In this process, assemblers built up "trim sandwiches," stacking materials in layers, using glue and bonding adhesives to hold them into place. These sandwiches were then molded in dielectric presses which operate much like stamping presses.[47] This technology turned cushion building on some model runs into an unskilled, high-speed operation. However, while the new method took critical operations out of the trimmers' hands, it still left them in control over the pacing of the process, because they built up the cushion layers and operated the presses by hand.[48]

Consequences for Wildcat Militancy

Thus, managements' capacities to control militant workers with deskilling and atomizing technologies proved to be rather limited. The only success was the gate-line technology which atomized operations performed previously by task-coordinating groups in stationary bucks.

Use of the technology that had the potential to both deskill and atomize solidary workers—in-line transfer—was constrained both by market changes requiring shorter production runs and by its own technical shortcomings. Hand-loading and activating proved to be more economical and cost-effective on most stamping and welding-press lines. This left operators' structural capacities for initiating outlawed work stoppages in tact. The same can be said for workers performing operations in component trim plants.

Perhaps an unintended consequence of these developments was to group such workers in plants that supplied the Big Three firms with necessary parts. This made these plants critical to the operations of their respective firms' entire production system. While this uncoupled potentially militant workers who worked in team processes from those with more limited capacities for acting collectively as well as independently of the existing authority structure, it also increased the strategic costs of potential wildcat strikes in the supplier plants. A strike in one of the key stamping plants had the potential to quickly and effectively shut down a firm's entire production system. A wildcat strike here also had the potential to do so without advance warning.

We know this because stamping plant workers actualized this potential during the 1960s in each of the Big Three firms. In May 1963, for example, workers at Ford's Chicago Heights stamping plant wildcatted over health and safety issues for eleven days, forcing Ford to close eight assembly plants, four other stamping plants, two glass plants, engine plants, foundries, and a frame plant. In all, forty thousand Ford workers were idled by the strike.[49] In February 1967, workers "brandishing baseball bats and tossing rocks and beer bottles" wildcatted at GM's Mansfield, Ohio, stamping plant for eight days over the outsourcing of dies to other plants.[50] As a result, 240,000 GM workers were idled. In January 1967, workers at Chrysler's Sterling Heights, Michigan, stamping plant went out on an authorized strike for seven days over production-standard issues and to protest the disciplining of workers leading a previous wildcat. Actual layoffs totaled twenty-one thousand, but had the strike continued a few days longer, it would have threatened one hundred thousand workers.[51]

The point here is that solidary workers' capacities for inflicting harm to management increased considerably with the concentration of body production operations in the stamping and trim plants. Body workers' structural capacities to fight management assaults on their shop customs and production standards were enhanced, rather than muted, by these developments.

Even so, we know that body workers wildcatted less often after 1958 than they had prior to that year. How did managements tame these workers' militant propensities? To answer this question we must turn to labor-relations developments that affected the authority systems governing work activities.

Labor-Relations Developments

The UAW International's policy toward militant locals protesting managements' assaults on production standards shifted notably after 1958. This shift was a strategic response to the coordinated local strike activity of the 1955 and 1958 contract negotiations. This activity forced the UAW International to participate in negotiating contract gains for its workers at the local level. In national contract negotiations of 1961, 1964, and 1967, militant GM and Ford locals went out on coordinated strikes for local gains after the UAW International reached contract agreements. In each case, the respective UAW department authorized the walkouts and then won contract gains that went a long way toward legitimating—at least on paper—the type of quota-based authority system that the local militants were fighting to defend. Chrysler followed the lead of its GM and Ford counterparts and ceded its locals the same concessions. We first examine these paper victories, and then assess the extent to which they affected shop-floor relations in final-assembly and body-supplier plants.

The Paper Victories

The UAW International went into the 1961 contract negotiations determined to win production standard relief for its GM, Ford, and Chrysler locals. The International Executive

Board set up a Comprehensive Production Standards Subcommittee on 21 January 1960. At the UAW Special Bargaining Convention in April 1961, the committee vowed to fight managements' broad definition of managerial prerogative, and to place limitations upon their abilities to speed up production at will. Managements' exchange-value-equivalency notion of a fair day's work was at issue here. The UAW resolved to force managements' acceptance of a provision restricting their capacities to increase production standards once set, unless they changed technologies, materials, or methods of operation. It also resolved to win contract language prohibiting speedups after line stoppages caused by technical problems, and to win extra relief time.[52]

After reaching an agreement over economic issues on 7 September 1961, the UAW/GM department authorized 92 of its 129 locals to strike for production standard relief. Walter Reuther championed the cause of the local militants by proclaiming to reporters that

> This strike is 99 percent about working conditions, the practical everyday problems the workers have in plants. We told General Motors Corporation that the economic package was fit, liberal, and attractive, but that it was not a substitute for a solution of the everyday problems which the workers have to live with.[53]

On 21 September, GM made key concessions to the militants' demands.

The UAW/Ford department approved twenty local strikes on 11 October 1961, claiming that it wanted to settle local issues before negotiating an economic package. Ford also capitulated to the union's production standard demands.[54] In November, Chrysler followed suit.[55]

In essence, the UAW had won a "pattern bargain." Besides added relief time for all production workers, and resolutions to the numerous local demands, three key contract gains were won. These were clauses that (1) prohibited management from changing set production standards unless it changed its "method, layout, tools, equipment, materials, or product design;" (2) restricted use of disciplinary action against workers failing to meet production standards during "abnormal conditions;" and (3) prohibitions against speedups to make up for time lost to mechanical breakdowns.[56] The 1964 and 1967 contract gains built on those which had been won in 1961.

On paper, then, these contract victories went far in legitimating the type of quota-based authority system for which the local militants were fighting. They protected production standards from managements' arbitrary assaults. They also delegitimated managements' market-based conception of a fair day's work. How well did these paper gains translate into shop-floor practices? This is the question to which we now turn.

Dual Shop-Floor Responses

To understand this translation, we must be aware of two things. The first is the ambiguity of formal language cast in a generalizable mode. What does the clause "unless and until the operation is changed as a result of a change in method, layout, tools, equipment, materials, or product design" actually mean on the shop floor and to the parties bound by it? What constitutes a legitimate change in operations? This phrase was critical in structuring and legitimating the authority systems that were to govern subsequent relations in production. Yet, its actual meaning was unclear and open to dispute.

From one point of view, the clause was quite limited in constraining managements. After all, with more frequent model changeovers and the proliferation of body styles, managements were constantly changing work methods, especially on final-assembly lines. This gave them leverage to justify tighter rates, and they used it throughout the period to do so.

The second point follows from the first. Given the ambiguity of the laws designed to regulate shop-floor activities of both management and workers regarding production standards, the party in control over the pacing of the work held the power to enforce its interpretation on the party that did not. For the most part, managements had this control in final assembly. Workers had it on the operator-paced, subassembly lines. With the increasing spatial separation of these types of operations, the stage was set for the development of two very different shop-floor authority systems.

In final assembly, managements controlled line speed. Speeding up production did not require workers' active consent. Managements had only to increase the control dials on the moving conveyor, and they used this control to impose a drive system on their assembly workers.

In contrast, workers controlled the speed at which work moved down the operator loaded and activated trim, stamping, and welding subassembly lines. Rather than the technology itself, production quotas paced these processes. All managements could do here was to increase quotas and hope that workers would increase their pace to meet them. If they did not—and if grievances were filed contesting the new rates—managements' options were limited. On the solidary lines, managements were forced to deal with the entire work group. To take action against one of these workers would run the risk of a collective response from them all. With the concentration of stamping and trim operations in a few large plants supplying firms' assembly lines with needed parts, managements were increasingly unlikely to take such risk.

The strike pattern presented in table 9.1 provides support for this dualism thesis. That table presents data specifying the issues motivating both wildcat and authorized strikes in stamping and final assembly during 1959–1973. The key finding here is that production standard issues provoked 78 percent of the strikes occurring in final assembly, while those same issues sparked only 43 percent of those called in stamping. This suggests that the patterns of strike activity in stamping and final-assembly plants were indeed different. Production standard issues were behind much more of the local strike activity occurring in final-assembly plants than in stamping. We know from the logistic regression analyses presented in chapter 4 that stamping plant workers were more likely to initiate wildcat strikes than were final-assembly plant workers. Yet, overall stamping and trim plants were struck less often than were final assembly plants during 1959–1973.

The reason for these differences, I suggest, is that managements tended to back away from the operator-paced production processes in stamping plants. Their actions tacitly legitimated a quota-based authority system in those plants and gave production workers little cause to wildcat. Managements accepted routinized production standards and did not change them until they changed the technological foundation of the labor process. They allowed workers to earn time

Table 9.1
Strike Behavior in Stamping and Final-Assembly Plants

*Stamping Plants Issues**			*Final Assembly Plants Issues**		
Type	Production** Standard	Other	Type	Production** Standard	Other
Wildcats	6	15	Wildcats	5	17
Authorized	9	5	Authorized	76	11
Total	15	20	Total	81	28

*Includes only strikes with a single and double issue reported.

**Includes production standard and contract strikes.

Source: Wall Street Journal and *New York Times* reports, various years.

on their operations, and allowed "running-for-time" shop cultures to thrive. In final assembly, managements tightened their grip over the labor process and attempted to force worker acceptance of the drive system.

Speedup for the Atomized

The paper gains won in the 1961 contracts did not usher in a new labor-relations practice for the industry's final-assembly workers. With the 1963 model run from late 1962 through 1963, managements assaulted production standards ruthlessly. Ken Bannon, the UAW/Ford department president, claims that the resulting production standard disputes at Ford were worse than any since 1947, and that similar developments were occurring in the GM plants. He stated that "they've tightened standards so much on our guys that a revolution is brewing."[57]

The speedups triggered a collective response from the UAW International. On 21 October 1963, the International approved strike notices in plants throughout the Ford, GM, and Chrysler systems in an apparent attempt to pressure the auto firms for speedup relief. When managements refused to respond to this threat, the International began authorizing local strikes throughout both the Ford and GM systems. In November, the UAW/Ford department struck final-assembly plants at Mahwah and Metuchen, New Jersey; Kansas City; and Wayne, Michigan. The UAW/GM department first struck Norwood, Ohio, in late October. From November through March, it struck final-assembly plants at South Gate and Fremont, California; Flint, Michigan; and Atlanta. Most of these strikes lasted from two to five weeks. Plant managements—undoubtedly under corporate-level pressure—were reluctant to budge from their hard line position on standards.

The UAW International was shocked by managements' dual responses to its locals' demands at this time. While managements took a hard line on production standard concessions in final assembly, they were apparently willing to concede them to supplier plant workers. This was especially striking at Ford. In May 1964, Bannon remarked that

> The company moves relatively quickly to resolve such [production standard] disputes at plants that manufacture components because strikes there can cut off the flow of parts to other plants and disrupt overall production. . . . When assembly plants are down, the company moves slower because other assembly plants continue to assemble cars and production is not stopped.[58]

Managements, of course, were playing strategically with their locals, imposing their production standard demands upon those that were most defenseless.

The UAW departments aided their locals as best they could. The GM and Ford departments were quick to grant strike authorization. In 1964, the UAW/Ford department even proposed bargaining to get all plants making the same model the right to strike in unison in response to production standard disputes.[59] However, it could not win this resolution in the contract.

Speedups continued in final-assembly plants throughout the 1960s, and the UAW authorized strikes throughout 1964, 1965, and 1966. In justification of the May 1966 strike at Ford's Metuchen, New Jersey plant, the president of UAW Local 980, stated that

> The company has piled unbearable work loads on the men. It's using a stopwatch with a minute breakdown into one hundred parts. They're trying in the 1960s to bring back conditions that existed in the 1930s.[60]

These strikes continued to drag on for weeks, as managements were reluctant to grant concessions.

In the 1967 negotiations, the UAW International responded strategically to managements' hardball tactics. Ford management began authorizing overtime and weekend work prior to their national contract negotiations with the UAW in an apparent attempt to build up its inventories in the case of a national strike. Outraged, the UAW began to authorize its locals to conduct waves of weekend plant strikes in apparent defiance of both the company and the contract. The UAW's success in using this tactic was to influence its subsequent responses to final assembly speedups.

In 1968, the UAW/GM department twisted to its own advantage the divergent capacities of its supplier and final-assembly locals to inflict damage to market outcomes. Production standard problems in GM final-assembly plants intensified during the new model run. The UAW/GM department issued strike deadlines to several final-assembly plants in February. However, management refused to back away from its tight standard position, and final-assembly workers walked out at Lordstown on 26 February. They also struck at Atlanta; Framingham, Massachusetts; and Van Nuys, California in early March; at Flint in mid-March; and at St. Louis in early April. The strikes at Atlanta and Framingham dragged on for more than six weeks without management budging on key issues. The strikes appeared to be lost.

Then, the UAW/GM department wielded a new weapon against GM. It authorized UAW Local 558, the local serving the Fisher Body stamping plant at Willow Springs, Illinois, to walk out on Friday, 18 April. The strike at Willow Springs was a suspicious one. The plant did not appear to be affected by the speedups. In fact, there were only fourteen local grievances on file at the time of the strike call, compared to the hundreds on file in the striking final-assembly plants.

However, this plant was a critical linchpin in the GM production system. The *Wall Street Journal* claimed that UAW used this strike to force GM to settle the strikes at Atlanta and Framingham. While GM called the strike an abuse of the contract, it moved quickly to settle its Atlanta and Framingham strikes immediately after Willow Springs shut down. Workers at Atlanta, Framingham, and Willow Springs all returned to work with settlements on Monday, April 21.[61]

Two major UAW/GM strike waves took place in 1969 and in 1972. Both were led by the UAW/GM department in reaction to speedups initiated by the new General Motors Assembly Division. In many ways, the GMAD approach represents the same approach that Chrysler and Studebaker managements tried in the late 1950s.

GMAD was hell-bent on imposing a managerial prerogative definition of a fair day's work on its shop floors, regardless of past customs and precedents, and regardless of contractual restrictions. Joseph E. Godfrey, GMAD's general manager, expressed the "get-tough" policy of the new division in an interview with *New York Times* reporters.[62] He proclaimed that management had a right to sixty minutes of work per hour paid. A member of GMAD's management team stated that the division anticipated strikes and local labor problems in response to its production standard policy. It decided to stick by its policy regardless of the strike possibilities.[63] As long as these stoppages followed contractual procedure, GMAD had strategic leverage to buffer their effects upon production and market outcomes.

GMAD's weapons were both organizational and technological. It instituted a computerized system to rank its plants monthly in terms of productivity and quality. Laggard plants were pressured to increase production performances.[64] This discouraged management from honoring past practices and customs likely to keep productivity stagnant. GMAD management also employed computerized time studies. Time-study data were fed into a central computer and average times were computed and used as the basis for standard revisions. However, these standards did not take the different plant-level contingencies affecting production into account.[65] Again, management based its shop-floor actions on knowledge obtained through an abstract, reified medium. Finally, GMAD committed itself to the use of the latest technological developments. It installed unimate robot welders in both its Norwood and Lordstown, Ohio, assembly plants.

The first wave of GMAD strikes took place in 1969, as GMAD consolidated its body and final assembly plants. These plants were built adjacent to one another or, in some cases, they were housed in the same building. They were managed, however, by different divisional managements—a Fisher Body group and a contingent from the respective car divisions. In many cases, two separate UAW locals represented the workers there. GMAD did away with dual plant managements and dual local contracts. It then violated long-standing traditions, speeding up production in the process. This produced a wave of strikes.

The most famous GMAD strike wave took place in 1972 and was when Lordstown gained its reputation and notoriety. However, the most significant of these strikes was the Norwood strike. GMAD reorganized production at Norwood, installing its first line of unimate robot welders there. It brought in outside management to force workers to produce at tighter production rates.[66] GMAD eliminated 749 jobs and maintained the same line speeds, forcing the remaining workers to increase their work pace considerably.

After its grievance backlog soared to four thousand cases, the UAW International authorized the Norwood local's strike. Norwood workers responded with a 174-day strike that began in early April 1972. This was the longest authorized local strike in the industry's history. The Norwood local clearly lost the strike, as the UAW International did little but stand by and watch. GMAD management refused to negotiate, and the local settled with slim concessions on seniority, overtime, and shift preferences. The problems with work loads on the assembly lines were still unresolved when the workers went back to work. As a local UAW official stated, "We got nothing on manpower. We lost on manpower, and we are losing more manpower now."[67]

The speedup at Norwood was followed by speedups in virtually all GMAD plants. The Lordstown strike was the most famous, and it followed the pattern set at Norwood, except that it was much shorter (twenty-two days) and the UAW International played a larger role in negotiating the resolution. The major reason for both was that GM had just introduced its Vega, and it could not afford to lose share in the highly competitive subcompact segment. While the union won reinstatement of four hundred laid-off workers, and while it managed to reduce the disciplinary penalties doled out during the dispute, the speedup issue was unresolved by the agreement.[68]

The UAW's losses in the Norwood and Lordstown strikes forced a shift in strike policy. The UAW International held an emergency meeting in October to discuss how it would deal with corporate-wide, final-assembly speedups. Leonard Woodcock, the UAW President succeeding Reuther, vowed that "we weren't going to let any local almost bleed to death."[69] The UAW resolved to throw its weight behind the fight for speedup relief and to counter GMAD's hardball tactics in kind. *Business Week* described these new tactics as "guerilla warfare."[70]

In many ways, the new tactics simply followed the precedent established in the inventory strikes during the 1967 negotiations. The UAW authorized its GM locals to conduct a series of short strikes at Wilmington, Delaware; St. Louis; Atlanta; Kansas City; Janesville, Wisconsin; and Arlington, Texas. These strikes were quite short—typically lasting less than a week—and workers often went back to their jobs without resolving the issues allegedly provoking them. These strikes signaled to GMAD that the UAW International was willing to provide leadership and organization to its locals. They were a show orchestrated to persuade GMAD to negotiate speedup issues.[71]

On 13 October, the UAW International wielded the same weapon against GM that it used to settle the 1968 strikes at Atlanta and Framingham. This time, it used the Fisher Body stamping plant at Mansfield, Ohio, as its smoking gun. Jerry Flint, a *New York Times* reporter, suggested that the UAW authorized this strike to pressure GM for speedup relief in the assembly plants. He labeled the Mansfield strike a "leverage strike." This plant made parts for all GM models, except Firebirds and Camaros. Again, it threatened to grind the GM production machine to a standstill. The International called the strike off quickly without a production standard settlement.[72]

In early November, the UAW International employed the same tactic. It authorized a strike at the GM steering-gear plant in Saginaw, Michigan. It also called off this strike after one day.[73] Because neither the Mansfield nor Saginaw plants were managed by GMAD, these strikes are best interpreted as attempts by the International to send louder signals to GM corporate management, giving it a glimpse of what might transpire if it were to continue to balk on negotiating its final-assembly-plant production-standard disputes.

The UAW International, of course, claimed that its innovative strike tactic was effective. Indeed, it used it frequently during contract negotiations after 1972. This strategy had advantages.

For one, it spread strike costs more evenly among affected workers, relieving local union members of having to forego wages for long periods of time. It also checked firms' abilities to choose plants that were least capable of upsetting its market position for speedup and strike targets. However, by posting strike deadlines—and thus signaling to management in advance of the impending walkout—these strategies gave managements the option of negotiating the contested grievances favorably in order to avoid critical and massive system shutdowns. Favoring compromise rather than confrontation, this was, of course, the UAW International's primary aim.

Thus, labor relations in final assembly continued along the conflictual path that was blazed during the late 1950s. The paper gains made in the national contracts did not reestablish the quota-based authority system defined in chapter 5. The strike evidence for the period shows that management assaulted production standards frequently. In the case of GM and Ford, these assaults were corporate-wide, and often instigated by a centralized management. Final-assembly managements did not honor or respect past custom and precedent as a legitimate brake on their capacities to impose their designs on the shop floor. The evidence suggests that managements responded to the profit squeeze discussed in chapter 8 with a strategic assault on the production standards in its final-assembly plants.

This tendency reached its fullest expression with the formation of GMAD which refused to pay even lip service in honoring any notions of customary shop practices, informally negotiated agreements between foremen and workers, or earned time. GMAD management claimed ownership of every minute of workers' on-the-job time, and it attempted to translate this ownership into increased productivity. The GMAD production-standard assaults and the reactions they produced can be viewed as struggles over the reimposition of a managerial-prerogative definition of a fair day's work. Viewed from the corporate level, these assaults were strikingly similar to those of the late 1950s.

However, three features distinguish them and the struggles they sparked from the earlier struggles. First, the latter conflicts occurred in plants with labor processes that: (1) inhibited the mobilization of militant collective action outside of the legitimated authority structure, (2) left management in control of pacing, and (3) atomized and fragmented work groups. These structural conditions left workers vulnerable.

Second, in contrast to the earlier period, the UAW International provided leadership for its distressed locals, and developed innovative strategies with which to respond to both GM's and Ford's corporatewide speed ups. The International led strategically planned campaigns against both Ford and GM, coordinating strike waves in an effort to force management concessions to local demands. Such leadership, for the most part, had been absent in the late 1950s. Then, the atomized workers on the machine-paced lines remained rather passive victims, while the solidary workgroups rebelled.

Third, I have characterized the revolts against the 1950s speedup as essentially normative and reactionist. From the standpoint of a rational, utilitarian, cost-benefit analysis, they were nonrational responses. Workers revolted to redeem shop practices which they had come to define as just, regardless of the risks involved or their probabilities of winning concessions. This was not the case with the authorized strikes led by the UAW International in the 1960s and early 1970s. They were strategically rational, as the UAW aimed to bring managements to the bargaining table. They were quick, often one-day affairs, and waged more as a show of force than as redemption for an injustice.

Earned Time for Solidary Workers

The story was much different in the component-supplier plants where operations were paced collectively by workers. To increase production, managements had to elicit the active consent of those workers by introducing viable technological changes on the line that enabled workers both to increase production and preserve the capacities for earning time with which they had grown accustomed. Because workers controlled pacing, they had power to force management to set realistic rates. This was illustrated to me in an interview I conducted with a seasoned press-line operator. She stated

> The union negotiates the rates on each press. First, the company sets a rate that is always too high, and nobody ever reaches it. There's a grievance. They write up what they call [a contract paragraph number]. I think that's the number in the contract. Then, they renegotiate the rate. . . . What they [workers] do is just slow down. They will run so slow [that] when the rates are down, they'll drive management crazy. Once they get a rate that they can make time on, people will run fast.

Lacking control over pacing—and faced with a strike threat capable of shutting down the firm's entire production system completely and unpredictably—I argue that such managements backed away from confrontation and conformed to expectations legitimated in the quota-based authority system. I use bits and pieces of archival and oral-history data to illustrate this.

First, key informants from the stamping plant where I interviewed workers and union officials clearly suggest this trend. In this plant, earned time was defined as a legitimate pursuit. The local contract stated that management would consider workers' assignments as completed once they finished the production rates specified in their shift standards. Time saved from meeting shift totals was defined as workers' "earned time."

A seasoned press operator reported that managements' policies regarding earned time had changed gradually from the early 1960s. In the past management forced workers to remain at their machines after they met their rates, even though they could not contractually force them to produce beyond their established quotas. Sometime thereafter, management allowed workers to leave their workstations for the friendlier confines of the breakroom and cafeteria. This had long become common practice.

The contractual legitimation of earned time was not a meaningless gain for these workers. Informants reported that they had earned time regularly, day in and day out, over the course of their careers. One informant, for example, claimed that she began on a welding-press line that typically ran at a speed of 167 percent of that specified in the rate. At this running speed, the line could finish its production quota in less than five hours. Other informants, while more guarded in disclosing specific details, claimed that meeting or beating production rates was an accepted shop-floor practice, although they could point to particular areas in which rates were much tighter. As discussed previously, these informants claimed that workers acted to assure that their lines ran fast enough to beat the rates. They were active in teaching one another the angles involved in making time, in pressuring slower workers to run fast, and in recruiting so-called speed merchants to their lines. These informants claimed that management both accepted and encouraged these practices in order to meet their production schedules consistently.

A *Fortune Magazine* article concerning work rule changes instituted at Chrysler's Vernor Avenue Trim Plant suggests similar developments.[74] Informants suggest that, prior to the massive work-rule changes instituted in the early 1980s, quota-based authority governed relationships between workers and management. Both management and union officials claimed that "running-for-time" shop practices were commonplace practices, including workers finishing production quotas long before the end of shifts, and at least the appearance of over-manning on the lines. A plant steward representing salaried workers there claims that some production quotas were so lax in some areas that workers were working only three to four hours per day.[75]

Finally, the Memorandum of Understanding reached between management and UAW Local 212 in September 1964 suggests the legitimation of quota-based authority in the Chrysler Body division stamping plants governed by the local. This agreement contained a provision requiring management to post standards on all production lines in the plant. This victory transferred the authority to determine production outputs from shop management's prerogative to the routinized and reified symbols posted on the machines. It restricted evaluative and disciplinary functions of supervision to monitoring overt compliance to the posted standards, rather than to the appearance of working hard or loafing. Once stamping-press operators met the posted rates, managers were left powerless to force more production out of them. The type of routinization legitimated by this contract victory would encourage and legitimate "running for time."

Thus, I have documented that auto managements (1) separated their atomized and solidary workers in different plants at the onset of the period; (2) selectively mounted corporate-wide speedup campaigns in GM and Ford final-assembly plants throughout the period, and in Chrysler final-assembly plants in the early years of the period; and (3) avoided corporate-wide production standard confrontations in key supplier plants where workers held some collective control over their work pace. I have suggested, further, that managements tended to allow quota-based authority to become legitimated in the body supplier plants. While I take the logic leading to this conclusion to be powerful in its own right, I have supported the thesis with suggestive evidence from a few critical cases. I encourage researchers to amass more of the rich, case-based data needed to explore, modify, and expand this thesis accordingly.

Summary

Thus, the historical evidence suggests that auto managements did stumble upon a program that was successful in reducing the incidence of wildcat activity in the industry after 1958. This program did not involve a successful deskilling technology, nor did it win workers' active commitments to managements' market goals. Managements simply separated those solidary work groups which they could not atomize from those that they could. They then responded to them in different ways. Managements backed off the shop floors of the solidary workers and allowed the quota-based authority system to become legitimated. At the same time, they played hardball on the shop floors of the atomized workers, attempting to increase their productivity in response to market pressures.

While effective in reducing the incidence of wildcat strikes, this program lacked the dynamism necessary to win workers' active commitments to the productivity increases needed to maintain the competitive position of the industry. The shop-floor program adopted in the 1960s was not hegemonic because it was established through fiat. I contend that, more than anything else, solidary workers' shop-floor power forced managements to respect the ends valued in their "running-for-time" cultures. Had these workers failed to preserve their collective control over work pace in the supplier plants, their lot would have been similar to that of the atomized in final assembly.

I have argued that the emergence of Sloanist market regulation during 1959–1973 enabled managements to stumble upon this shop-floor program by providing them with relief from the intense market competition of the late 1950s. This structure offered room for experimentation, trials, and a good many errors, before managements arrived at a viable program. It also provided space for uncoupling their most strategically vital plants from the immediate swings of the market. Without the protection of this benign market structure, managements would likely have been driven to assault production standards in the plants housing solidary work crews, as well as in those housing the atomized. Such an assault—and the reactions it would have stirred—might have had important consequences for industrial relations and class formation.

CHAPTER 10

Toward a General Theory of Postwar Industrial Development

This study began as a historical examination of how the U.S. auto firms developed structures taming, on the one hand, the more destructive features of price competition on the market and workers' shop-floor militancy on the other. I assumed that these structures existed in a systemic relationship to one another. By way of conclusion, I first review the account of this relationship's development presented in this book, specifying the major forces determining its course. Then, I draw upon the findings to specify guidelines for orienting further research on the relationship between market and shop-floor developments.

The History of Postwar Market Regulation

I constructed an ideal type definition of Sloanism in chapter 1 to show how market-level structures functioned to regulate interfirm competition in the automobile industry. I defined Sloanism as a program for orienting the market actions of individual firms. In theory, Sloanist firms' pursuit of their self-interests functioned to produce and maintain an industrial structure that avoided destructive price competition. The end which Sloanist firms pursue is the stabilization of market environments so that they can earn high and predictable returns on their investments. Sloanist firms develop accurate means of forecasting market conditions. They invest only in production for stable markets in which fierce price competition is unlikely to occur. When all of the major firms in the industry adopt these risk-avoiding practices, competition is minimized and firms earn high return rates.

Chapter 1 also linked Sloanism to the interests of distinct management groups. The Sloanist program is most appealing to the interests of outside financiers, whose primary interests are high, stable profit rates. It is, of course, also appealing to firms' finance managements, who are hired primarily to promote the interests of capital owners. Sloanism's compatibility with the interests of the product-bound management groups, however, was questioned. These groups define their interests as linked to the expansion of the particular product or product lines that they produce and sell. They tend to view Sloanism's cautious investment strategies as overly restrictive. They also tend to ignore them once they win dominance in corporate power structures.

In Part III, I traced the influence of Sloanist regulation on the automobile industry's development in the postwar period. The evidence suggests that Sloanism proved to be incapable of winning—for very long—voluntary commitment to its prescriptions by management factions leading the major auto firms. Both Ford and GM abandoned Sloanist marketing policies almost immediately after Eisenhower's election in 1952, setting off some of the most vicious market competition experienced in the industry. Without the specter of antitrust action haunting GM's market performance throughout the 1960s and early 1970s, it is also doubtful that GM would have backed away from its campaign to increase its market share. Even when Sloanism was most effective at regulating competition during 1947-1952 and 1959-1973, key market segments remained unstable. Why, then, was Sloanist regulation so precarious?

To understand the problem with Sloanism, we must understand finance capital's inevitable dilemma. Finance capital was not typically competent to manage the affairs of the auto firms which it controlled. Its representatives in the auto industry were uninvolved in the making and selling of automobiles, in organizing production processes, or in the management of labor. However ingenious the statistical systems which they developed for monitoring production schedules and markets might have been, they were nothing more than monitoring systems. At best, they could tell firms when and where they could earn desirable profit rates on the market. However, they were useless in informing firms of how to make and sell automobiles profitably.

For these production and sales operations, finance capital was dependent upon those who had acquired knowledge and skill through direct experience in the automobile business. The interest of this product-bound management group proved to be rather difficult to reconcile with the interests of those best served by Sloanism. The history of the U.S. auto industry after the stock market crash of 1929 bears this out.

This aspect surfaced most tellingly in the case of GM. In the mid-1920s GM's outside financiers ceded operating control of the business to operations management after the copper-cooled engine fiasco had threatened the viability of the firm.[1] During the 1930s, GM's operations management consolidated its power in the corporation and began to pursue expansionary policies deviating from Sloanist marketing prescriptions. These policies played a role in driving GM's competitors out of the market during the Great Depression. Only when the state threatened to take antitrust action against GM after 1938 did GM begin to put brakes to its market-share expansion.

Operations managements were also behind the expansionary drives of both Ford and GM during the 1950s. Operations managements in both firms embarked upon campaigns to increase market share. Again, these drives were halted only when the state intervened with antitrust action against GM.

Perhaps a requisite to the emergence and functioning of the Sloanist regulatory structure in the 1959-1973 period was the development of centralized managerial structures which stifled operations managements' autonomy and leverage in defining and carrying out the auto firms' operational policies. In each of the Big Three firms in the 1959-1973 period, finance managements came to dominate policy. They muted operations managements' influence over production scheduling, engineering, and investment decisions.

Thus, we must conclude that Sloanism failed to unite the interests of finance and operations managements behind a dynamic plan of action, as would a truly hegemonic program. It won ascendance in the industry only as finance managers expropriated operations managers' hold on corporate practice.

Finance capital's unwitting ally in increasing its domination over the industry proved to be the state. While the state committed itself to a more active role in industrial regulation after 1958, the exact nature of this commitment was contradictory. The ideology underlying much of the state's regulatory activities during the period was that of free-market competition. Yet, when the industry's firms were most free to pursue their self-interests in the market, the outcome was greater concentration. By the end of World War II, General Motors' size and market power had given it an incredible advantage over its competition. Had it been free to use it, most industry analysts agree that the outcome would have been complete monopolization.

The state took antitrust action against GM to prevent this, even when it meant interfering with the free play of market forces. The consequences of this action were: (1) the consolidation of corporate power in the hands of GM's finance management; (2) the emergence of a Sloanist, self-regulated market environment which supported four producers rather than one; and (3) pricing and marketing policies deviating considerably from those expected in a truly competitive free-enterprise system.

While this unwitting alliance between finance capital and the state paved the way toward Sloanist self-regulation in the auto industry during the 1959–1973 period, we should not impute a particularly rosy hue to it. This alliance marked the industry's decline as a dynamic force in the U.S. economy. By the 1970s, the industry was failing to react effectively to stagnating productivity levels, to profit margin declines, and to international competition. In retrospect, this peculiar form of Sloanist regulation proved to be little more than a palliative to the 1950s crises. It was not a permanent resolution to the problems, nor to the interest-group conflicts spawning them.

The History of Shop-Floor Regulation in the Auto Industry

I addressed the theme of shop-floor regulation in Part II. I located the source of the outlawed wildcat activity during the postwar period in the organization of specific labor processes. These processes organized workers in solidary work groups and provided them with some collective control over their work. They functioned unintentionally to create group consciousness and commitment. I labeled these processes *solidarity-generating.*

I also discussed how these processes led to the emergence of "running-for-time" shop cultures and to the development of a valued work goal that was different from that defined by management. This goal was beating managements' production quotas and earning free time in the workplace.

I wove together market and shop-floor developments in chapter 5 and developed a conceptualization of the authority structure taming solidary workers' propensities to initiate militant collective action. I labeled the authority structure compatible with both solidary workers' desires to earn time on the job and with the demands of firms operating in Sloanist-regulated markets as the *quota-based authority system.* In this system, management accepts routinized production quotas legitimated through custom and past precedent as a fair day's work.

I labeled the authority structure that was incompatible with solidary workers' interests in earning time as the *drive system.* Here, managements refuse to accept routinized production quotas as legitimate and attempt to establish a prerogative to set and change output expectations at will. I hypothesized that the imposition of this system upon workers who were accustomed to earning time on the job would trigger militant protest action.

I also linked both authority systems to market conditions. I hypothesized that operating in unregulated, competitive markets would propel managements to embrace the drive system. I hypothesized further that operating in Sloanist-regulated markets would encourage them to legitimate quota-based authority.

Did shop-floor developments in the postwar auto industry conform to these hypotheses? This was the major question addressed in Part III. From 1946–1958, I showed that, when market segments became increasingly competitive, managements attempted to replace quota-based authority systems with the drive system. This, in turn, triggered increased protest action from the solidary workers whose work expectations developed in the quota-based systems. I also examined some archival evidence suggesting that, when market environments stabilized during the period, firms did tend, over time, to develop features of the quota-based system. Thus, for a thirteen-year period, the expected market/ shop-floor relationships materialized.

From 1959–1973, however, auto managements moved to buffer the effect of market forces upon the labor processes spawning outlawed worker militancy. They separated the solidary labor processes from those that atomized workers in final assembly plants. Then, they reacted to the two types of workers in different ways. In the final-assembly plants, managements attempted to force workers to accept their right to set and change production standards at will. They subjected them to corporatewide speedups and authoritarian crackdowns.

In the stamping and body plants—where workers collectively controlled their work pace—auto managements appear to have accepted and legitimated quota-based authority. I argued that the gains won in the 1961 national collective-bargaining negotiations legitimated "earned time" for these workers by contractually prohibiting managements from changing established production rates on jobs without changing technology. Workers were able to translate these paper gains into actual shop-floor practice because they had the collective power to do so.

The evidence suggests, then, that market developments played only a limited role in taming workers' propensities to wildcat in the U.S. auto industry after 1958. The major market segments in the industry did stabilize considerably. Yet, we should not make too much of this, for other market segments had become increasingly competitive, and all firms' profit margins began to decline somewhat by the end of the period. This situation pressured firms to increase productivity. The emergence of the Sloanist regulatory structure did not abate these pressures.

What, then, was the precise role of this structure then in taming workers' propensities to wildcat? My argument is simply that this structure gave managements space for experimentation, trial, and a good many errors until they happened upon a remedy that worked. It enabled them, for example, to (1) experiment with technological remedies that failed—such as the automatic transfer and loading devices tried on the Ford, GM, and Chrysler stamping lines; (2) spend a considerable amount of time and money in reorganizing their production systems, and (3) accept the emergence of quota-based authority systems in key body-supplier plants.

Had market competition intensified, continuing the course blazed in the 1950s, I question whether the auto firms would have had the luxury of stumbling as much as they did in arriving at a resolution to the labor militancy occurring in their plants. I doubt whether they would have been able to succumb to the shop-floor demands of their militant, solidary workers.

From the Case to a General Theory of Development

How might this detailed historical account inform a general understanding of industrial development? To address this question, I first divide the explanatory account into its component parts—the theory of noninstitutionalized shop-floor militancy, and the theory of market regulation. I discuss separately each theory's generalizing power and its implications for further industrial research. Then, I discuss the theory of the relationship between shop-floor and market developments.

The Theory of Noninstitutionalized Militancy

I cast the theory of shop-floor militancy in chapter 3 as a general theory. The basic hypothesis is that a certain type of labor process will generate more wildcat militancy than will others. The militancy-generating labor process (1) encourages workers to form primary, functional work groups in order to accomplish their tasks; (2) provides workers with leverage for collectively controlling either their work pace or their working procedures; and (3) provides workers with leverage for redefining the ends to which their workplace activities are directed as their own ends—that is, as ends other than those which management intended.

I have confidence in the generalizing power of this simple hypothesis. I feel that it has much intuitive appeal. The quantitative and historical evidence reviewed here strongly support it. The hypothesis held up when tested across postwar periods, firms, plants, and strike incidents. It was also supported by Lichtenstein's pioneering research on the auto militancy of the 1930s and 1940s, and by Sayles' case-study evidence.[2] The fact that labor processes employed in the auto industry were quite diverse—involving raw materials as varied as cloth and steel, and employing technologies with considerable variations in labor and capital intensity, layout, and the like—also supports the generalizing power of the hypothesis. I am confident that future research across industrial contexts will support it, if the measures used are sensitive to the detailed labor-process variation existing within them.

The Theory of Market Regulation

The Sloanist ideal type developed here has proven to be useful over time in analyzing market developments in the case of the auto industry. Yet, it is not cast in a form that is amenable to generalization. It is unclear whether this concept will be useful in explaining market developments in other industries. I suspect that much more case-based theorizing must be done before we are ready to move to a more general theory of postwar market regulation. At this level, I chose to sacrifice generalizability for specificity.

However, I suspect that the structural forces responsible for selecting Sloanism as the auto industry's regulatory structure affected the selection of market-regulating structures in other industries as well. I state two of these forces here as general variables, in the hope that they might inspire further replication and development.

The first variable which I theorize to determine the general course of market regulation emerging in industries follows Fligstein's general argument.[3] This is the outcome of struggles between distinct management groups for control over firms' marketing policies. One of these management groups' interests are tied directly to finance capital's interests. The other's interests apply to the expansion of a specific product or industry. How this struggle played itself out in the various auto firms determined their predisposition toward Sloanism which, in turn, limited and/or enhanced its hegemonic appeal. I suggest that this type of struggle and its outcome might have been decisive in determining the type of industrial regulation emerging in other industries as well. However, it is not often accounted for in studies linking shop-floor and market developments.

The second variable that I theorize to determine the course of market regulation also follows Fligstein's argument.[4] This is simply the state's orientation to the various types of industrial regulation competing for dominance in an industry. The U.S. Department of Justice's antitrust policies precluded full monopolization in the postwar auto industry. I have suggested further that the political culture's antagonism toward state regulation may have further precluded the viability of socialist or state corporatist forms of industrial regulation. I suggest, following Fligstein, that state policy and political culture may have been important in determining the course of industrial regulation in other industries as well.

The Theory of Shop-Floor Regulation

The explanation I developed to explain the decline in wildcat militancy in the auto industry—the explanation linking market and shop-floor developments—is quite historically bounded. Its generalizing power may well be limited to the particular case. Yet, I feel that the structure of the explanation has value in informing further research on the market/shop-floor relationship. I will use it myself to conduct future studies. Again, I specify the variables that might determine this relationship generally in the hope that they will inspire future hypothesis testing and generation.

I theorize that three variables are critical in determining the type of structures emerging to tame shop-floor militancy. The first is the identity of the occupational groups initiating the militancy and the organizational foundations enhancing their capacities for engaging in collective action. Differentiating militant from passive work groups is a necessary first step in developing an explanation for militancy declines.

The failure to make this distinction has severe theoretical ramifications. Most importantly, it prevents us from accounting for the decoupling option, or the possibility that managements might isolate their militant work groups from their passive ones and respond to each group differently. This oversight might lead us to generalize structural developments to the entire labor force that could possibly affect only a small minority.

The second critical variable in determining the type of structure emerging to tame shop-floor militancy is managements' orientations to the work goals which the militant groups value and fight to uphold. In the case of the auto industry, solidary workers valued and often fought for earned time on the job. When managements adopted and respected a definition of a fair day's work which accepted earned time as a legitimate workers' right, levels of wildcat activity declined. When managements refused to do so—and attempted to impose its will arbitrarily on the shop floor—solidary workers tended to initiate more wildcats. I suspect that managements' orientations to the work goals valued by their militant occupational groups would be critical in determining courses of shop-floor developments in other industries.

The third critical variable in determining the emergence of shop-floor regulatory structures is their compatibility with the structures emerging to regulate interfirm competition in the product market. In the postwar auto industry, a market environment regulated by firm-level commitments to Sloanism appears to have been a requisite for the emergence of quota-based shop-floor authority, albeit in limited form and scope. I feel that theoretically specifying the functional compatibility of these market/shop-floor systems, and historically documenting their interrelationships, will be critical to understanding industrial developments elsewhere.

Yet, the analysis presented warns against overstating the effect of market development on shop-floor relations. I found that decoupling militant work groups from the passive ones—and making concessions only to the militants—might enable managements to buffer the effect of competitive market forces on shop-floor militancy. Obviously, the types of concessions required to passify a minority of workers (with militant structural capacities) will not demand the same level of market stabilization as needed to make those concessions throughout the workforce.

Probably the most important lesson to be drawn from this study is that the market/shop-floor relationship is not easy to specify historically, and that the type of detailed account developed here might be necessary for the generation of meaningful theory. To presume, at this point, that we know enough in general about market/shop-floor relationships to specify quantifiable values on key variables to be researched in "quick-and-dirty" fashion—or to formulate sweeping, general, society-wide theories of these relationships—is to presume much too much. In light of our current limitations, I suggest that industrial analysts work inductively, building cautious generalizations through comparative, historical case studies.

I suggest that the rather crude variables already defined serve only as sensitizing reference points for the development of more refined, general hypotheses concerning the relationship between market and shop-floor regulation. Comparative analyses that capture the complexity of actual case developments are sorely needed. Such analyses should lead us toward a more insightful and generalizable theory than currently exists. This study is meant to serve as a necessary prologue to this larger comparative agenda.

Notes

Introduction

1. See, for example, Burawoy, *Manufacturing Consent*; Gordon, Edwards, and Reich, *Segmented Work, Divided Workers*; Piore and Sabel, *Second Industrial Divide*.

2. Burawoy, *Manufacturing Consent*; Gordon, Edwards, and Reich, *Segmented Work, Divided Workers*; Piore and Sabel, *Second Industrial Divide*. See also Stone, "The Origin of Job Structures."

3. See Burawoy, *Manufacturing Consent*, "Between the Labor Process and the State."

4. See Calhoun, "The Radicalism of Tradition"; Conell and Voss, "Formal Organization and the Fate of Social Movements"; Haydu, *Between Craft and Class*; Katznelson and Zolberg, eds., *Working-Class Formation*; Tilly, "Solidary Logics."

5. See Babson, *Building the Union*; Friedlander, *Emergence of a UAW Local*; Lichtenstein, "Auto Worker Militancy."

6. See, for example, Edwards, *Contested Terrain*, ch. 7.

7. See, for example, Piore and Sabel, *Second Industrial Divide*; Wood, ed., *Degradation of Work?*

8. See, for example, Burawoy, "Between the Labor Process and the State."

9. Ibid. Also Gordon, Edwards, and Reich, *Segmented Work, Divided Workers*; Piore and Sabel, *Second Industrial Divide*.

10. Gordon, Edwards, and Reich, *Segmented Work, Divided Workers*, ch. 4.

11. Burawoy, *Manufacturing Consent*.

12. Lichtenstein, "Auto Worker Militancy"; Sayles, *Behavior of Industrial Work Groups*.

13. The argument here follows the general argument developed by Fligstein in *Transformation of Corporate Control.*

Chapter 1. Sloanist Market Regulation

1. See Baran and Sweezy, *Monopoly Capital*; Galbraith, *New Industrial State*; O'Connor, *Fiscal Crisis of the State*; Piore and Sabel, *Second Industrial Divide.*
2. See Galbraith, *New Industrial State*; Piore and Sabel, *Second Industrial Divide.* See also Chandler, *Visible Hand.*
3. Hofstadter, *American Political Tradition*, xxx.
4. May, *R.E. Olds*, 220–221.
5. See Cray, *Chrome Colossus*; Fine, *Automobile Under the Blue Eagle*; Nevins, *Ford*; Seltzer, *Financial History of the American Automobile Industry.*
6. See May, *R.E. Olds*; Nevins, *Ford.*
7. See Fine, *Automobile Under the Blue Eagle.*
8. Ibid.; Sorensen, *My Forty Years with Ford*, ch. 18.
9. Gramsci, *Selections from the Prison Notebooks.*
10. See Sloan, *My Years with General Motors.*
11. Ibid., xxiv–xxv.
12. Ibid., 66.
13. See Brown, *Reminiscences*; Sloan, *My Years with General Motors.*
14. Ibid.
15. See Bell, "The Subversion of Collective Bargaining."
16. Sloan, *My Years with General Motors*, ch. 8.
17. Ibid.
18. Ibid.
19. Ibid., ch. 9.
20. See Chandler, *Strategy and Structure*; Drucker, *Concept of the Corporation*; Fligstein, *Transformation of Corporate Control*; Sloan, *My Years with General Motors*; Stinchcombe, *Information and Organizations.*
21. See Brown, *Reminiscences*; Sloan, *My Years with General Motors.*
22. See Ford, *My Life and Work* and *Today and Tomorrow.*
23. See Piore and Sabel, *Second Industrial Divide.*
24. See Fligstein, *Transformation of Corporate Control.*
25. See Edwards, *Dynamics of the United States Automobile Industry*; White, *Automobile Industry Since 1945*; Wright, *On a Clear Day*, 269.
26. Fligstein, *Transformation of Corporate Control.*
27. For a similar treatment of interest group dynamics among

managerial factions, see Fligstein, *Transformation of Corporate Control*. My analysis of the auto industry collapses manufacturing and sales management factions into a single "operations management" category because the conflict between operations and finance management was most notable in the auto industry. See Cray, *Chrome Colossus* for a historical account of this type of conflict in General Motors' history.

28. See Fligstein, *Transformation of Corporate Control*.

29. Cray, *Chrome Colossus*, 314.

30. Sloan, *My Years with General Motors*, 172–177.

31. Ibid., 178–179.

32. Ibid., 177–181.

33. Ibid., 177–181.

34. Fine, *Automobile Under the Blue Eagle*.

35. Bernstein, *Turbulent Years*; Fraser, *Labor Will Rule*.

36. See Brody, *Workers in Industrial America*; Fine, *Automobile Under the Blue Eagle*.

37. Cray, *Chrome Colossus*, 311–312.

38. Ibid.

39. See Chandler, *Giant Enterprises*; Galbraith, *Liberal Hour*.

40. Nevins and Hill, *Ford*, chs. 12 and 13.

41. See Hickerson, *Ernie Breech*, 140–142; Schnapp, *Corporate Strategies*, vol. 2, 36–37.

42. See Schnapp, *Corporate Strategies*, vol. 2.

Chapter 2. Sloanist Labor Regulation

1. See John W. Scoville's comments cited in MacDonald, *Collective Bargaining in the Automobile Industry*, 319.

2. Brody, *Workers in Industrial America*. See also Piore and Sabel, *Second Industrial Divide*.

3. Edsforth, *Class Conflict and Cultural Consensus*, chs. 6 and 7.

4. Fine, *Automobile Under the Blue Eagle*, 20.

5. Edsforth, *Class Conflict and Cultural Consensus*, chs. 6 and 7; Fine, *Automobile Under the Blue Eagle*, 20–21; Serrin, *Company and the Union*, 105.

6. See Edsforth, *Class Conflict and Cultural Consensus*, 164; Gartman, *Auto Slavery*.

7. Edsforth, *Class Conflict and Cultural Consensus*, 140–142. See also Weir, "Rebellion in American Labor's Rank and File."

8. Edsforth, *Class Conflict and Cultural Consensus*, 165–166. See also Cole, *Work, Mobility and Participation*; Thompson, *Making of the English Working Class*.

9. Fine, *Automobile Under the Blue Eagle*, 85-95, 195-202, 259-266, 274, 400-401.

10. Ibid.
11. See Cray, *Chrome Colossus*, 295–296. See also Fine, *Sit-Down*.
12. See Beasley, *Knudsen*, 175–176.
13. Edsforth, *Class Conflict and Cultural Consensus*, 177.
14. Cited in Frank Marquart, *Auto Worker's Journal*, 78.
15. Cited in ibid., 94.
16. Herring and Thrasher, "UAW Sit-down Strike," 180.
17. Sloan, *My Years with General Motors*, 406.
18. Edsforth, *Class Conflict and Cultural Consensus*.
19. Ibid., 193.
20. Ibid., ch. 8.
21. Ibid.
22. See Halpern, *UAW Politics*; Lichtenstein, *Labor's War at Home*.
23. See Herding, *Job Control and Union Structure*; Jennings, "Wildcat!"
24. See Gartman, *Auto Slavery*, Ph.D. dissertation, 711–712.
25. Ibid. See also Harbison and Dubin, *Patterns of Union-Management Relations*.
26. See Burawoy, *Manufacturing Consent*, ch. 7.
27. See Piore and Sabel, *Second Industrial Divide*, ch. 4.
28. Offe and Wiesenthal, "Two Logics of Collective Action". See also Haydu, *Between Craft and Class*.
29. Offe and Wiesenthal, "Two Logics of Collective Action."
30. Ibid., 75. For a discussion of the general effects of working-class diversity on political outcomes, see Form, *Divided We Stand*.
31. Offe and Wiesenthal, "Two Logics of Collective Action," 75.
32. Ibid., 87.
33. Ibid., 78–79.
34. Ibid., 103–109.
35. For a distinction between wildcat and bureaucratic strikes, see Fantasia, *Cultures of Solidarity*, 48–72.

Chapter 3. Work Organization and Work-Group Solidarity

1. See Jenkins and Perrow, "Insurgency of the Powerless"; Shorter and Tilly, *Strikes in France*.
2. Lippert, "Fleetwood Wildcat."
3. See Lichtenstein, "Auto Worker Militancy"; Sayles, *Behavior of Industrial Work Groups*; Scott and Homans, "Reflections on the Wildcat Strikes"; Weir, "Rebellion in American Labor's Rank and File."
4. See Kerr and Siegel, "The Inter-industry Propensity to Strike."

5. Friedlander, *Emergence of a UAW Local.*

6. See Halle, *America's Working Man.*

7. See Edwards, *Contested Terrain*; Gordon, Edwards, and Reich, *Segmented Work, Divided Workers*; Stone, "Origin of Job Structures."

8. Lukács, *History and Class Consciousness*, 83–222.

9. Braverman, *Labor and Monopoly Capital.*

10. For extended discussion, see Burawoy, "Toward a Marxist Theory of the Labor Process."

11. See Halle, *America's Working Man.* See also Vallas, *Power in the Workplace.*

12. See Blauner, *Alienation and Freedom.* ch. 3; Marx, *Capital*; Walker and Guest, *Man on the Assembly Line*, ch. 5.

13. See Lichtenstein, "Auto Worker Militancy"; Sayles, *Behavior of Industrial Work Groups.*

14. See Sayles, *Behavior of Industrial Work Groups*, 45.

15. See, for example, Walker and Guest, *Man on the Assembly Line.*

16. Ibid., 71–73.

17. Faunce, "Automation in the Automobile Industry" and "Automation and the Automobile Worker."

18. Walker and Guest, *Man on the Assembly Line*, 47.

19. For similar arguments applying to nineteenth-century rebellions, see Calhoun, "Radicalism of Tradition." See also Wolf, *Peasant Wars.*

20. See Sayles, *Behavior of Industrial Work Groups*, ch. 3.

21. See Lichtenstein, "Auto Worker Militancy"; Sayles, *Behavior of Industrial Work Groups*, 64.

22. For review and critique of such theories, see Piore and Sabel, *Second Industrial Divide.*

23. See Fountain, *Union Guy*, 26–29. See also "Fabric Trim Assemblies Produced by the Millions," *Automotive Industries*, 1 Nov. 1959, 46.

24. Studebaker and some supplier firms worked on piece-rate systems rather than nonmonetary quota systems. See *Oral History Interview of Mr. George Hupp.*

25. See "New Speedup Method Devised by Company," *Ford Facts*, 9 Oct. 1948, 2; "Company Answers Union Demands," *Ford Facts*, 13 Dec. 1952, 2; "Co. Gives Partial Answer to Demands," *Ford Facts*, 17 Jan. 1953. See also MacDonald, *Collective Bargaining in the Automobile Industry*, 272–275. For a description of practices in the Studebaker stamping department, see *Oral History Interview of Mr. George Hupp*, 34. For a description of the Dodge Main Trim department, see Patricia Cayo Sexton, "A Feminist Union Perspective," 21–22. For a description of production standard practices in a trim-

component plant, see "Anatomy of an Auto Plant Rescue," *Fortune*, 4 Apr. 1983. For descriptions of the welding-press subassembly operation, see Walker and Guest, *Man on the Assembly Line*, 74; "Spot Welding Mass Produces Body Panels," *American Machinist*, 28 Aug. 1947; "Cost-Cutting Methods of Producing 'Henry J.' Car Bodies," *Machinery*, Feb. 1951; "Welding the Lincoln Uniframe Body," *Machinery*, Dec. 1957.

26. Blauner, *Alienation and Freedom*, 95–98.

27. See Lippert, "Fleetwood Wildcat" and "Shopfloor Politics at Fleetwood."

28. See "Ford Strike Cuts Lincoln Output," *New York Times*, 19 Nov. 1946, 5; "For Poll on Lincoln Halt," *New York Times*, 4 Feb. 1947, 21; "First Post-War Walkout at Ford's Lincoln Plant Settled in a Few Hours," *Wall Street Journal*, 19 Nov. 1946.

29. Lichtenstein, "Auto Worker Militancy," 338.

30. For an interesting discussion on the relationship between back stages on the job and consciousness see, Vallas, *Power in the Workplace*, 170–173.

31. "Welding the Lincoln Uniframe Body," *Machinery*, Dec. 1957.

32. Roy, "Quota Restriction and Goldbricking" and "Efficiency and the Fix."

33. Burawoy, *Manufacturing Consent*.

34. See Roy, "Work Satisfaction and Social Reward."

35. See Collins, Dalton, and Roy, "Restrictions of Output."

36. Ibid.

37. Studebaker, and some supplier firms, worked on piece-rate systems rather than nonmonetary quota systems. But, as in Roy's and Burawoy's piece-rate shops, workers tended to honor quota ceilings and earn free time from production requirements. This made these systems quite similar to those employed at GM, Ford, and Chrysler. See, for example, *Oral History Interview of Mr. George Hupp*.

38. I do not mean to imply that management is unaware of these goals, nor that, under some circumstances, they are unable to manipulate them to serve their production ends.

39. Lippert, "Fleetwood Wildcat."

40. Lippert, "Shopfloor Politics at Fleetwood."

41. For a description and analysis of similar practices in longshore work, see Finlay, *Work on the Waterfront*.

42. Sayles, *Behavior of Industrial Work Groups*, 32.

43. Goffman, *Asylums*.

44. See Burawoy, "Toward a Marxist Theory of the Labor Process."

45. Lippert, "Fleetwood Wildcat."

46. Lippert reports that it took him a while to develop this reading game. The trick was to figure out how to hold his place in the book and return to it quickly without wasting earned seconds.

47. See Aronowitz, *False Promises*, ch 1.

48. Descriptions culled from *UAW Local 5*, "Strike Vote—March 16, 1956."

49. For an interesting theoretical discussion of this type of dealmaking, see Finlay, *Work on the Waterfront*.

Chapter 4. Evidence Supporting the Solidary Work-Group Thesis

1. See Ragin, *Comparative Method*; Ragin and Zaret, "Theory and Method"; Weber, *Economy and Society*.

2. Friedlander, *Emergence of a UAW Local*; Lichtenstein, "Auto Worker Militancy."

3. See Babson, *Building the Union*.

4. Freidlander, *Emergence of a UAW Local*, 75-76. See also Babson, *Building the Union*.

5. Freidlander, *Emergence of a UAW Local*, 116-131.

6. For a discussion of the strategic-location thesis, see Perrone, "Positional Power, Strikes, and Wages"; Wallace, Griffin, and Rubin, "Positional Power of American Labor." For a discussion of the militant-craft-worker thesis, see Tilly, "Solidary Logics," and other articles in the issue. For a discussion of the militant community thesis, see Kerr and Siegel, "The Inter-industry Propensity to Strike."

7. I chose these papers, rather than the *Detroit News* or *Detroit Free Press*, because their reports were indexed throughout most of the period in question. The *Wall Street Journal Index* began in 1955. I was forced to scan every daily issue from 1946 to 1954 to complete the data set. As Paige warns in *Agrarian Revolution* (88-89), the labor intensive nature of locating newspaper articles without a reliable index proved to be an immense undertaking, with thousands of pages to scan per year of interest. Collecting data from other unindexed papers over an extended span was not feasible.

8. For our purposes, multiple-operation sites are those where more than one type of process is located—such as sites where a foundry, a final-assembly, and an engine plant are located. Sites omitted from the target sample include engine and transmission plants, steel foundries, electrical-parts plants, glass plants, and so forth. The occupations represented in these plants were too difficult to categorize with confidence.

9. Compare to the statistics presented in Edwards, *Strikes in the United States*, 281; and Lichtenstein, "UAW Bargaining Strategy and Shop-Floor Conflict."

10. There are problems with this preliminary categorization. Some of the occupations grouped in the craft-worker category—such as maintenance workers—also held strategic positions. Some of the occupations grouped in the solidary-worker category were more skilled than others. These problems are corrected in the multivariate analyses by ranking each occupational group along separate dimensions.

11. Based on plant counts reported by the Motor Vehicle Manufacturers Association in *Plants of U.S. Motor Vehicle Manufacturers in the U.S. and Canada*, I estimate that roughly one half of the total labor force employed in the industry worked in the target-plant population. Population percentages for occupations are based on statistics reported in "Wage Structure in Motor Vehicles, February 1950," and "Wages in the Motor Vehicle Industry, 1957." For assemblers and solidary workers, these are: occupational frequencies reported in *MLR* divided by total workers in the industry x 2. Strategic workers estimates are not adjusted for the targeted sample under the assumption that such workers would be evenly distributed through the industry's plants. The craft-category estimate = 2 x the number of toolbuilders + the number of workers in the general craft categories ÷ total workers. This estimate assumes that general-maintenance craft workers would be evenly distributed throughout the sample, while tool-building workers would all be included in the target sample's body plants.

12. See Charles Tilly, "Solidary Logics."

13. The plant-sized measure is the natural logarithm of the average number of workers employed in the plant divided by 1,000. These numbers were reported in strike articles published in the *Wall Street Journal*'s and *New York Times*'s reports.

14. The periodization employed in subsequent chapters is longer and more irregular: 1946 to 1952, 1953 to 1958, and 1959 to 1973. The latter periodization is used to break down history by general market-level tendencies. The one employed here reflects trends in labor-relations developments. The period from 1946 to 1950 represents the uncertain era within which the union's postwar role in industrial relations was uncertain. Contracts during this period tended to last from one to two years. While the bureaucratic alternative to open shop-floor conflict was in place, its legitimacy was not secured. The period from 1951 to 1955 was the period of relative labor peace ushered in by the five-year collective bargaining agreement signed by GM and the UAW. This set a precedent for longer contract periods and secured both management's and union's commitment to the bureaucratic structure. The period from 1956 to 1959 was a period of heightened management/union conflict. In response to intense product market competition, management

assaulted existing production standards and relationships. The period from 1960 to 1963 is one of structural reorganization in the industry, during which body-building operations were separated from final assembly in centralized supplier plants.

15. See Lichtenstein, "Auto Worker Militancy." See also "Wage Structure in Motor Vehicles, February 1950"; "Wages in the Motor Vehicle Industry, 1957."

16. Census data were employed for this categorization. The solidary communities had less than one hundred thousand people; were at least 90 percent white; had 25 percent of their firms involved in durable goods manufacture; and were located at least twenty-five miles from a large urban area. These criteria would, most likely, force plant managements to draw their labor force from homogeneous residential communities similar to those which Clark Kerr and Abraham Siegel specify in "The Inter-industry Propensity to Strike."

Chapter 5. The Market/Shop-Floor Conjunctures

1. Burawoy, *Manufacturing Consent.*

2. See Burawoy, "Between the Labor Process and the State." See also the discussion and critique in Vallas, *Power in the Workplace*, ch. 2.

3. For related argument, see Godard, "Strikes as Collective Voice"; Halaby, "Worker Attachment and Workplace Authority." See also Montgomery, *Workers' Control in America*, ch. 1; Thompson, *Making of the English Working Class.*

4. See Jefferys, *Management and Managed*, 13–16, for similar conceptualization. See also Gouldner, *Patterns of Industrial Bureaucracy.*

5. Burawoy, *Manufacturing Consent*, 133.

6. See also *Oral History Interview of Mr. Lester Fox*, 23–24; "Planning Assembly Lines for Volume Production," *SAE Journal*, December 1953, 33–34.

7. See Burawoy, *Manufacturing Consent*; Mathewson, *Restrictions of Output*; Nelson, "Scientific Management and the Workplace," 85–89; Roy, "Efficiency and the Fix."

8. See, for example, Littler, *Development of the Labour Process.* See also Vallas, *Power in the Workplace*, 156–157.

9. For the definition of the foreman's role in labor unrest held by the liberal wing of the personnel management movement, see Jacoby, *Employing Bureaucracy*. For a discussion of the foremen's position during the period of unionization, see Lichtenstein, "Man in the Middle."

Chapter 6. The Skittish Emergence of a Hegemonic Order, 1946–1952

1. *UAW Local 5*, "Production Standards Undated: 1948-1958."

2. *Oral History Interview of Mr. George Hupp*, 34.

3. See MacDonald, *Collective Bargaining in the Automobile Industry*, ch. 6.

4. See Edwards, *Dynamics of the United States Automobile Industry*, 107-108; MacDonald, *Collective Bargaining in the Automobile Industry*, 258, 357-362; Mahoney, *Story of George Romney*, 161-163.

5. See MacDonald, *Collective Bargaining in the Automobile Industry*, 357-369.

6. *Oral History Interview of Mr. George Hupp*, 34; "Local 154, Jan. 1953-Feb. 1967," *UAW President: Walter P. Reuther Collection.*

7. MacDonald, *Collective Bargaining in the Automobile Industry*, 314.

8. Sloan, *My Years with General Motors*, 394-395.

9. Cited in MacDonald, *Collective Bargaining in the Automobile Industry*, 350.

10. Ibid.

11. "Local 3, April 1946-Oct. 1954," *UAW President: Walter P. Reuther Collection.*

12. *Oral History Interview of Mr. Elmer Yenney*. See also Asher, "The 1949 Ford Speedup Strike"; MacDonald, *Collective Bargaining in the Automobile Industry*, 337.

13. "Planning Assembly Lines for Volume Production," *SAE Journal*, Dec. 1953, 33-34.

14. Schnapp, *Corporate Strategies*, vol. 3.

15. MacDonald, *Collective Bargaining in the Automobile Industry*, 333.

16. Sloan, *My Years with General Motors*, 258.

17. Jefferys, *Management and Managed.*

18. Ibid.

19. Ibid.

20. See Nash, "Job Satisfaction: A Critique," 82-85. See also Sexton, "A Feminist Union Perspective."

21. Sexton, "A Feminist Union Perspective," 21.

22. "Briggs Charged With Violating Contract," *Voice of Local 212*, 19 Apr. 1946; "Briggs Workers Vote for Strike Action," *Voice of Local 212*, 24 May 1946.

23. "This, the Company Refuses to Do," *Voice of Local 212*, 24 May 1946.

24. "Negotiations Report to Membership," *Voice of Local 212*, 9 Aug. 1946.

25. "President's Column," *Voice of Local 212*, Jan. 1949; "Speedup Issue Settled," *Voice of Local 212*, May 1949.

26. See Nevins and Hill, *Ford*, 298–311.

27. Printed in "Kay a Victim of the New Speedup Communique," *Ford Facts*, 12 June 1948.

28. "President Mike Donnelly Reports on Conditions of Speedup Lines," *Ford Facts*, 19 Mar. 1949.

29. "President Mike Donnelly Reports to Dearborn Assembly Workers," *Ford Facts*, 22 Jan. 1949; "President's Column," *Ford Facts*, 12 Mar. 1949; "Top Job Merry-go-round Locked at Standards," *Ford Facts*, 23 Apr. 1949.

30. "President's Column," *Ford Facts*, 4 June 1949, 1. See also Asher, "The 1949 Ford Speedup Strike."

31. Ibid.

32. Ibid.

33. "President's Column," *Ford Facts*, 16 July 1949, 1.

34. Abernathy, *Productivity Dilemma*, 36.

35. Nevins and Hill, *Ford*.

36. See "Ford Handles by Automation," *American Machinist*, 21 Oct. 1948; "How Ford Automates Production Lines," *American Machinist*, 17 Mar. 1952. See also Nevins and Hill, *Ford*, 352–355.

37. See especially "Auditorium Packed at General Council Session," *Ford Facts*, 20 May 1950; "Stellato's Inaugural Speech," *Ford Facts*, 20 May 1950; "Most Foremen Unqualified to Handle Labor Problems," *Ford Facts*, 20 May 1950; "Production Crazy," *Ford Facts*, 7 July 1951; "Executive Board Maps Plan to Curb Speedup," *Ford Facts*, 7 July 1951.

38. All divisions are grouped according to price ranges reported in "Car Prices, Weight and Bodies," *Automotive Industries*, 15 Mar. 1951.

39. Jefferys, *Management and Managed*.

40. See Nevins and Hill, *Ford*, chs. 12 and 13.

41. For an interesting discussion suggesting differences between the ideologies of corporate management and line-based supervisors, see Lichtenstein, "Man in the Middle."

42. Asher, "The 1949 Ford Speedup Strike."

43. "Most Foremen Unqualified to Handle Labor Problems," *Ford Facts*, 20 May 1950. As suggested by the title of the article, the UAW local leaders initially viewed this change in policy with suspicion. From their experiences with belligerent foremen during the Bennett days, and the days of instability during the early years of the new management, they had learned to be distrustful and suspicious of direct supervision. My view is that the belligerent orientation of Ford's foremen in the early postwar years was encouraged and supported by Bugas's industrial relations department. With the new directives from this department urging stabilized industrial relations in the 1950s, the pressures pushing foremen to the drive

position likely subsided. The incentive to get the product out smoothly and efficiently would likely encourage foreman to honor stable, predictable production standards, as the new Ford management's proficiency at planning production increased.

44. "Company Answers Union Demands," *Ford Facts*. 13 Dec. 1952; "Co. Gives Partial Answer to Demand," *Ford Facts*, 17 Jan. 1953.

45. "Grievances Bog Down as Chrysler (ABD) Nixes Bargaining," *Voice of Local 212*, Oct. 1954.

46. Edwards, *Dynamics of the United States Automobile Industry*, 119–124.

47. Cray, *Chrome Colossus*.

48. Langworth, *Kaiser-Frazer*, 32–39.

49. Edwards, *Dynamics of the United States Automobile Industry*, 124–125.

50. Nevins and Hill, *Ford*, 362–363.

51. Ibid., 363.

52. See Schnapp, *Corporate Strategies*, vol. 3, 52–55.

53. See Brown, *Reminiscences*, ch. 7.

54. See White, *Automobile Industry since 1945*, 124–125.

Chapter 7. Bursting Two Seams in the Early Hegemonic Order: Market Breakdown and Shop-Floor Responses, 1953–1958

1. Nevins and Hill, *Ford*, 382–387; Schnapp, *Corporate Strategies*, vol. 3, 58–59; Sloan, *My Years With General Motors*, 205–211.

2. See Cray, *Chrome Colossus*, 353.

3. Schnapp, *Corporate Strategies*, vol. 3.

4. Edwards, *Dynamics of the United States Automobile Industry*, 70–71; Schnapp, *Corporate Strategies*, vol. 3, 6–7.

5. All percentages of market-share gains or losses reported here are absolute values. They are the percentage of market share at time one minus the percentage of market share at time two. Percentage of market share is simply the firm's percentage of the annual auto sales transacted in the domestic market.

6. AMC and Studebaker survived by reentering the low-priced market with new compact models, a strategy that proved to be quite successful for AMC.

7. See MacDonald, *Collective Bargaining in the Automobile Industry*, 270–275, 323–324.

8. Ibid., 325.

9. "Chrysler Re-evaluating Every Job in Plant," *Voice of Local 212*, July 1956.

10. See *Arthur Hughes Collection*, "UAW-Chrysler Department Meeting with L. L. Colbert, 13 Aug. 1956."

11. MacDonald, *Collective Bargaining in the Automobile Industry*, 280–283.

12. Ibid., 325

13. See "Grievances Bog Down as Chrysler (ABD) Nixes Bargaining," *Voice of Local 212*, Oct. 1954.

14. *UAW Local 212*, "Correspondences of Shop Committee."

15. "Grievances Bog Down as Chrysler (ABD) Nixes Bargaining," *Voice of Local 212*, Oct. 1954.

16. Ibid. See also "Mazey Spells Out Strike Issues," *Voice of Local 212*, Nov. 1954; "212 Members Vote Strike Action to Safeguard Union," *Voice of Local 212*, Nov. 1954; "Management Uses Tricks to Cut Down Manpower," *Voice of Local 212*, May 1955; "Chrysler Re-evaluating Every Job in Plant," *Voice of Local 212*, July 1956.

17. "Chrysler Re-evaluating Every Job in Plant," *Voice of Local 212*, July 1956.

18. See "Strike of 10,000 at Dodge Main Halt Chrysler Unit's Output, Idle 75,000," *Wall Street Journal*, 20 July 1954, 2; *UAW President: Walter P. Reuther Collection*, "Local 3, April 1946–Oct. 1954."

19. Jefferys, *Management and Managed*, 129.

20. Ibid., 137.

21. "Chrysler, UAW President to Seek End of Work Standards Dispute," *Wall Street Journal*, 3 March 1958, 6.

22. See MacDonald, *Collective Bargaining in the Automobile Industry*.

23. See *Oral History Interview of Mr. William Ogden*, 22–31.

24. Moritz and Seaman, *Going for Broke*, 11.

25. *Arthur Hughes Collection*, "UAW-Chrysler Negotiations, Jan.-Feb. 1958."

26. "Wildcat Strike Halts Hudson Assembly," *Wall Street Journal*, 17 March 1949, 2; "Slowdown Shuts Hudson," *New York Times*, 16 March 1949, 54.

27. *UAW President: Walter P. Reuther Collection*, "Local 154, Jan. 1953–Feb. 1967."

28. "Hudson Truce Hangs on Study," *Business Week*, 18 June 1951, 32. See also "Lay-offs Affect 16,700," *New York Times*, 11 July 1951, 15; "Hudson Accord Reached," *New York Times*, 13 Aug. 1951, 17; "Hudson Asks 1,500,000 in Suit Against UAW," *New York Times*, 27 Oct. 1951, 22; "Hudson Motor Production Again Halted," *Wall Street Journal*, 13 June 1951, 4; "Hudson Motor Shift Again Sent Home," *Wall Street Journal*, 14 June 1951, 2; "Hudson Motor Car Plant Closed Again," *Wall Street Journal*, 30 June 1951, 2; "Hudson Plant Down Again," *Wall Street Journal*, 3 July 1951, 2; "Hudson Down Once More," *Wall Street Journal*, 18 July 1951, 2; "UAW

Charges Hudson Deliberately Stirs Up Disputes to Curb Output," *Wall Street Journal*, 20 July 1951, 2; "Hudson Makes Charge Against Union," *Wall Street Journal*, 27 July 1951, 2; "Hudson Work Stoppage Ends with Plan for Time Study of Operations," *Wall Street Journal*, 15 Aug. 1951, 2.

29. *Marianna Wells Collection*, "Production Standards Agreement: Hudson and Local 154, Aug. 11, 1951."

30. From *Marianna Wells Collection*, "Working Rules—Hudson."

31. From *UAW Local 154*, "Correspondences."

32. *UAW President: Walter P. Reuther Collection*, "Local 154, May 1946–Feb 1952."

33. "Eight Miles of Conveyor in New DeSoto Plant," *American Machinist*, 18 Sept. 1950, 147.

34. "One of Three Struck Chrysler Plants Reopens," *Wall Street Journal*, 23 Aug. 1950, 2.

35. "DeSoto Assemblies Halted," *Wall Street Journal*, 7 June 1951, 2; "DeSoto Assemblies Stopped," *Wall Street Journal*, 23 June 1951, 2.

36. "Plymouth and DeSoto Plants Hit," *Wall Street Journal*, 11 July 1951, 2; "Lay-offs Affect 16,700," *New York Times*, 11 July 1951, 15.

37. "Chrysler Back to Normal," *Wall Street Journal*, 21 July 1951, 2.

38. *UAW President: Walter P. Reuther Collection*, "September 1946–December 1961."

39. *UAW President: Walter P. Reuther Collection*, "Local 3, April 1946–Oct. 1954"; "Strike of 10,000 at Dodge Main Halt Chrysler Unit's Output, Idle 75,000," *Wall Street Journal*, 20 July 1954, 2; "Dodge Plant Shut Down," *New York Times*, 20 July 1954, 11; "More Are Made Idle by Chrysler Strike," *New York Times*, 22 July 1954, 24; "UAW Orders Strikers Back to Work," *New York Times*, 24 July 1954, 6. See also *Arthur Hughes Collection*, "UAW-Chrysler Negotiations, March–Dec. 1954."

40. "Dodge Workers Return," *New York Times*, 17 Jan. 1957, 19.

41. *Arthur Hughes Collection*, "Chrysler Corporation Settlements with UAW Locals, Jan.–Feb. 1958."

42. *Arthur Hughes Collection*, "UAW-Chrysler Negotiations, Jan.–Feb. 1958."

43. "Work Stops for 6,000," *New York Times*, 7 Feb. 1958, 10; "Chrysler Pact Sets a Full Week Ford Needed Men, Layoff for Rest," *New York Times*, 4 March 1958, 39; "Detroit Dodge Plant Closes Again in Fight on Work Standards," *Wall Street Journal*, 12 Feb. 1958, 7.

44. *Arthur Hughes Collection*, "UAW-Chrysler Negotiations, March–April, 1958."

45. *Arthur Hughes Collection*, "Contract Negotiations, Press Releases, 1958."

46. "Plymouth Car Making Halted After Another Dispute in Body Plant," *Wall Street Journal*, 17 May 1955, 4.

47. "Auto Strikes Continue," *New York Times*, 15 June 1955, 34.

48. "Wildcat Walkout at Chrysler Detroit Plant Idles 11,225," *Wall Street Journal*, 24 Feb. 1956, 3.

49. "Wildcat Walkout Idles 8,810 Chrysler Corp. Workers," *Wall Street Journal*, 12 June 1956, 2; "New Chrysler Walkouts Idle 16,000 in Detroit Area," *Wall Street Journal*, 14 June 1956, 3; "Workers at Chrysler's Mack Avenue Plant Slate Poll on Strike," *Wall Street Journal*, 19 June 1956, 3; "Wildcat Walkout Idles 8,810 Chrysler Corp. Workers," *Wall Street Journal*, 25 June 1956, 2; "Strike Slows Chrysler," *New York Times*, 12 June 1956, 7; "16,000 Idle at Chrysler," *New York Times*, 14 June 1956, 66; "Chrysler Plants Halted Again," *New York Times*, 16 June 1956, 11.

50. "Chrysler Local Plans Quick Action on Strike," *Wall Street Journal*, 8 May 1957, 2; "Chrysler Files $5 Million Damage Suit Against Auto Workers Local 212," *Wall Street Journal*, 9 May 1957, 26; "Chrysler UAW Reach Accord on Equipment Transfer," *Wall Street Journal*, 13 May 1957, 2; "Chrysler Delayed by 2 New Walkouts," *New York Times*, 7 May 1957, 26; "Chrysler Files Suit Against UAW Unit," *New York Times*, 9 May 1957, 24; "Chrysler Settles Fight with UAW," *New York Times*, 12 May 1957, 44; "Chrysler is Ready to Push Production," *New York Times*, 13 May 1957, 21; *UAW President: Walter P. Reuther Collection*, "Local 212, June 1947 to October 1962"; "Twinsburg Agreement—Here's How It Works," *Voice of Local 212*, May 1957.

51. *Arthur Hughes Collection*, "Chrysler Corporation Settlements with UAW Locals, Jan.-Feb. 1958."

52. "Five Chrysler Plants Due To Reopen Today," *Wall Street Journal*, 3 Feb. 1958; "Chrysler Sputnik Approach Puts Production Standards in Orbit," *Voice of Local 212*, Feb. 1958; "Chrysler Uses Whip," *Voice of Local 212*, Feb. 1958.

53. "Auto Workers May Revive Shorter Work Week Plea," *Wall Street Journal*, 17 Feb. 1958, 3.

54. *Arthur Hughes Collection*, "Contract Negotiations, Press Releases, 1958."

55. "2 Chrysler Units Closed in Dispute," *New York Times*, 7 June 1958, 23; "Chrysler Closes Plant After 400 Walk Off Jobs," *Wall Street Journal*, 11 June 1958, 7.

56. "GM Offers Reward in Sabotage of Cars," *New York Times*, 2 July 1958, 9.

57. "New Chrysler Tie-up," *New York Times*, 29 July 1958, 49.

58. *Arthur Hughes Collection*, "Contract Negotiations, Press Releases, 1958"; "Local 212 Files 'Unfair Labor Practices' Against Chrysler Corporation," *Voice of Local 212*, July 1958, 1, "Attention All Chrysler ABD Members of Local 212," *Voice of Local 212*, July 1958, 1.

59. "Strike Vote is Taken at Studebaker Plant," *Wall Street Journal*, 21 Jan 1955, 2.

60. *UAW Local 5*, "Production Standards Undated; 1948–1958."

61. "Strike Vote Set Tomorrow Over Studebaker Layoff of 1,700 Workers," *Wall Street Journal*, 11 July 1955, 2; "Studebaker Plant Shut by Wildcat Strike," *Wall Street Journal*, 15 July 1955, 2; "Studebaker Plant Resumes Output as Assembly Workers End Walkout," *Wall Street Journal*, 21 July 1955, 2; "Studebaker is Closed Again by Assembly Line Walkout," *Wall Street Journal*, 27 July 1955, 2; "Studebaker Assemblers Walk Out Again Over Issue of Seniority," *Wall Street Journal*, 28 July 1955, 2; "Studebaker Strike Ends as Firm Grants Seniority to 55 Assembly Workers, Agrees to Recall Up to 500 Others," *Wall Street Journal*, 3 Aug. 1955, 2; "Studebaker to Lay-off 1,700," *New York Times*, 7 Ju. 1955, 9; "Auto Dispute Settled," *New York Times*, 2 Aug. 1955, 12. See also MacDonald, *Collective Bargaining in the Automobile Industry*, 280–282.

62. "UAW Local Strikes at Studebaker's Main Plant in South Bend," *Wall Street Journal*, 2 Sept. 1955, 2; "Studebaker Strikers Ordered Back to Work on Monday by UAW Chiefs," *Wall Street Journal*, 8 Sept. 1955, 2; "Some Strikers Return to Studebaker Plant Following Union Order," *Wall Street Journal*, 9 Sep 1955, 2; "Layoff Pact Ends Auto Strike," *New York Times*, 3 Sept. 1955, 32; "Men at Studebaker Boo End-strike Bid," *New York Times*, 11 Sept. 1955, 46.

63. MacDonald, *Collective Bargaining in the Automobile Industry*, 280–282.

64. *Oral History Interview of Mr. Elmer Yenney*, 12.

65. "Series of Ford Plants Close as Workers Walk Out in Protest of Contract," *Wall Street Journal*, 8 June 1955, 2; "GM to Close 20 Plants Because of Parts Shortage Brought on by Wave of UAW-CIO Wildcat Walkouts," *Wall Street Journal*, 10 June 1955, 2; "Pickets Appear at Some Plants," *New York Times*, 6 June 1955, 18.

66. "GM, Despite New Contract, Still Has 18 Plants Idle," *Wall Street Journal*, 16 June 1955, 3; "Twelve GM Plants Stay Shut Down," *Wall Street Journal*, 17 June 1955, 2; "Most GM Plants to be Operating Today as Wildcat Strikers Return," *Wall Street Journal*, 20 June 1955, 2; "Parts Shortage, Strike Cut Output at 12 GM Plants," *Wall Street Journal*, 21 June 1955, 2; "G.M. Battle Won, Union Will Widen Wage Plans Drive," *New York Times*, 14 June 1955, 1; "Auto Strikes Continue," *New York Times*, 15 June 1955, 34; "Contract Ratified by GM Workers," *New York Times*, 29 June 1955, 21.

67. "GM Offers Reward in Sabotage of Cars," *New York Times*, 2 July 1958, 9.

68. Weir, "Rebellion in American Labor's Rank and File."

Chapter 8. Repairing the Seams of the Hegemonic Order: State-Inspired, Sloanist-Regulated Market Relations, 1959–1973

1. Schnapp, *Corporate Strategies*, vol. 3, 11-66.
2. Ibid., 11-66.
3. Fligstein, *Transformation of Corporate Control.*
4. "Antitrusters Start Firing at GM," *Business Week*, 7 Feb. 1959.
5. "Washington Outlook," *Business Week*, 2 Sept. 1961; Cray, *Chrome Colossus*, 444-448.
6. "How GM Did It," *Fortune*, June 1963, 97-98.
7. Schnapp, *Corporate Strategies*, vol. 3, 11-42.
8. See, for example, Mahoney, *Story of George Romney.*
9. Ibid., 25.
10. See Wright, *On a Clear Day.*
11. "Can GM's New Top Team Cope with the '70s?" *Business Week*, 11 Dec. 1971.
12. Wright, *On a Clear Day*, 245-248.
13. See Ibid.
14. See Ibid., 123.
15. Abernathy, *Productivity Dilemma*, 38.
16. See Schnapp, *Corporate Strategies*, vol. 3, 11-39.
17. See Ibid., 18-19, 40-41, 69.
18. See Ibid., 259.
19. Wright, *On a Clear Day.*
20. Schnapp, *Corporate Strategies*, vol. 3, 11-59, 107-108.
21. Ibid. See White, *Automobile Industry Since 1945.*

Chapter 9. Repairing the Seams of the Hegemonic Order: Labor Process Dualism, 1959–1973

1. Braverman, *Labor and Monopoly Capital.*
2. See Gartman, *Auto Slavery.*
3. See Ibid.
4. Noble, *Forces of Production.*
5. See Piore and Sabel, *Second Industrial Divide.*
6. See Attewell, "Deskilling Controversy"; Littler, *Development of the Labour Process.*
7. See Zetka, "Automated Technologies."
8. Noble, *Forces of Production*, ch. 11.
9. See Attewell, "Deskilling Controversy;" Littler, *Development of the Labor Process*; Wood (ed.), *Degradation of Work?.*

10. "How Ford Automates Production Lines," *American Machinist*, 17 March 1952.

11. "On the Assembly Line," *Iron Age*, 3 Nov. 1949; "New Transfer Machines Shown to Pay Their Way," *SAE Journal*, Dec. 1949.

12. "How Ford Automates Production Lines," *American Machinist*, 17 Mar 1952.

13. "New Transfer Machines Shown to Pay Their Way," *SAE Journal*, Dec. 1949; "Automation: How to Apply It and Where It Works" *SAE Journal*, Oct. 1954. See also Shaiken, *Work Transformed.*

14. "Automatic Materials Handling at Ford's New Parts Plant," *Automotive Industries*, 1 Dec. 1951.

15. "Ford's New Engine and Stamping Facilities at Cleveland," *Automotive Industries*, 1 Dec. 1955; "Automated Press Lines in Ford's Cleveland Stamping Plant," *Automotive Industries*, 1 Apr. 1956.

16. "New Plant, New Presses Stamp Chrysler Bodies," *American Machinist*, 4 Nov. 1957; "Chrysler Automates Stamping Plant," *Machinery*, Dec. 1957.

17. "New Press Line, New Handling Equipment, New Car," *Machinery*, Dec. 1958.

18. "Company Answers Union Demands," *Ford Facts*, 13 Dec. 1952; "Frame Plant: Things Are Looking Up," *Ford Facts*, 2 Feb. 1970.

19. See, for example, "Frame and Cold Heading Building: Hell's Little Acre, Buck Job," *Ford Facts*, 5 June 1954.

20. "It Doesn't Always Pay to Put All Your Chips on Automation," *Business Week*, 10 Aug. 1957.

21. Gartman, *Auto Slavery.*

22. "It Doesn't Always Pay to Put All Your Chips on Automation," *Business Week*, 10 Aug. 1957.

23. "Transportation Unit: FOMOCO Going Automation Crazy," *Ford Facts*, 8 Sept. 1956.

24. "Frame and Cold Heading: Institute New Work Standards," *Ford Facts*, 8 Sept. 1956.

25. "Frame and Cold Heading: Confusion on Frame Line," *Ford Facts*, 13 Oct. 1956.

26. "Ford Negotiations on Frame Plant Problems," *Ford Facts*, 21 Sept. 1957.

27. "Settle Health and Safety Problems," *Ford Facts*, 2 June 1960.

28. "Moving Chases Replace Shuttles in Automated Framing Line," *Iron Age*, 10 Nov. 1960.

29. "GM Heads for Annual Retooling," *Iron Age*, 22 May 1958; "Automation Isn't Always Best," *Iron Age*, 5 June 1958.

30. See White, *Automobile Industry Since 1945*, 22.

31. "Latest Techniques at New Fisher Body Plant at Mansfield," *Automotive Industries*, 1 Jan. 1959.

32. "Moving Bolster Press Line Handles with Wide Variety of

Parts," *Automotive Industries,* 1 March 1961; "Rolling Bolster Press Line at Fisher Body Plant," *Automotive Industries,* 1 July 1961; "Versatile Rolling Bolster Presses at Fisher Body Cleveland Plant," *Automotive Industries,* 1 Feb. 1963.

33. "Moving Bolster Presses at Ford's Cleveland Plant," *Automotive Industries,* 15 Sept. 1962; "New Production and Plant Equipment," *Automotive Industries,* 1 March 1962; "Ford Woodhaven Stamping Plant," *Automotive Industries,* 1 Aug. 1966.

34. "Chrysler Warren Stamping Plant Expansion," *Automotive Industries,* 15 Feb. 1965.

35. "Ford Handles by Automation," *American Machinist,* 21 Oct. 1948.

36. See "Automation Welding Helps Build Valiant," *Welding Engineer,* March 1960. See Thomas, *Citizenship, Gender and Work,* for discussion of a similar technology in lettuce harvesting.

37. Abernathy, *Productivity Dilemma,* 214-215.

38. "Latest Body Assembly Techniques by Fisher," *Automotive Industries,* 15 Sept. 1947.

39. "Futurama Bodies Require Major Change-Over," *Automotive Industries,* 1 May 1948.

40. *Arthur Hughes Collection,* "UAW-Chrysler Department Meeting with L. L. Colbert, 13 Aug. 1956."

41. "Assembling the Dart," *Automotive Industries,* 1 Dec. 1959; "Latest Production Methods at Plymouth Assembly," *Automotive Industries,* 1 April 1960; "Efficiency Conveyor Setup for Valiant Production at Chrysler's Hamtramck Plant," *Automotive Industries,* 15 May 1960; "Rolling Bolster Press Line at Fisher Body Plant," *Automotive Industries,* 1 July 1961; "Automation Welding Helps Build Valiant," *Welding Engineer,* March 1960.

42. Leonard Sayles, *Behavior of Industrial Work Groups,* 30.

43. Ibid., 30.

44. See Sexton, "A Feminist Union Perspective," 22.

45. See Abernathy, *Productivity Dilemma,* 143.

46. See *Arthur Hughes Collection,* "UAW-Chrysler Negotiations, 1960."

47. "Molding Eliminates Sewing," *Modern Plastics,* Dec. 1952, 105-108.

48. See "Fabric Trim Assemblies Produced by the Millions," *Automotive Industries,* 1 Nov. 1959.

49. "Ford Will Layoff 4,500 Because of Wildcat Strike," *New York Times,* 18 May 1963, 18; "Ford Plant Warns Men to End Strike Tomorrow," *New York Times,* 19 May 1963, 49; "9-day Ford Strike Halted in Chicago," *New York Times,* 21 May 1963, 41; "Ford Plant Strike Cutting Industry's Output This Week," *Wall Street Journal,* 17 May 1963, 7; "Ford Has Laid Off 12,500 Workers Because of Strike," *Wall Street*

Journal, 20 May 1963, 2; "Ford Hopes Production Will Rise by Friday to Near Normal Levels," *Wall Street Journal*, 22 May 1963, 2.

50. "New Layoff Set in Auto Industry," *New York Times*, 18 Feb. 1967, 37; "GM Asserts Strike in Ohio Will Close 22 Plants by Friday," *New York Times*, 21 Feb. 1967, 26; "GM Begins Layoff of 80,000 This Week as Strike Continues," *New York Times*, 22 Feb. 1967, 16; "Strikers at G.M. Agree to Return," *New York Times*, 23 Feb. 1967, 1; "Strikers Return to Work at G.M. Plant," *New York Times*, 24 Feb. 1967, 23; "GM Says Effect of Parts Strike Hits Other Units," *Wall Street Journal*, 21 Feb. 1967, 2; "Mid-February Car Sales Off 21% from '66," *Wall Street Journal*, 23 Feb. 1967, 3; "More GM Plants to Close Despite Ending of Strike," *Wall Street Journal*, 24 Feb. 1967, 4.

51. "Strike at Chrysler Perils 100,000 Jobs," *New York Times*, 29 Jan. 1966, 22; "Chrysler and Union Reach Pact to End 2-day Strike," *New York Times*, 30 Jan. 1966, 24; "Chrysler and Union Reach Agreement," *New York Times*, 3 Feb. 1966, 32; "Chrysler Strike Ended," *New York Times*, 5 Feb. 1966, 17; "Chrysler Workers Bar Stamping-plant Pact, Imperil All Production," *Wall Street Journal*, 1 Feb. 1966, 3; "Snow, Strike to Cut Week's Car Output 11%," *Wall Street Journal*, 4 Feb. 1966, 2; "Chrysler Corp. to Start Resuming Output of Cars at Plant Shut by Strike," *Wall Street Journal*, 7 Feb. 1966, 5.

52. "Company Stalls in Negotiations," *Ford Facts*, 16 Sept. 1961. Also *Arthur Hughes Collection*, "Special Collective Bargaining Convention, April 1961."

53. "U.A.W. on Strike at 92 G.M. Plants," *New York Times*, 12 Sept., 1.

54. "Ford-Union Talks Seek Local Pacts," *New York Times*, 9 Oct. 1961, 22; "Ford and U.A.W. Agree to 3-year National Pact," *New York Times*, 12 Oct. 1961, 1.

55. *Arthur Hughes Collection*, "UAW National Chrysler Council: Production and Maintenance Agreement, Nov. 1961."

56. Ibid. See also *Oral History Interview with Mr. Arthur Hughes*; "Details of UAW-Ford Economic Agreement," *Ford Facts*, 21 Oct. 1961, 1; "UAW Calls Off Last GM Strike," *New York Times*, 25 Sept. 1961, 33.

57. "Tough Standards Decried by U.A.W.," *New York Times*, 16 Nov. 1963, 11.

58. "Ford Union Sets Contract Goals," *New York Times*, 23 May 1964, 56.

59. "Contract Report," *Ford Facts*, 20 July 1964; "Ford Union Sets Contract Goals," *New York Times*, 23 May 1964, 56.

60. "New Jersey Plant Struck," *Wall Street Journal*, 12 May 1966, 4; "Strike Ends at Ford's Metuchen, N.J., Plant," *Wall Street Journal*, 20 June 1966, 3.

61. "At GM Plant in Illinois 1,300 Workers Walk Out," *New York*

Times, 19 April 1968, 66; "Slated Fisher Body Strike Could Cripple GM Output,"*Wall Street Journal*, 18 April 1968, 28; "Auto Workers, GM Reach Accord to End Stamping-plant Strike," *Wall Street Journal*, 22 April 1968, 17.

62. "GM's Toughest Division," *New York Times*, section 3, 16 April 1972, 1.

63. "A Day's Work," *Wall Street Journal*, 6 Dec. 1972, 1.

64. "GM's Toughest Division," *New York Times*, section 3, 16 April 1972, 1.

65. "A Day's Work," *Wall Street Journal*, 6 Dec. 1972, 1.

66. Ibid.

67. Ibid. See also "Spread of GM's Lordstown Syndrome," *Business Week*, 7 Oct. 1972, 27; "UAW Strikes GM at Norwood, Ohio, Over Job Standards," *Wall Street Journal*, 10 April 1972, 4; "UAW Refuses to Meet with GM on Walkout at Norwood, Ohio Unit," *Wall Street Journal*, 12 April 1972, 8; "GM Says Negotiations Have Resumed at Plant Struck Since Friday," *Wall Street Journal*, 13 April 1972, 23; "GM Offers Concessions to End Norwood Strike, but Union Wants Pact," *Wall Street Journal*, 29 June 1972, 15; "Record GM Strike Near End as Firm, UAW Set Accord," *Wall Street Journal*, 26 Sept. 1972, 2; "Talks Held in G.M. Strike at Ohio Assembly Plant," *New York Times*, 10 April 1972, 11; "G.M. Strike Talks Recessed," *New York Times*, 13 April 1972, 12; "Tentative Accord is Reached in Longest General Motors Strike," *New York Times*, 26 Sept. 1972, 20; "Longest Strike at G.M. is Ended at Plant in Ohio After 174 Days," *New York Times*, 28 Sept. 1972, 42.

68. "GM Efficiency Move That Backfired," *Business Week*, 25 March 1972; "Union Strikes G.M. Facility in Work Methods Dispute," *New York Times*, 5 March 1972, 36; 5 March 1972, 36; "Talks Show Gain in G.M. Ohio Strike," *New York Times*, 6 March 1972, 65; "G.M.'s Vega Plant Closed by Strike," *New York Times*, 7 March 1972, 42; "Auto Talks Continue," *New York Times*, 9 March 1972, 31; "G.M. Talks Resume," *New York Times*, 13 March 1972, 1; "U.A.W. and G.M. Agree on Ending Vega Plant Strike," *New York Times*, 25 March 1972, 63; "GM Plant in Ohio is Producing Again," *New York Times*, 28 March 1972, 33; "General Motors, UAW Make Progress in Talks Over Struck Vega Plant," *Wall Street Journal*, 6 March 1972, 4; "GM Layoffs Seen at Some Other Sites After Lordstown," *Wall Street Journal*, 7 March 1972, 14; "GM Resuming Output at Lordstown, Ohio, as Striking UAW Local Ratifies Accord," *Wall Street Journal*, 27 March 1972, 2. See also Widick (ed.), *Auto Work and Its Discontents*.

69. "UAW Tells GM of 3 More Possible Strikes," *Wall Street Journal*, 17 Oct. 1972, 7.

70. "UAW Hits GM with Guerilla Tactics," *Business Week*, 28 Oct. 1972.

71. "Strike is Halted at Key G.M. Plant," *New York Times*, 17 Oct. 1972, 82; "3 More G.M. Factories Struck," *New York Times*, 21 Oct. 1972, 11; "UAW Begins New Strike Strategy at GM in Intensified Battle Over Job Standards," *Wall Street Journal*, 16 Oct. 1972, 6; "GM Labor Trouble Appear Key Factor in Production Lag," *Wall Street Journal*, 20 Oct. 1972, 3; "GM Hit by Strikes at 3 Assembly Units," *Wall Street Journal*, 23 Oct. 1972, 6.

72. "Ohio G.M. Plant Struck," *New York Times*, 13 Oct. 1972, 35; "G.M. and Union Set Talks on Weekend Walkout in Ohio," *New York Times*, 14 Oct. 1972, 3; "G.M. to Scrap 1,000 Cars Stranded During Strike," *New York Times*, 14 Oct. 1972, 31; "UAW Begins New Strike Strategy at GM in Intensified Battle Over Job Standards," *Wall Street Journal*, 16 Oct. 1972, 6; "GM Labor Trouble Appear Key Factor in Production Lag," *Wall Street Journal*, 20 Oct. 1972, 19.

73. "GM Struck by UAW at 3 More Plants," *Wall Street Journal*, 6 Nov. 1972, 4; "GM Workers at Saginaw Return to Their Jobs," *Wall Street Journal*, 7 Nov. 1972, 3.

74. "Anatomy of an Auto Plant Rescue," *Fortune*, 4 April 1983.

75. Ibid., 112.

Chapter 10. Conclusion

1. Cray, *Chrome Colossus*; Sloan, *My Years with General Motors*.

2. Lichtenstein, "Auto Worker Militancy"; Sayles, *Behavior of Industrial Work Groups*.

3. Fligstein, *Transformation of Corporate Control*.

4. Ibid.

Bibliography

Abernathy, William J. *The Productivity Dilemma.* Baltimore: John Hopkins University Press, 1978.

Aronowitz, Stanley. *False Promises.* New York: McGraw-Hill, 1973.

Arthur Hughes Collection. Detroit: Archives of Labor and Urban Affairs, Wayne State University.

——. "Chrysler Corporation Settlements with UAW Locals, Jan.-Feb., 1958." Box 12, File. 14.

——. "Contract Negotiations, Press Releases, 1958." Box 14, File 1.

——. "Special Collective Bargaining Convention, April 1961." Box 16, File 7.

——. "UAW-Chrysler Department Meeting with L. L. Colbert, 13 August 1956." Box 12, File 8.

——. "UAW-Chrysler Negotiations, Jan.-Feb. 1958." Box 12, File 15.

——. "UAW-Chrysler Negotiations, March-April, 1958." Box 13, File 1.

——. "UAW-Chrysler Negotiations, March-Dec., 1958." Box 11, File 4.

——. "UAW-Chrysler Negotiations, 1960." Box 15, File 9.

——. "UAW National Chrysler Council: Production and Maintenance Agreement, Nov. 1961." Box 18, File 16.

Asher, Robert. "The 1949 Ford Speed Up Strike and the Post-War Social Compact, 1946-1961." Ch. 5 in *Autowork*, edited by Robert Asher and Ronald Edsforth. Albany: State University of New York Press, forthcoming.

Attewell, Paul. "The Deskilling Controversy." *Work and Occupations* 14 (1987): 323-346.

Babson, Steve. *Building the Union*. New Brunswick, N.J.: Rutgers University Press, 1991.

Baran, Paul A., and Paul M. Sweezy. *Monopoly Capital*. New York: Monthly Review Press, 1966.

Beasley, Norman. *Knudsen*. New York: McGraw-Hill, 1947.

Bell, Daniel. "The Subversion of Collective Bargaining," *Commentary* 29 (1960): 185–197.

Bernstein, Irving. *Turbulent Years*. Boston: Houghton Mifflin Company, 1970.

Blauner, Robert. *Alienation and Freedom*. Chicago: University of Chicago Press, 1964.

Braverman, Harry. *Labor and Monopoly Capital*. New York: Monthly Review Press, 1974.

Brody, David. *Workers in Industrial America*. New York: Oxford University Press, 1980.

Brown, Donaldson. *Some Reminiscences of an Industrialist*. Easton, PA: Hive Publishing, 1977.

Burawoy, Michael. "Toward a Marxist Theory of the Labor Process." *Politics and Society* 8 (1978):247–312.

——. *Manufacturing Consent*. Chicago: University of Chicago Press, 1979.

——. "Between the Labor Process and the State." *American Sociological Review* 48 (1983):587–605.

Calhoun, Craig Jackson. "The Radicalism of Tradition." *American Journal of Sociology* 88 (1983):886–913.

Chandler, Alfred D. *Strategy and Structure*. Cambridge: MIT Press, 1962.

——. *Giant Enterprise*. New York: Harcourt, Brace and World, 1964.

——. *The Visible Hand*. Cambridge: Belknap Press, 1977.

Cole, Robert E. *Work, Mobility and Participation*. Berkeley: University of California Press, 1979.

Collins, Orvis, Melville Dalton, and Donald Roy. "Restrictions of Output and Social Cleavage in Industry," *Applied Anthropology* 5 (1946):1–14.

Conell, Carol, and Kim Voss. "Formal Organization and the Fate of Social Movements." *American Sociological Review* 55 (1990): 255–269.

Cray, Ed. *Chrome Colossus*. New York: McGraw-Hill, 1980.

Drucker, Peter. *Concept of the Corporation*. New York: John Day, 1946.

Edsforth, Ronald. *Class Conflict and Cultural Consensus*. New Brunswick, N.J.: Rutgers University Press, 1987.

Edwards, Charles E. *Dynamics of the United States Automobile Industry*. Columbia: University of South Carolina Press, 1965.

Edwards, Richard. *Contested Terrain*. New York: Basic Books, 1979.

Edwards, P. K. *Strikes in the United States, 1881-1974*. New York: St. Martin's Press, 1981.

Fantasia, Rick. *Cultures of Solidarity*. Berkeley: University of California Press, 1988.

Faunce, William A. "Automation in the Automobile Industry." *American Sociological Review* 23 (1958a):401–414.

——. "Automation and the Automobile Worker." *Social Problems* 6 (1958b):68–78.

Fine, Sidney. *The Automobile Under the Blue Eagle*. Ann Arbor: University of Michigan Press, 1963.

——. *Sit-Down*. Ann Arbor: University of Michigan Press, 1969.

Finlay, William. *Work on the Waterfront*. Philadelphia: Temple University Press, 1988.

Fligstein, Neil. *The Transformation of Corporate Control*. Cambridge: Harvard University Press, 1990.

Ford, Henry in collaboration with Samuel Crowther. *My Life and Work*. Garden City, N.Y.: Doubleday, Page and Co., 1922.

——. *Today and Tomorrow*. Cambridge, Mass.: Productivity Press, 1988 [1926].

Form, William. *Divided We Stand*. Urbana: University of Illinois Press, 1985.

Fountain, Clayton W. *Union Guy*. New York: Viking Press, 1949.

Fraser, Steve. *Labor Will Rule*. New York: Free Press, 1991.

Friedlander, Peter. *The Emergence of a UAW Local, 1936-1939*. Pittsburg: University of Pittsburg Press, 1975.

Galbraith, John K. *The Liberal Hour*. Boston: Houghlin Mifflin, 1960.

——. *The New Industrial State*. Boston: Houghton Mifflin, 1973 [1967].

Gartman, David. "Auto Slavery." Ph.d. Dissertation. Department of Sociology, University of California at San Diego, 1980.

——. *Auto Slavery*. New Brunswick, N.J.: Rutgers University Press, 1986.

Godard, John. "Strikes as Collective Voice." *Industrial and Labor Relations Review* 46(1992):161–175.

Goffman, Erving. *Asylums*. Garden City, N.Y.: Anchor Books, 1961.

Gordon, David M., Richard Edwards, and Michael Reich. *Segmented Work, Divided Workers*. New York: Cambridge University Press, 1982.

Gouldner, Alvin W. *Patterns of Industrial Bureaucracy.* New York; Free Press, 1954.

———. *Wildcat Strike.* Yellow Springs, Ohio: Antioch Press, 1954.

Gramsci, Antonio. *Selections from the Prison Notebooks of Antonio Gramsci.* New York: International Publishers, 1971.

Halaby, Charles N. "Worker Attachment and Workplace Authority." *American Sociological Review* 51 (1986):634–649.

Halle, David. *America's Working Man.* Chicago: University of Chicago Press, 1984.

Halpern, Martin. *UAW Politics in the Cold War Era.* Albany: State University of New York Press, 1988.

Harbison, Frederick H., and Robert Dubin. *Patterns of Union-Management Relations.* Chicago: Chicago Science Research Associates, 1947.

Haydu, Jeffrey. *Between Craft and Class.* Berkeley: University of California Press, 1988.

Herding, Richard G. *Job Control and Union Structure.* Amsterdam: Rotterdam University Press, 1972.

Herring, Neill, and Sue Thrasher. "UAW Sit-down Strike," in *Working Lives,* ed. Marc S. Miller. New York: Pantheon Books, 1980, 172–183.

Hickerson, J. Mel. *Ernie Breech.* New York: Meredith Press, 1968.

Hofstadter, Richard. *The American Political Tradition and the Men Who Made It.* New York: Dodd, Mead, and Company, 1948.

Jacoby, Sanford M. *Employing Bureaucracy.* New York: Columbia University Press, 1985.

Jefferys, Steve. *Management and Managed.* New York: Cambridge University Press, 1986.

Jenkins, J. Craig and Charles Perrow. "Insurgency of the Powerless." *American Sociological Review* 305 (1977):278–287.

Jennings, Ed. "Wildcat! The Wartime Strike Wave in Auto." *Radical America* 9 (1975):77–105

Katznelson, Ira, and Aristide R. Zolberg, eds. *Working-Class Formation.* New York: Princeton University Press, 1986.

Kerr, Clark, and Abraham Siegel. "The Inter-industry Propensity to Strike," in *Industrial Conflict,* ed. A. Kornhauser, R. Dubin, and A. Ross. New York: McGraw-Hill, 1954, 189–212.

Langworth, Richard M. *Kaiser-Frazer.* New York: E.P. Dutton, 1975.

Lichtenstein, Nelson. "Auto Worker Militancy and the Structure of Factory Life, 1937-1955." *Journal of American History* 67 (1980):335–353.

——. *Labor's War at Home.* New York: Cambridge University Press, 1982.

——. "UAW Bargaining Strategy and Shop-Floor Conflict: 1946-1970." *Industrial Relations* 24 (1985):360-381.

——. "'The Man in the Middle': A Social History of Automobile Industry Foreman," in *On the Line,* ed. Nelson Lichtenstein and Stephen Meyer. Ch. 7. Urbana: University of Illinois Press, 1989.

Lippert, John. "Fleetwood Wildcat." *Radical America* 11 (1977):7-38.

——. "Shopfloor Politics at Fleetwood." *Radical America* 12 (1978):53-70.

Littler, Craig R. *The Development of the Labour Process in Capitalist Societies.* London: Heinemann Educational, 1982.

Lukács, Georg. *History and Class Consciousness.* Cambridge: MIT Press, 1971.

MacDonald, Robert M. *Collective Bargaining in the Automobile Industry.* New Haven: Yale University Press, 1963.

Mahoney, Tom. *The Story of George Romney.* New York: Harper, 1960.

Marianna Wells Collection. Detroit: Archives of Labor and Urban Affairs, Wayne State University.

——. "Production Standards Agreement: Hudson and Local 154, August 11, 1951." Box 1, File 6.

——. "Working Rules—Hudson." Box 1, File 6.

Marquart, Frank. *An Auto Worker's Journal.* University Park: Pennsylvania State University Press, 1975.

Marx, Karl. *Capital,* vol. 1. New York: Vintage Books, 1977.

Mathewson, Stanley B. *Restriction of Output Among Unorganized Workers.* New York: Viking Press, 1931.

May, George S. *R.E. Olds.* Grand Rapids, Mich.: William B. Eerdmans Publishing, 1977.

Montgomery, David. *Workers' Control in America.* New York: Cambridge University Press, 1979.

Moritz, Michael and Barrett Seaman. *Going for Broke.* New York: Doubleday, 1981.

Motor Vehicle Manufacturers Association. *Plants of U.S. Motor Vehicle Manufacturers in the United States and Canada.* Detroit: Statistics Department, MVMA, 1974.

Nash, Al. "Job Satisfaction: A Critique," in *Auto Work and Its Discontents,* ed. B. J. Widick. Ch. 6. Baltimore: Johns Hopkins University Press, 1976.

Nelson, Daniel. "Scientific Managment and the Workplace, 1920-1935," in *Masters to Managers: Historical and Comparative*

Perspectives on American Employers, ed. Sanford Jacoby. Ch. 4. New York: Columbia University Press, 1991.

Nevins, Allan. *Ford: The Times, the Man, the Company*. New York: Charles Scribner's Sons, 1954.

Nevins, Allan, and Frank E. Hill. *Ford: Decline and Rebirth, 1933-1962*. New York: Charles Scribner's Sons, 1963.

Noble, David. *The Forces of Production*. New York: Alfred A. Knopf, 1984.

O'Connor, James. *The Fiscal Crisis of the State*. New York: St. Martin's Press, 1973.

Offe, Claus, and Helmut Wiesenthal. "Two Logics of Collective Action," in *Political Power and Social Theory*, vol. 1, ed. Maurice Zeitlin. Greenwich, Conn.: JAI Press, 1980, 76–115.

Oral History Interview of Mr. Lester Fox, 12 June 1971. Detroit: Archives of Labor and Urban Affairs, Wayne State University.

Oral History Interview of Mr. Arthur Hughes, 3 March 1963. Detroit: Archives of Labor and Urban Affairs, Wayne State University.

Oral History Interview of Mr. George C. Hupp, 15 May 1972. Detroit: Archives of Labor and Urban Affairs, Wayne State University.

Oral History Interview of Mr. William Ogden, 12 May 1972. Detroit: Archives of Labor and Urban Affairs, Wayne State University.

Oral History Interview of Mr. Elmer Yenney, 27 April 1961. Detroit: Archives of Labor and Urban Affairs, Wayne State University.

Paige, Jeffery M. *Agrarian Revolution*. New York: Free Press, 1975.

Perrone, Luca. "Positional Power, Strikes, and Wages." *American Sociological Review* 49 (1984):412–426.

Piore, Michael J., and Charles F. Sabel. *The Second Industrial Divide*. New York: Basic Books, 1984.

Ragin, Charles C. *The Comparative Method*. Berkeley: University of California Press, 1987.

Ragin, Charles C., and David Zaret. "Theory and Method in Comparative Research." *Social Forces* 61 (1983):731–54.

Roy, Donald. "Quota Restriction and Goldbricking in a Machine Shop." *American Journal of Sociology* 57 (1952):427–442.

——. "Efficiency and the Fix." *American Journal of Sociology* 60 (1954):255–266.

——. "Work Satisfaction and Social Reward in Quota Achievement," in *Labor and Trade Unionism*, eds. Walter Galenson and Seymour M. Lipsett. New York: John Wiley and Sons, 1960, 301–369.

Sayles, Leonard R. *Behavior of Industrial Work Groups*. New York: Wiley, 1958.

Schnapp, John B. *Corporate Strategies of the Automotive Manufacturers*, vols. 2 and 3. Boston: Harbridge House, 1978.

Scott, Jerome F., and George C. Homans. "Reflections on the Wildcat Strikes." *American Sociological Review* 12 (1947):278–292.

Seltzer, Lawrence H. *A Financial History of the American Automobile Industry*. Boston: Houghton Mifflin, 1928.

Serrin, William. *The Company and the Union*. New York: Vintage Books, 1973.

Sexton, Patricia Cayo. "A Feminist Union Perspective," in *Auto Work and Its Discontents*, ed. B. J. Widick. Baltimore: John Hopkins University Press, 1976, 18–33.

Shaiken, Harley. *Work Transformed*. New York: Holt, Rinehart, and Winston, 1984.

Shorter, Edward, and Charles Tilly. *Strikes in France, 1830-1968*. New York: Cambridge University Press, 1974.

Sloan, Alfred P., Jr. *My Years with General Motors*. Garden City, N.Y.: Doubleday, 1964.

Sorensen, Charles, with Samuel T. Williamson. *My Forty Years with Ford*. New York: W. W. Norton, 1956.

Stinchcombe, Arthur L. *Information and Organizations*. Berkeley: University of California, 1990.

Stone, Katherine. "The Origin of Job Structures in the Steel Industry." *Review of Radical Political Economics* 6 (1974):113–173.

Thomas, Robert J. *Citizenship, Gender and Work*. Berkeley: University of California Press, 1985.

Thompson, E. P. *The Making of the English Working Class*. New York: Vintage Books, 1966 [1963].

Tilly, Charles. "Solidary Logics." *Theory and Society* 17 (1988): 451–458.

UAW Local 5. Detroit: Archives of Labor and Urban Affairs, Wayne State University.

——. "Production Standards Undated: 1948–1958." Boxes 2 and 18.

——. "Strike Vote—March 16, 1956." Box 21.

UAW Local 154. Detroit: Archives of Labor and Urban Affairs, Wayne State University.

——. "Correspondences."

UAW Local 212. Detroit: Archives of Labor and Urban Affairs, Wayne State University.

——. "Correspondences of Shop Committee." Box 16.

UAW President: Walter P. Reuther Collection. Detroit: Archives of Labor and Urban Affairs, Wayne State University.

——. "Local 3, April 1946–Oct. 1954." Box 229, File 3.

——. "Local 154, May 1946–Feb. 1952." Box 234, File 16.

——. "Local 154, Jan. 1953–Feb. 1967." Box 234, File 15.

——. "Local 212, June 1947–Oct. 1962." Box 236, File 40.

——. "September 1946–December 1961." Box 237, File 21.

Vallas, Stephen P. *Power in the Workplace.* Albany: State University of New York Press, 1993.

Walker, Charles R., and Robert H. Guest. *The Man on the Assembly Line.* New York: Arno Press, 1979 [1952].

Wallace, Michael, Larry J. Griffin, and Beth A. Rubin. "The Positional Power of American Labor, 1963–1977." *American Sociological Review* 54 (1989):197–214.

Weber, Max. *Economy and Society.* Berkeley: University of California Press, 1976 [1922].

Weir, Stanley. "Rebellion in American Labor's Rank and File," in *Worker's Control,* ed. Gerry Hunnius, C. David Gerson, and John Case. New York: Random House, 1973, 45–61.

White, Lawrence J. *The Automobile Industry since 1945.* Cambridge, Mass.: Harvard University Press, 1971.

Widick, B. J., ed. *Auto Work and Its Discontents.* Baltimore: Johns Hopkins University Press, 1976.

Wolf, Eric R. *Peasant Wars of the Twentieth Century.* New York: Harper and Row, 1969.

Wood, Stephen, ed. *The Degradation of Work?* London: Hutchinson, 1982.

Wright, J. Patrick. *On a Clear Day You Can See General Motors.* New York: Avon Books, 1979.

Zetka, James R. Jr., "Automated Technologies, Institutional Environments, and Skilled Labor Processes." *Sociological Quarterly* 32 (1991):557–574.

Newspapers, Magazines, and Union and Trade Periodicals

American Machinist
Automotive Industries
Business Week
Chicago Tribune
Ford Facts
Fortune
Iron Age
Machinery
Modern Plastics
Monthly Labor Review
New York Times
SAE Journal
Voice of Local 212
Wall Street Journal
Welding Engineer

Index